TEXAS TEST PREP
Student Quiz Book
STAAR Mathematics
Grade 3

© 2015 by Test Master Press Texas

All rights reserved. No part of this book may be reproduced or transmitted in any form or by any means, electronic, mechanical, photocopying, recording, or otherwise without prior written permission.

ISBN 978-1522983309

CONTENTS

Introduction	5
Understanding, Representing, and Comparing Whole Numbers	6
Quiz 1: Composing and Decomposing Whole Numbers	8
Quiz 2: Identifying Place Value	12
Quiz 3: Understanding Place Value Relationships	14
Quiz 4: Using Place Value to Compare Numbers	18
Quiz 5: Representing Numbers on Number Lines	22
Quiz 6: Rounding Whole Numbers	24
Quiz 7: Comparing and Ordering Whole Numbers	28
Representing and Using Fractions	32
Quiz 8: Representing Fractions with Diagrams	34
Quiz 9: Modeling Fractions	38
Quiz 10: Representing Fractions on Number Lines	40
Quiz 11: Understanding Unit Fractions	44
Quiz 12: Composing and Decomposing Fractions	48
Quiz 13: Using Fractions to Solve Problems	52
Quiz 14: Understanding Equivalent Fractions	56
Quiz 15: Representing Equivalent Fractions	60
Quiz 16: Comparing Fractions	64
Computing with Whole Numbers	68
Quiz 17: Adding Whole Numbers	70
Quiz 18: Subtracting Whole Numbers	74
Quiz 19: Solving Word Problems Using Addition and Subtraction	78
Quiz 20: Solving Two-Step Word Problems	82
Quiz 21: Using Estimation and Rounding	86
Quiz 22: Finding the Value of Money	90
Quiz 23: Representing Multiplication	92
Quiz 24: Using Multiplication Facts	96
Quiz 25: Solving Word Problems Using Multiplication	98
Quiz 26: Representing Division	102
Quiz 27: Using Division Facts	106
Quiz 28: Solving Word Problems Using Division	108
Quiz 29: Identifying Even and Odd Numbers	112
Quiz 30: Using Properties of Numbers to Multiply and Divide	114
Analyzing and Creating Patterns and Relationships	118
Quiz 31: Representing Word Problems with Equations	120
Quiz 32: Representing Word Problems with Diagrams	124
Quiz 33: Representing Multiplication and Division with Arrays	128
Quiz 34: Representing Multiplication and Division with Equations	130

Quiz 35: Understanding Multiplication as a Comparison	134
Quiz 36: Finding Missing Numbers in Equations	137
Quiz 37: Understanding Patterns	140
Quiz 38: Representing Real-World Relationships	144
Quiz 39: Using Tables to Represent Relationships	148

Understanding and Analyzing the Properties of Shapes — 152

Quiz 40: Classifying Two-Dimensional Shapes	154
Quiz 41: Comparing and Sorting Two-Dimensional Shapes	158
Quiz 42: Understanding and Using the Properties of Shapes	162
Quiz 43: Classifying Three-Dimensional Shapes	166
Quiz 44: Comparing and Sorting Three-Dimensional Shapes	170
Quiz 45: Identifying and Drawing Quadrilaterals	174
Quiz 46: Finding the Area of Shapes	178
Quiz 47: Finding the Area of Rectangles	182
Quiz 48: Using Area to Solve Problems	186
Quiz 49: Finding the Area of Composite Shapes	190
Quiz 50: Dividing Shapes into Parts	194

Solving Measurement Problems — 198

Quiz 51: Understanding and Measuring Perimeter	200
Quiz 52: Solving Problems Involving Perimeter	204
Quiz 53: Writing and Measuring Time	208
Quiz 54: Adding and Subtracting Time	210
Quiz 55: Measuring and Estimating Liquid Volume	214
Quiz 56: Solving Word Problems Involving Liquid Volume	216
Quiz 57: Measuring and Estimating Weight	218
Quiz 58: Solving Word Problems Involving Weight	220

Displaying and Interpreting Data — 222

Quiz 59: Using Frequency Tables to Represent Data	224
Quiz 60: Using Dot Plots to Represent Data	228
Quiz 61: Using Pictographs to Represent Data	232
Quiz 62: Using Bar Graphs to Represent Data	236
Quiz 63: Using Frequency Tables to Solve Problems	240
Quiz 64: Using Dot Plots to Solve Problems	244
Quiz 65: Using Pictographs to Solve Problems	248
Quiz 66: Using Bar Graphs to Solve Problems	252

Developing Personal Financial Literacy — 256

Quiz 67: Understanding Labor and Income Relationships	258
Quiz 68: Understanding Scarcity and Cost Relationships	262
Quiz 69: Understanding Credit and Interest	266
Quiz 70: Understanding Saving and Savings Plans	270

Answer Key — 274

INTRODUCTION
For Parents, Teachers, and Tutors

About the Texas State Standards

In 2014-2015, the state of Texas introduced the Revised TEKS for Mathematics. These are a set of standards that describe what students are expected to know. Student learning is based on these standards throughout the year, and the STAAR mathematics tests determine whether students have the skills described in the standards. This quiz book covers all the skills listed in the Revised TEKS for Mathematics that are assessed on the STAAR tests.

Developing Mathematics Skills

The quizzes are divided into the main subject areas of the TEKS standards. There are sections covering all the subject areas listed below.

- Understanding, Representing, and Comparing Whole Numbers
- Representing and Using Fractions
- Computing with Whole Numbers
- Analyzing and Creating Patterns and Relationships
- Understanding and Analyzing the Properties of Shapes
- Solving Measurement Problems
- Displaying and Interpreting Data
- Developing Personal Financial Literacy

For each subject area, the TEKS lists specific skills the student should have. These skills are listed at the start of each section. Within each section, there is one quiz for each specific skill that students need. For each quiz, the difficulty of questions increases from simple to complex. This format introduces the skill, and then encourages students to apply the skill and to develop complete understanding of the skill. Many quizzes also include guided questions that will help students understand what is expected in answers. This will ensure that students gain a thorough and complete understanding of each skill.

Preparing for the STAAR Mathematics Assessments

Students in Texas are assessed each school year by taking the STAAR mathematics assessments. The assessments include questions that test the student's knowledge of the skills, as well as the student's ability to apply the skills to solve a range of mathematical and real-world problems.

This quiz book will provide students with the knowledge and skills required to perform well on the assessments. Students will gain the mathematical knowledge that the tests measure. Students will gain the thorough understanding needed to show knowledge of the mathematics skills, as well as the ability to apply the skills to solve problems. Students will also have experience answering multiple-choice and open-response questions. This will ensure that students have the skills, knowledge, and experience needed to perform well on the tests.

Quizzes 1 to 7

Understanding, Representing, and Comparing Whole Numbers

Directions

Read each question carefully. For each multiple-choice question, fill in the circle for the correct answer. For other types of questions, follow the directions given in the question.

You may use a ruler to help you answer questions. You should answer the questions without using a calculator.

MATHEMATICS SKILLS LIST
For Parents, Teachers, and Tutors

Quizzes 1 through 7 cover these skills from the Texas Essential Knowledge and Skills (TEKS).

Number and Operations

The student applies mathematical process standards to represent and compare whole numbers and understand relationships related to place value.

The student is expected to be able to complete the following tasks.

- Compose and decompose numbers up to 100,000 as a sum of so many ten thousands, so many thousands, so many hundreds, so many tens, and so many ones using objects, pictorial models, and numbers, including expanded notation as appropriate.

- Describe the mathematical relationships found in the base-10 place value system through the hundred thousands place.

- Represent a number on a number line as being between two consecutive multiples of 10; 100; 1,000; or 10,000 and use words to describe relative size of numbers in order to round whole numbers.

- Compare and order whole numbers up to 100,000 and represent comparisons using the symbols >, <, or =.

Student Quiz Book, STAAR Mathematics, Grade 3

Quiz 1: Composing and Decomposing Numbers

1. There are 709 students at Mike's school. Which of these is another way to write 709?

   Ⓐ 7 + 9 Ⓑ 70 + 9 Ⓒ 700 + 9 Ⓓ 700 + 90

2. Which of these shows the number 62,058 in expanded form?

   Ⓐ 620 + 58

   Ⓑ 62,000 + 5 + 8

   Ⓒ 60,000 + 200 + 50 + 8

   Ⓓ 60,000 + 2,000 + 50 + 8

3. Which number is represented by the diagram below?

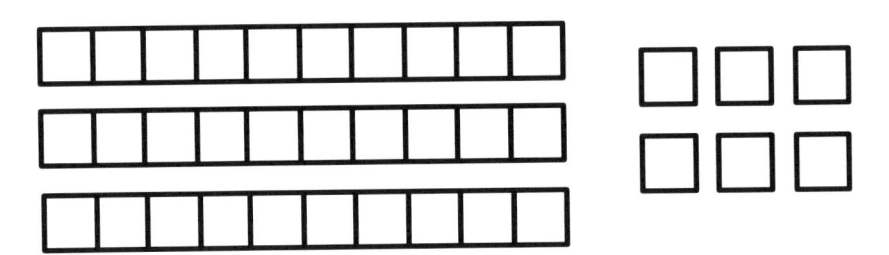

   Ⓐ 18 Ⓑ 36 Ⓒ 180 Ⓓ 360

4. Which number is represented by the place-value blocks below?

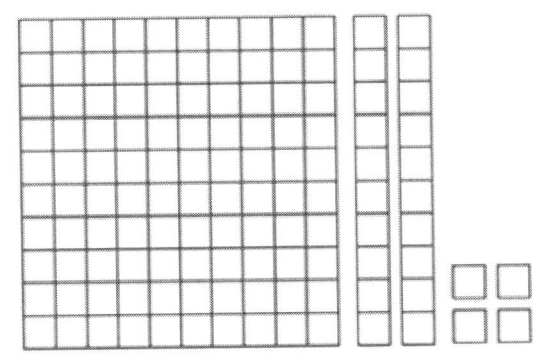

   Answer _____

5. Which of these is the same as 60,000?
   - Ⓐ six hundreds
   - Ⓑ six thousands
   - Ⓒ six ten thousands
   - Ⓓ six hundred thousands

6. Which expression could be used to find the sum of 256 and 71?
   - Ⓐ 2 + 5 + 6 + 7 + 1
   - Ⓑ 20 + 50 + 6 + 70 + 1
   - Ⓒ 200 + 700 + 50 + 6 + 1
   - Ⓓ 200 + 50 + 70 + 6 + 1

7. Write numbers on the lines to complete each sentence correctly.

   89 is the same as ____ tens and ____ ones.

   65 is the same as ____ tens and ____ ones.

   42 is the same as ____ tens and ____ ones.

   975 is the same as ____ hundreds, ____ tens, and ____ ones.

   703 is the same as ____ hundreds, ____ tens, and ____ ones.

   540 is the same as ____ hundreds, ____ tens, and ____ ones.

8. Fill in the chart to show how many hundreds, tens, and ones are in each number.

Number	Hundreds	Tens	Ones
684			
759			
403			
160			

9 Write each number described in words in number form.

forty thousand and six _____

forty thousand and sixty _____

forty thousand six hundred _____

forty-six thousand _____

four hundred thousand six hundred _____

four hundred and sixty thousand _____

four hundred thousand and six _____

four hundred and six thousand _____

four hundred thousand and sixty _____

10 Write numbers on the lines to show each number in expanded form.

1,682   (___ × 1,000) + (___ × 100) + (___ × 10) + (___ × 1)

3,295   (___ × 1,000) + (___ × 100) + (___ × 10) + (___ × 1)

4,083   (___ × 1,000) + (___ × 100) + (___ × 10) + (___ × 1)

62,867 (___ × 10,000) + (___ × 1,000) + (___ × 100) + (___ × 10) + (___ × 1)

91,304 (___ × 10,000) + (___ × 1,000) + (___ × 100) + (___ × 10) + (___ × 1)

86,570 (___ × 10,000) + (___ × 1,000) + (___ × 100) + (___ × 10) + (___ × 1)

11 Write each number represented below on the line.

$7 \times 1{,}000 + 3 \times 100 + 5 \times 10 + 2 \times 1$ _____

$6 \times 1{,}000 + 8 \times 100 + 4 \times 10 + 8 \times 1$ _____

$2 \times 10{,}000 + 7 \times 1{,}000 + 6 \times 10 + 9 \times 1$ _____

$8 \times 10{,}000 + 1 \times 1{,}000 + 6 \times 100 + 8 \times 1$ _____

$4 \times 10{,}000 + 8 \times 1{,}000 + 3 \times 10 + 4 \times 1$ _____

$3 \times 100{,}000 + 5 \times 1{,}000 + 8 \times 100 + 2 \times 10 + 5 \times 1$ _____

$9 \times 100{,}000 + 8 \times 10{,}000 + 3 \times 100 + 5 \times 10$ _____

$5 \times 100{,}000 + 6 \times 10{,}000 + 5 \times 1{,}000 + 7 \times 1$ _____

12 Adam has place-value blocks with the shape shown below.

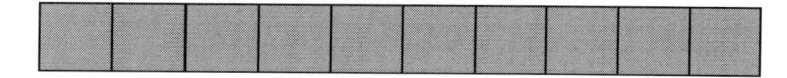

How many of these blocks would Adam need to represent the number 70?

Answer _____ blocks

How many of these blocks would Adam need to represent the number 300?

Answer _____ blocks

How many of these blocks would Adam need to represent the number 370?

Answer _____ blocks

Quiz 2: Identifying Place Value

1. What is the value of the digit 3 in 53,987?

   Ⓐ thirty

   Ⓑ three hundred

   Ⓒ three thousand

   Ⓓ thirty thousand

2. Which number has a 7 in the hundreds place?
   Ⓐ 7,386   Ⓑ 3,879   Ⓒ 2,782   Ⓓ 1,937

3. Which digit is in the ten thousands place in the number 461,823?
   Ⓐ 4   Ⓑ 6   Ⓒ 1   Ⓓ 8

4. Cecilia writes a five-digit number with a 5 in the thousands place. Which number could Cecilia have written?
   Ⓐ 15,368   Ⓑ 52,763   Ⓒ 38,597   Ⓓ 64,350

5. Look at the place-value blocks below.

   Which digit is in the tens place of the number represented?

   Answer _____

   Which digit is in the ones place of the number represented?

   Answer _____

6 Circle all the numbers that have a 6 in the tens place.

36	67	16	60
680	206	365	600
1,674	6,087	5,364	3,426

7 Complete the table below with the missing information.

Number	Digit in the Thousands Place	Digit in the Hundreds Place	Digit in the Tens Place	Digit in the Ones Place
1,289				
6,859				
	1	3	5	6
	7	9	2	4

8 Write a number that meets each description given below.

a two-digit number with a 6 in the tens place _____

a three-digit number with a 2 in the hundreds place _____

a four-digit number with a 7 in the hundreds place _____

a four-digit number with a 1 in the thousands place _____

a five-digit number with a 9 in the thousands place _____

a five-digit number with a 5 in the ten thousands place _____

Quiz 3: Understanding Place Value Relationships

1 How many times greater is 35,000 than 35?

    Ⓐ 10   Ⓑ 100   Ⓒ 1,000   Ⓓ 10,000

2 Which number has a 6 that represents a value ten times greater than the value represented by the 6 in 21,608?

    Ⓐ 63,852   Ⓑ 26,701   Ⓒ 48,269   Ⓓ 21,846

3 In the number 78,721, how much greater is the value represented by the 7 in the ten thousands place than the value represented by the 7 in the hundreds place?

    Ⓐ 1   Ⓑ 10   Ⓒ 100   Ⓓ 1,000

4 In the number below, how many times greater is the number represented by the digit in the thousands place than the number represented by the digit in the hundreds place?

$$182,235$$

    Ⓐ 1   Ⓑ 10   Ⓒ 100   Ⓓ 1,000

5 Which pair of numbers correctly completes the equation?

$$\_\_\_\_ \times 100 = \_\_\_\_$$

    Ⓐ 53 and 53,000   Ⓑ 530 and 5,300

    Ⓒ 53 and 530   Ⓓ 530 and 53,000

6 What is the value of the expression below?

$$28,000 \div 280$$

    Ⓐ 1   Ⓑ 10   Ⓒ 100   Ⓓ 1,000

7. In which pairs of numbers does the 5 in the first number represent a value 10 times greater than the 5 in the second number? Select all the correct answers.

- ☐ 500 and 523
- ☐ 503 and 57
- ☐ 5,860 and 2,050
- ☐ 3,547 and 6,185
- ☐ 15,948 and 26,579
- ☐ 27,582 and 37,950

8. In which of these does a missing number of 100 make the equation true? Select all the correct answers.

- ☐ 67 × _____ = 6,070
- ☐ 3,406 × _____ = 34,600
- ☐ 25 × _____ = 2,500
- ☐ 7,854 × _____ = 78,540
- ☐ 823 × _____ = 80,023
- ☐ 6,002 × _____ = 600,200
- ☐ 107 × _____ = 107,000
- ☐ 33,025 × _____ = 330,250

9. Complete the table below with the missing numbers.

Number	Number × 10	Number × 100	Number × 1000
42			
685			
271			
	350		
	2,840		
		309,500	
		22,400	

10 For each pair of numbers, list how much greater the value of the 9 is in the first number than the second.

397	359	_____ times greater
921	609	_____ times greater
3,698	2,509	_____ times greater
9,361	2,493	_____ times greater
1,975	8,349	_____ times greater
39,008	37,009	_____ times greater
96,112	76,903	_____ times greater
239,622	281,944	_____ times greater
950,001	590,001	_____ times greater

11 Write the missing number on the line to make each equation correct. Then write a multiplication equation that shows that the equation is correct. The first one has been completed for you.

300 ÷ __10__ = 30   __30__ × __10__ = __300__

600 ÷ _____ = 6   _____ × _____ = _____

2,400 ÷ _____ = 24   _____ × _____ = _____

11,000 ÷ _____ = 11   _____ × _____ = _____

68,000 ÷ _____ = 680   _____ × _____ = _____

12 Selma is putting pennies into piles of 100. Selma makes 15 piles of 100 pennies. How many pennies does Selma have in all?

Show your work.

Answer _____ pennies

13 A box of safety pins contains 1,000 pins. Damien buys 12 boxes of pins. How many safety pins did Damien buy?

Show your work.

Answer _____ safety pins

14 A teacher ordered 32 textbooks for $100 each. What would be the total cost of the order?

Show your work.

Answer $_____

15 Cameron completes the calculation below.

$$30{,}000 \div 3000 = 10$$

Explain how place value shows that the calculation is correct.

_____

_____

Quiz 4: Using Place Value to Compare Numbers

1. Which digit in 17,340 proves that the number is greater than 16,230?
   - Ⓐ 1
   - Ⓑ 7
   - Ⓒ 3
   - Ⓓ 4

2. Which digit in the number 4,829 proves that the number is greater than 4,357?
   - Ⓐ 4
   - Ⓑ 8
   - Ⓒ 2
   - Ⓓ 9

3. Which number is less than the number below?

   8 thousands + 6 hundreds + 9 tens

   - Ⓐ 8 thousands + 9 hundreds + 4 tens
   - Ⓑ 8 thousands + 5 hundreds + 7 tens
   - Ⓒ 9 thousands + 4 hundreds + 5 tens
   - Ⓓ 9 thousands + 6 hundreds + 2 tens

4. Samuel used place-value blocks to represent the number below. Jenna added 2 more hundreds blocks and 4 more ones blocks.

   Which number would be represented by all the blocks?

   Answer _____

5 Choose one number from each column to create each three-digit number described. Write the number on the blank line.

Hundreds	Tens	Ones
6	9	3
9	5	5
7	4	8
1	3	9

an even number greater than 980 _____

the lowest three-digit number possible _____

the greatest three-digit number possible _____

a number between 740 and 744 _____

a number less than 140 that is divisible by 5 _____

a number greater than 654 but less than 657 _____

a number 10 greater than 148 _____

a number 100 less than 759 _____

6 Write the correct number on each blank line.

Which number is ten less than 458? _____

Which number is two hundreds more than 365? _____

Which number is six more than 421? _____

Which number is three tens more than 147? _____

Which number is five hundreds less than 786? _____

Which number is one less than 564? _____

Which number is one hundred less than 836? _____

Which number is seven tens less than 978? _____

7 Complete the missing number to make each number sentence correct.

262 + _____ = 282	385 + _____ = 985	85 − _____ = 75
197 + _____ = 597	799 − _____ = 709	43 + _____ = 48
350 − _____ = 310	408 + _____ = 478	11 + _____ = 41
485 − _____ = 185	512 − _____ = 112	64 − _____ = 34
897 + _____ = 899	957 + _____ = 987	57 − _____ = 37

8 What are the two smallest 3-digit numbers that can be made using the digits 6, 3, and 7? Each digit must be used only once in each number.

Answer _____ and _____

On the lines below, explain how you found your answer.

_____

_____

_____

9 The table shows the number of sales a bookstore had on five days.

Day	Monday	Tuesday	Wednesday	Thursday	Friday
Sales	3,287	3,650	4,002	3,995	4,137

Which day had the least sales? _____

Which day had the most sales? _____

Which day had between 4,000 and 4,100 sales? _____

Which day had between 3,990 and 4,000 sales? _____

10 Complete the blank spaces to show four different ways to represent the number 26,573.

____ ten-thousands, ____ thousands, ____ hundreds, ____ tens, ____ ones

____ ten-thousands, ____ thousands, ____ hundreds, ____ ones

____ thousands, ____ hundreds, ____ tens, ____ ones

____ thousands, ____ tens, ____ ones

11 Kevin wrote the three numbers below on the board.

$$80{,}000 \qquad 3{,}000 \qquad 700$$

How many hundreds are in 80,000? _____ hundreds

How many thousands are in 80,000? _____ thousands

How many hundreds are in 3,000? _____ hundreds

How many thousands are in 3,000? _____ thousands

How many tens are in 700? _____ tens

How many hundreds are in 700? _____ hundreds

Use your answers to complete the equations below.

80,000 = _____ × 100   800,000 = _____ × 1,000

3,000 = _____ × 100   3,000 = _____ × 1,000

700 = _____ × 10   700 = _____ × 100

Quiz 5: Representing Numbers on Number Lines

1   Which point on the number line represents 24?

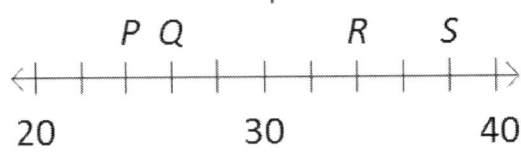

         P Q   R S
       20   30   40

Ⓐ point P   Ⓑ point Q   Ⓒ point R   Ⓓ point S

2   Which point on the number line represents 55?

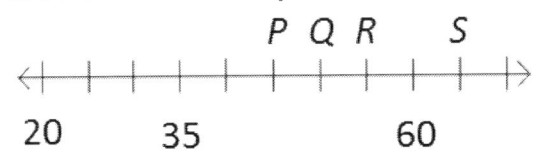

               P Q R   S
       20   35   60

Ⓐ point P   Ⓑ point Q   Ⓒ point R   Ⓓ point S

3   Which number is plotted on the number line below?

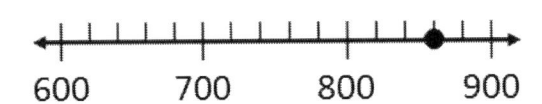

      600   700   800   900

Answer _____

4   What number does point Q represent?

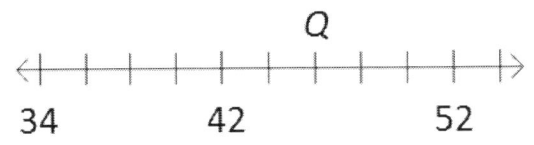

                        Q
       34   42   52

Answer _____

5   What number does point T represent?

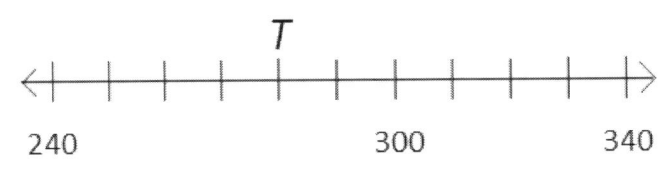

             T
      240   300   340

Answer _____

6 Plot the following points on the number line below.

- Point *X* at the number 55
- Point *Y* at the number 40 greater than 55
- Point *Z* at the number 30 less than 55

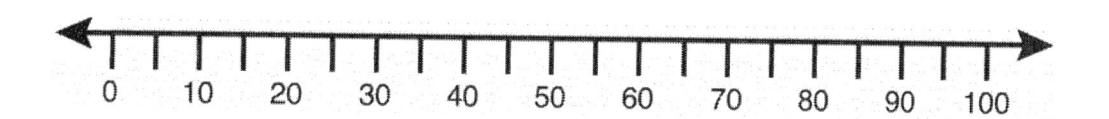

7 Plot the approximate positions of each of the points below.

- Point *J* at the number 23
- Point *K* at the number 41
- Point *L* at the number 68
- Point *M* at the number 96

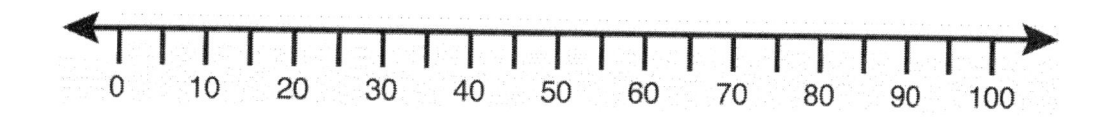

8 Plot the following points on the number line below.

- Point *A* at the number 2,400
- Point *B* at the number 2,560
- Point *C* at the number 2,680
- Point *D* at the number 2,820

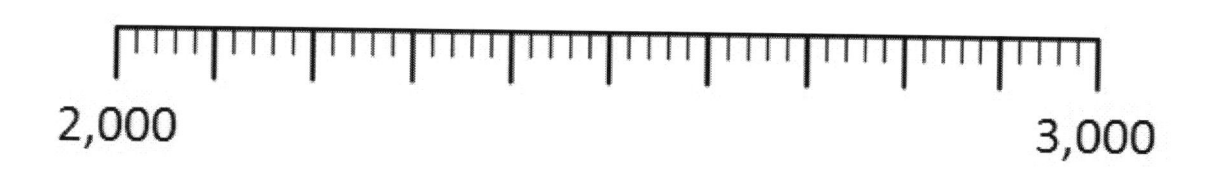

Quiz 6: Rounding Whole Numbers

1 What is 687 rounded to the nearest ten?

Ⓐ 600 Ⓑ 680 Ⓒ 690 Ⓓ 700

2 What is 374 rounded to the nearest hundred?

Ⓐ 300 Ⓑ 370 Ⓒ 380 Ⓓ 400

3 Select all the numbers that will equal 650 when rounded to the nearest ten.

☐ 643 ☐ 637 ☐ 647

☐ 659 ☐ 653 ☐ 665

☐ 652 ☐ 605 ☐ 651

4 Select all the numbers that will equal 800 when rounded to the nearest hundred.

☐ 842 ☐ 803 ☐ 861

☐ 870 ☐ 848 ☐ 817

☐ 894 ☐ 826 ☐ 855

5 What is 774 rounded to the nearest ten and nearest hundred?

Nearest ten _____   Nearest hundred _____

6 What is 1,227 rounded to the nearest ten and nearest hundred?

Nearest ten _____   Nearest hundred _____

7 Complete the table by rounding each number to the nearest 10 and the nearest 100.

Number	Nearest 10	Nearest 100
687		
524		
186		
359		
62		
725		
133		
805		
261		
909		

8 Complete the table by writing in a possible number for the original number.

Number	Nearest 10	Nearest 100
	430	400
	90	100
	680	700
	130	100
	110	100
	190	200
	690	700
	460	500
	340	300
	710	700

9 Complete each statement that describes which digit is used to decide whether to round the number up or down.

681 to the nearest ten   the digit ___, which is in the _____ place

7,486 to the nearest ten   the digit ___, which is in the _____ place

547 to the nearest hundred   the digit ___, which is in the _____ place

1,352 to the nearest hundred   the digit ___, which is in the _____ place

10 On the number line below, plot all the whole numbers that equal 90 when rounded to the nearest ten.

```
←——+——+——+——+——+——+——+——+——+——+——+——+——+——+——+——+——+——+——+——+——→
   80                             90                            100
```

11 Complete the table by filling in the missing numbers.

Number Rounded to the Nearest Ten	Lowest Possible Number	Highest Possible Number
50		
280		
400		
1,760		

12 Round 8,782 to the nearest ten and the nearest hundred.

Nearest ten _____   Nearest hundred _____

Explain how you worked out whether to round the number up or down.

_____

_____

_____

13 The table shows how many points Greg's basketball team scored in each game. Greg rounds the scores to the nearest ten.

Game	1	2	3	4	5	6	7	8
Score	87	76	92	72	81	66	94	79

In which two games did the team score 70 points, to the nearest ten?

_____ and _____

In which three games did the team score 90 points, to the nearest ten?

_____ , _____ , and _____

In the next game, the score to the nearest ten was 60. What is the most the actual score could be? Explain your answer.

_____

_____

To estimate the total points scored, Greg rounds all the scores to the nearest hundred and adds them. Would the estimate be more or less than the actual total points scored? Explain your answer.

_____

_____

14 Michael states that to the nearest hundred, there are 700 students at his school. Jessica states that there must be at least 700 students, but no more than 749 students. Describe the mistake that Jessica made.

_____

_____

_____

Quiz 7: Comparing and Ordering Whole Numbers

1   Which number is between 5,137 and 5,341?

   Ⓐ 5,403   Ⓑ 5,068   Ⓒ 5,292   Ⓓ 5,730

2   Anderson's class took a history test. All the students finished the test in between 111 and 143 minutes. Which of these could have been Anderson's time?

   Ⓐ 109 minutes   Ⓑ 137 minutes   Ⓒ 148 minutes   Ⓓ 153 minutes

3   Which number could be placed on the blank line to complete the statement below correctly?

$$57{,}382 < _____$$

   Ⓐ 55,200   Ⓑ 57,295   Ⓒ 58,106   Ⓓ 56,999

4   Which number has the smallest digit in the thousands place?

   Ⓐ 47,386   Ⓑ 63,879   Ⓒ 12,782   Ⓓ 51,937

5   Which statements correctly compare two numbers? Select all the correct answers.

   ☐ 538 < 583   ☐ 385 > 358

   ☐ 835 > 853   ☐ 538 > 835

   ☐ 385 < 583   ☐ 358 > 583

6   Place the numbers below in order from lowest to highest. Write 1, 2, 3, and 4 on the lines to show the order.

   ___ 5,198   ___ 5,217   ___ 5,224   ___ 5,179

7 Write the correct number on each blank line.

Which number is ten less than 5,697? _____

Which number is four hundreds more than 24,137? _____

Which number is five more than 102,002? _____

Which number is three tens more than 2,145? _____

Which number is six hundreds less than 67,897? _____

Which number is one less than 333,648? _____

Which number is two hundreds less than 447,852? _____

Which number is six tens less than 999,887? _____

Which number is two thousands less than 376,845? _____

Which number is ten thousand more than 435,710? _____

8 Use the four digits below to create each number described. Each digit should be used exactly once in each number.

$$3 \quad 5 \quad 4 \quad 8$$

The lowest four-digit number possible. _____

The greatest four-digit number possible. _____

A number between 3,850 and 3,860. _____

An odd number between 5,400 and 5,500. _____

The lowest odd number possible. _____

An even number greater than 8,000. _____

9 Place-value blocks were used to represent a number.

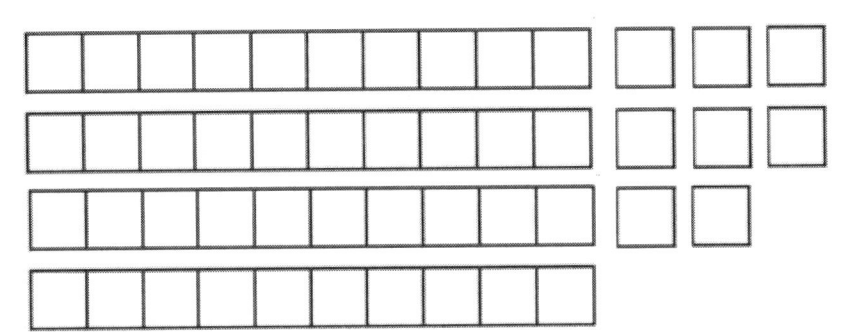

[place-value blocks diagram showing 3 tens rods and 8 ones, 2 tens rods and 3 ones, 2 tens rods and 2 ones, 1 tens rod — actual counts: row 1: ten-rod of 10 squares, ten-rod of 10 squares, and 3 single squares; row 2: ten-rod, ten-rod, 2 single squares; row 3: ten-rod, ten-rod, 1 single square; row 4: ten-rod]

In the space below, draw place-value blocks to represent a number 20 less than the number represented above.

What number is represented above? _____

10 Add the symbol <, >, or = to each empty box to make each statement true.

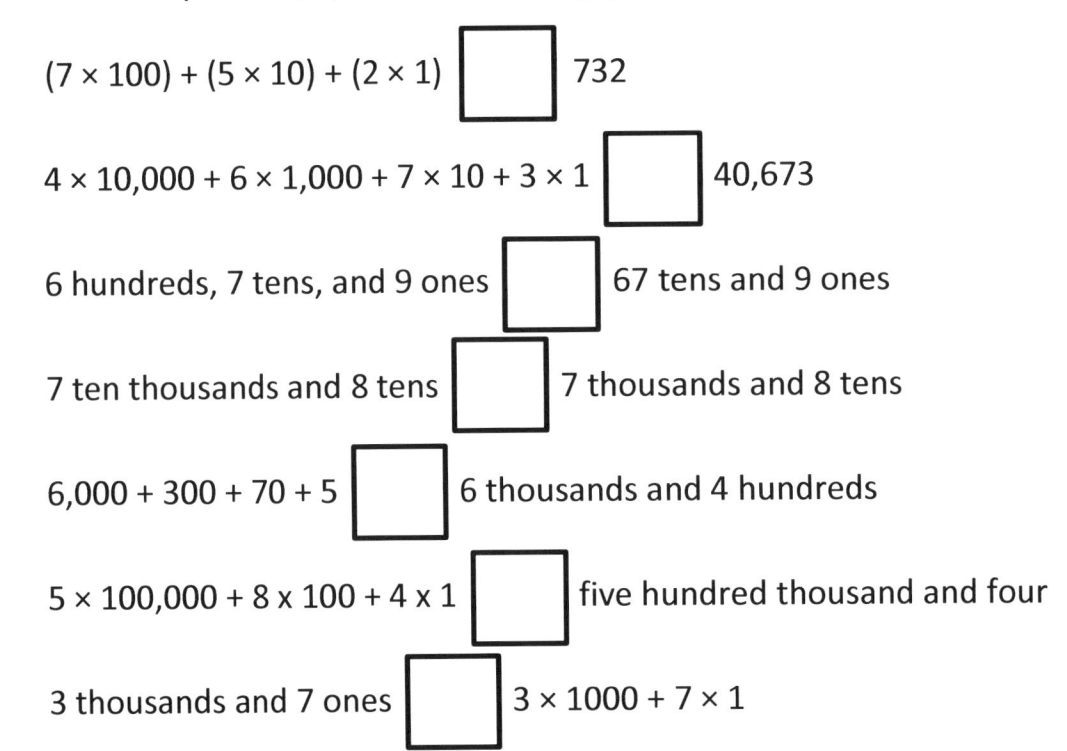

(7 × 100) + (5 × 10) + (2 × 1) ☐ 732

4 × 10,000 + 6 × 1,000 + 7 × 10 + 3 × 1 ☐ 40,673

6 hundreds, 7 tens, and 9 ones ☐ 67 tens and 9 ones

7 ten thousands and 8 tens ☐ 7 thousands and 8 tens

6,000 + 300 + 70 + 5 ☐ 6 thousands and 4 hundreds

5 × 100,000 + 8 × 100 + 4 × 1 ☐ five hundred thousand and four

3 thousands and 7 ones ☐ 3 × 1000 + 7 × 1

11 Write numbers on the lines to complete each sentence correctly.

60 is the same as _____ tens.

64 is the same as _____ tens and _____ ones.

Explain how this shows that 64 is greater than 60.

_____

_____

12 Write numbers on the lines to complete each sentence correctly.

385 is the same as _____ hundreds, _____ tens, and _____ ones.

345 is the same as _____ hundreds, _____ tens, and _____ ones.

Explain how this shows that 345 is less than 385.

_____

_____

13 The table shows the number of steps taken by five students one day.

Graham	Leanna	Ryder	Warren	Rosie
12,058	12,854	11,965	11,530	12,507

Place the numbers in order from the least to the greatest.

_____ < _____ < _____ < _____ < _____

Jayla took more steps than Warren, but fewer steps than Ryder. List four possible numbers that could be the number of steps that Jayla took.

_____ _____ _____ _____

Quizzes 8 to 16

Representing and Using Fractions

Directions

Read each question carefully. For each multiple-choice question, fill in the circle for the correct answer. For other types of questions, follow the directions given in the question.

You may use a ruler to help you answer questions. You should answer the questions without using a calculator.

MATHEMATICS SKILLS LIST
For Parents, Teachers, and Tutors

Quizzes 8 through 16 cover these skills from the Texas Essential Knowledge and Skills (TEKS).

Number and Operations

The student applies mathematical process standards to represent and explain fractional units.

The student is expected to be able to complete the following tasks.

- Represent fractions greater than zero and less than or equal to one using concrete objects and pictorial models, including strip diagrams and number lines.
- Determine the corresponding fraction greater than zero and less than or equal to one given a specified point on a number line.
- Explain that the unit fraction $1/b$ represents the quantity formed by one part of a whole that has been partitioned into b equal parts where b is a non-zero whole number.
- Compose and decompose a fraction a/b with a numerator greater than zero and less than or equal to b as a sum of parts $1/b$.
- Solve problems involving partitioning an object or a set of objects among two or more recipients using pictorial representations of fractions.
- Represent equivalent fractions using a variety of objects and pictorial models, including number lines.
- Explain that two fractions are equivalent if and only if they are both represented by the same point on the number line or represent the same portion of a same size whole for an area model.
- Compare two fractions having the same numerator or denominator in problems by reasoning about their sizes and justifying the conclusion using symbols, words, objects, and pictorial models.

Geometry and Measurement

The student applies mathematical process standards to select appropriate units, strategies, and tools to solve problems involving customary and metric measurement.

The student is expected to be able to complete the following tasks.

- Represent fractions of halves, fourths, and eighths as distances from zero on a number line.

Quiz 8: Representing Fractions with Diagrams

1 Which of these has $\frac{2}{3}$ shaded?

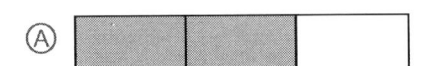

Ⓐ Ⓑ

Ⓒ Ⓓ

2 Which diagram is shaded to represent $\frac{1}{4}$?

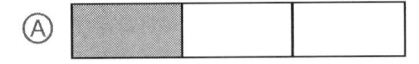

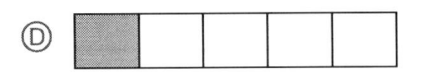

Ⓐ Ⓑ

Ⓒ Ⓓ

3 What fraction of the circle below is shaded?

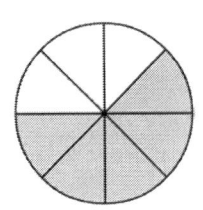

Ⓐ $\frac{5}{8}$ Ⓑ $\frac{3}{5}$ Ⓒ $\frac{2}{3}$ Ⓓ $\frac{3}{4}$

4 What fraction of the hexagon below is shaded?

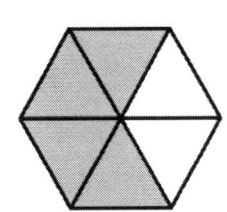

Ⓐ $\frac{2}{4}$ Ⓑ $\frac{3}{2}$ Ⓒ $\frac{2}{6}$ Ⓓ $\frac{2}{3}$

Student Quiz Book, STAAR Mathematics, Grade 3

5 A pizza was cut into 8 equal pieces. The picture below shows the pieces of pizza left. What fraction of the pizza is left?

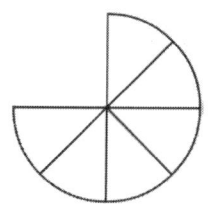

Ⓐ $\frac{1}{8}$ Ⓑ $\frac{1}{4}$ Ⓒ $\frac{3}{4}$ Ⓓ $\frac{3}{8}$

6 Which shapes have $\frac{1}{2}$ the squares shaded? Select all the correct answers.

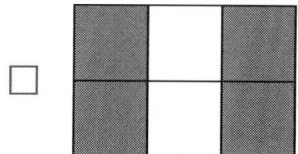

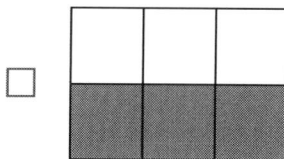

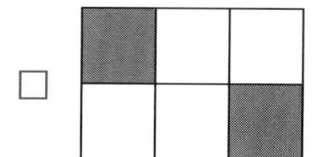

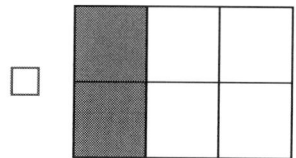

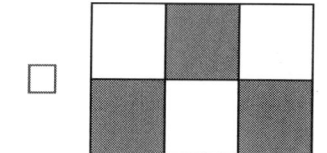

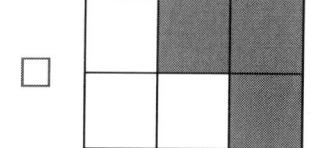

7 Vernon bought a carton of eggs and used 1 egg. The eggs left in the carton are shown below.

What fraction of the eggs are left in the carton? _____

8 Duncan's gas tank gauge shows how empty or full the tank is. Which statement describes the gas tank when the gauge is as below?

Ⓐ The gas tank is half full.

Ⓑ The gas tank is one quarter full.

Ⓒ The gas tank is three quarters full.

Ⓓ The gas tank is one third full.

9 For each shape below, shade the fraction of squares given.

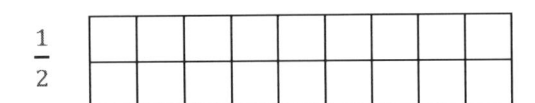

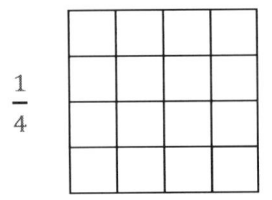

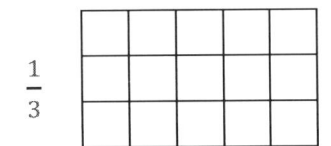

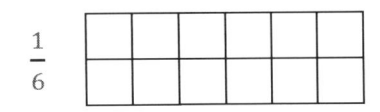

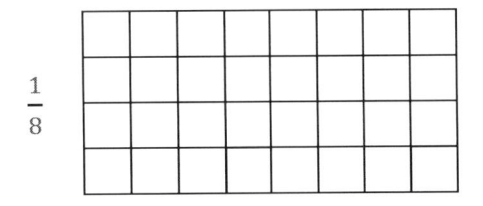

$\frac{1}{2}$

$\frac{1}{4}$

$\frac{1}{3}$

$\frac{1}{6}$

$\frac{1}{8}$

10 The flags of 12 different countries are shown below. Circle all the flags that are divided into equal thirds.

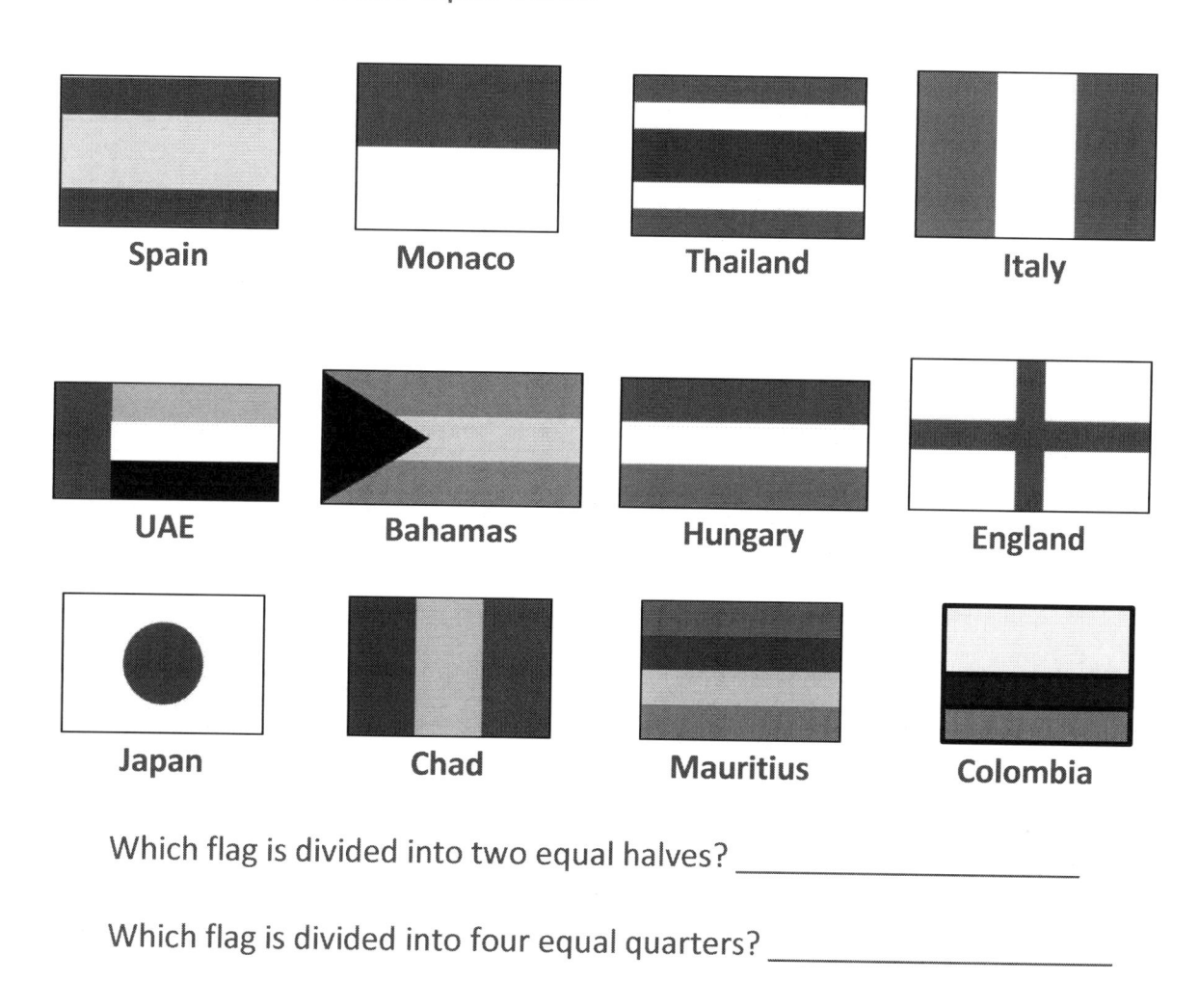

Spain   **Monaco**   **Thailand**   **Italy**

UAE   **Bahamas**   **Hungary**   **England**

Japan   **Chad**   **Mauritius**   **Colombia**

Which flag is divided into two equal halves? _____

Which flag is divided into four equal quarters? _____

11 Koby divided a triangle into equal pieces and then cut out one piece of the triangle, as shown below.

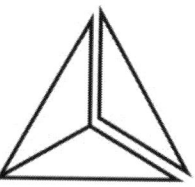

What fraction of the whole is the piece he cut out? _____

What fraction of the whole remains? _____

Quiz 9: Modeling Fractions

1 What fraction of the shape below is shaded?

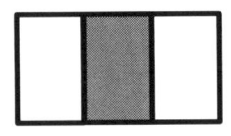

Ⓐ $\frac{1}{2}$ Ⓑ $\frac{1}{3}$ Ⓒ $\frac{1}{4}$ Ⓓ $\frac{1}{6}$

2 Harriet made a bookmark by drawing stripes on a piece of cardboard, as shown below.

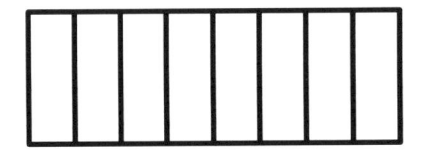

What fraction of the cardboard does each stripe cover?

Ⓐ $\frac{1}{2}$ Ⓑ $\frac{1}{4}$ Ⓒ $\frac{1}{6}$ Ⓓ $\frac{1}{8}$

3 Which of these shows one way to divide a hexagon into two parts with equal areas?

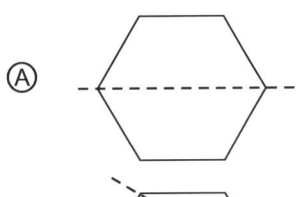

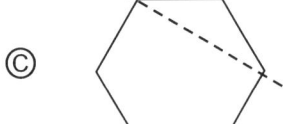

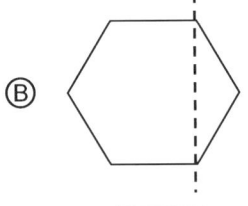

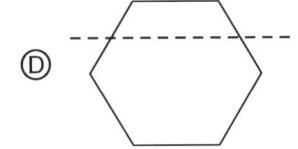

Ⓐ   Ⓑ   Ⓒ   Ⓓ

4 Which of these shapes can be divided into two equal triangles? Select all the correct answers.

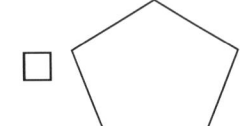

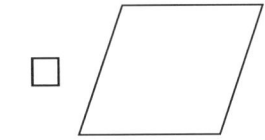

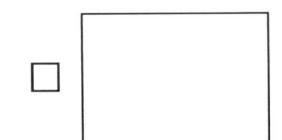

5 Divide each shape below into two triangles of equal areas.

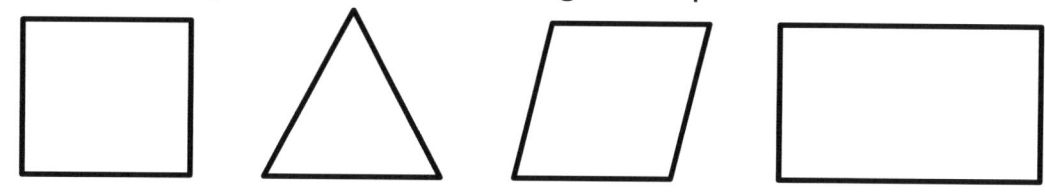

6 Bailey divided circles into two equal parts, as shown below. Draw additional lines to divide the other circles into the number of parts given.

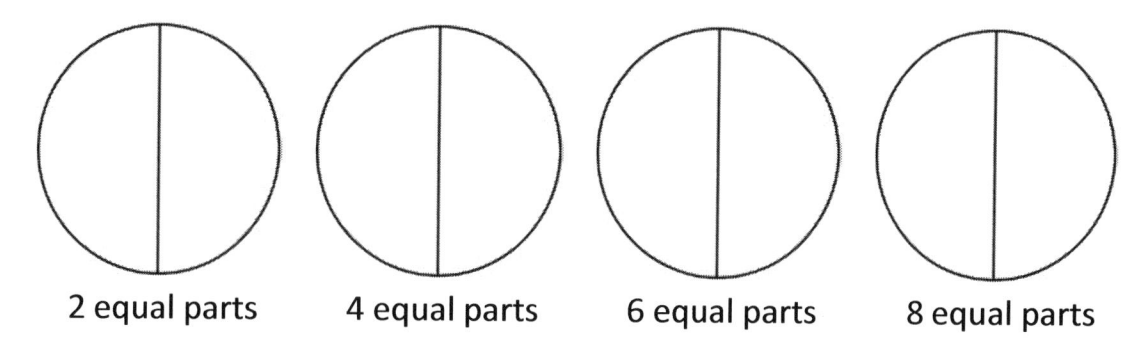

2 equal parts   4 equal parts   6 equal parts   8 equal parts

7 Divide each rectangle shown below into the number of parts given.

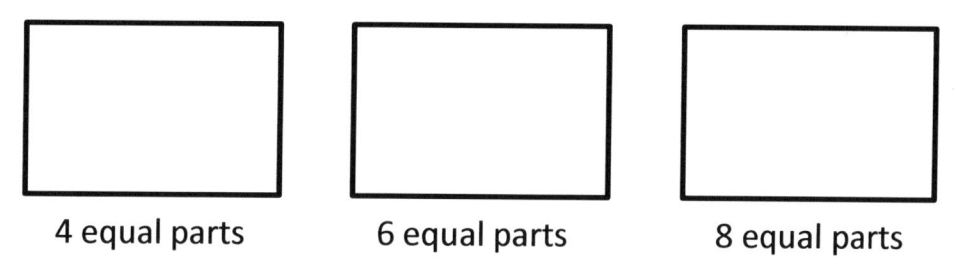

4 equal parts   6 equal parts   8 equal parts

8 For each shape shown below, divide it into 3 parts with equal areas.

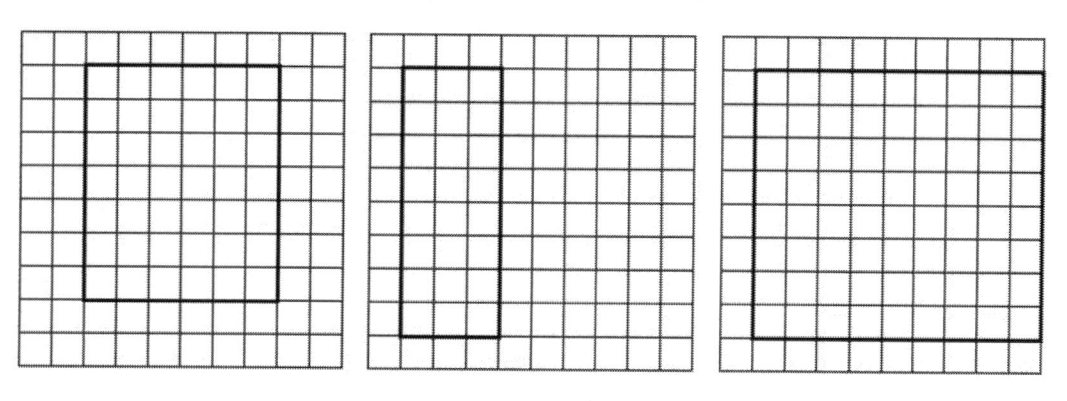

Quiz 10: Representing Fractions on Number Lines

1 Which fraction is represented on the number line below?

Ⓐ $\frac{5}{6}$ Ⓑ $\frac{4}{5}$ Ⓒ $\frac{1}{6}$ Ⓓ $\frac{1}{5}$

2 Which fraction is represented on the number line below?

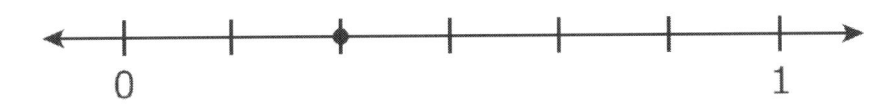

Ⓐ $\frac{2}{3}$ Ⓑ $\frac{2}{4}$ Ⓒ $\frac{2}{5}$ Ⓓ $\frac{2}{6}$

3 What fractions is the number line below divided into?

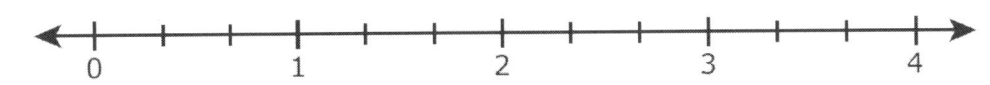

Ⓐ halves   Ⓑ thirds   Ⓒ quarters   Ⓓ eighths

4 Plot the fractions $\frac{1}{4}, \frac{1}{2}, 1\frac{1}{4}$, and $1\frac{3}{4}$ on the number line below.

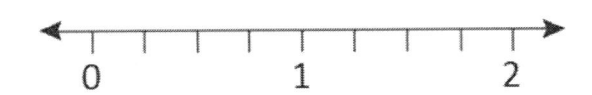

5 Divide the number line below into the same fractions as the rectangle below. Then plot the point that represents the fraction of the rectangle that is shaded.

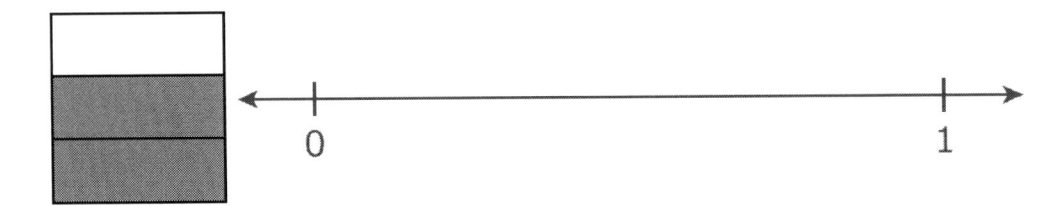

6 Plot the fractions $\frac{1}{8}, \frac{4}{8}, \frac{5}{8}$, and $\frac{7}{8}$ on the number line below. Then use the number line to answer the questions below.

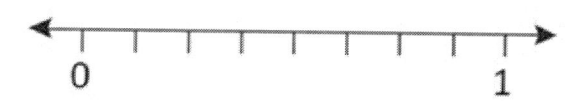

Which two fractions have a distance of $\frac{1}{8}$ between them? _____ and _____

Which two fractions have a distance of $\frac{2}{8}$ between them? _____ and _____

Which fraction is equivalent to $\frac{1}{2}$? _____

What is the distance between $\frac{7}{8}$ and 1? _____

7 Plot the fractions $\frac{1}{3}, 1\frac{1}{3}, 1\frac{2}{3}$, and $2\frac{1}{3}$ on the number line below. Then use the number line to answer the questions below.

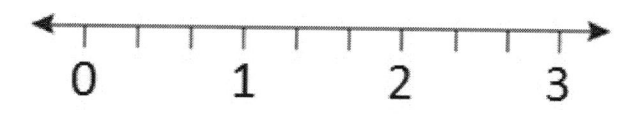

Which two fractions have a distance of $\frac{1}{3}$ between them? _____ and _____

At which whole number would $\frac{3}{3}$ be plotted? _____

Which fraction plotted is closest to 1? _____

Which two fractions plotted would $\frac{2}{3}$ be plotted between? _____ and _____

What is the distance between $2\frac{1}{3}$ and 3? _____

8 Plot the fractions $\frac{1}{6}, \frac{2}{6}, \frac{5}{6}, 1\frac{3}{6}$ and $1\frac{5}{6}$ on the number line below. Then use the number line to answer the questions below.

Which two fractions have a distance of $\frac{2}{6}$ between them? ____ and ____

Which fraction plotted is closest to 1? ____

Which fraction is equivalent to $\frac{1}{3}$? ____

Which fraction is equivalent to $1\frac{1}{2}$? ____

Which fraction plotted is $\frac{2}{3}$ less than 1? ____

What is the distance between $1\frac{5}{6}$ and 1? ____

9 The points on the number line represent the distances of four streets from Main Street. James Street is 1 mile from Main Street.

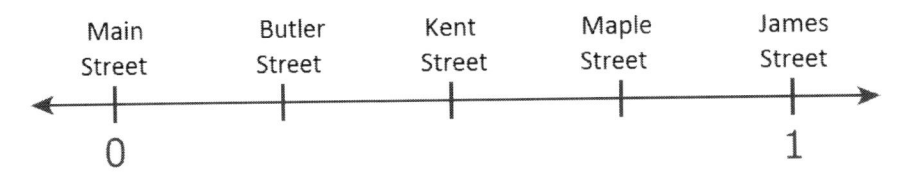

Which street is $\frac{1}{2}$ mile from Main Street? _____

Which street is $\frac{3}{4}$ mile from Main Street? _____

How far is the walk from Butler Street to Kent Street? _____ mile

How far is the walk from Kent Street to James Street? _____ mile

Which street is $\frac{1}{2}$ mile from Maple Street? _____

Student Quiz Book, STAAR Mathematics, Grade 3

10   Plot the fractions listed on the number line below.

$$\frac{1}{2}, \frac{2}{3}, \frac{1}{6}, 1\frac{1}{3}, 1\frac{5}{6}$$

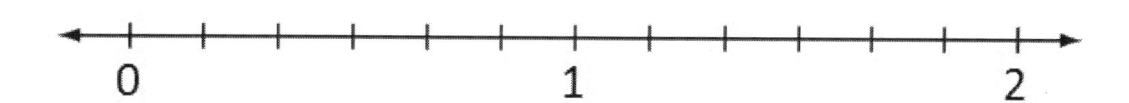

<-----+----+----+----+----+----+----+----+----+----+----+----->
0   1   2

11   A charity run has checkpoints at equal distances. The number line below shows the distance of checkpoints A through G.

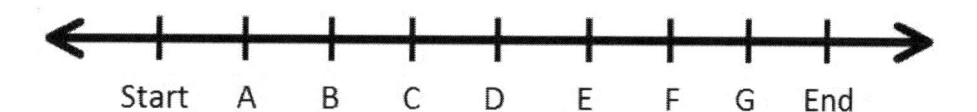

<-----+----+----+----+----+----+----+----+----->
   Start A   B   C   D   E   F   G   End

What fraction of the run is completed at Checkpoint A? _____

Explain how you found the answer on the lines below.

_____

_____

_____

At which checkpoint is half the run complete? _____

Explain how you found the answer on the lines below.

_____

_____

_____

43

Quiz 11: Understanding Unit Fractions

1 What fraction of the figure below is shaded?

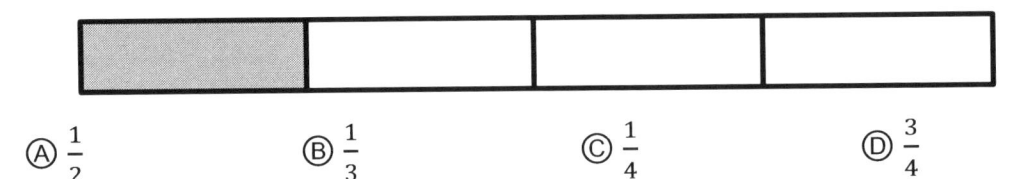

Ⓐ $\frac{1}{2}$ Ⓑ $\frac{1}{3}$ Ⓒ $\frac{1}{4}$ Ⓓ $\frac{3}{4}$

2 Moira cut a length of ribbon into 3 equal pieces. What fraction of the whole is each piece?

Ⓐ $\frac{1}{3}$ Ⓑ $\frac{3}{3}$ Ⓒ $\frac{1}{1}$ Ⓓ $\frac{3}{1}$

3 Justine divided a brownie into equal pieces, as shown below.

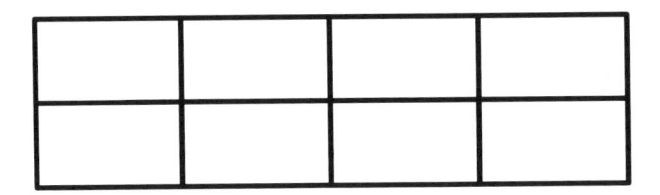

What fraction of the whole is each piece? _____

Justine ate 3 pieces. What fraction of the whole did Justine eat? _____

4 Draw lines to divide the rectangle below into 3 equal parts.

What fraction of the whole is each part? _____

5 Draw lines to divide the hexagon into 6 equal parts.

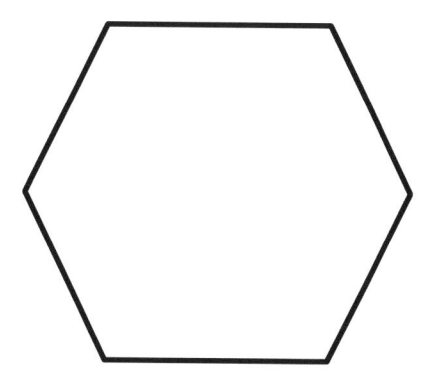

What fraction of the whole is each part? _____

6 Draw a line to divide each shape shown below into two equal halves.

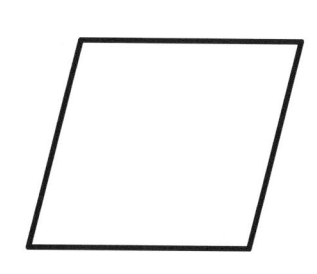

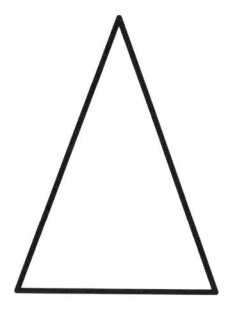

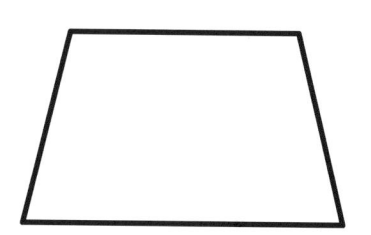

7 The shaded squares on the grid are a third of a rectangle. Shade squares to complete the whole rectangle.

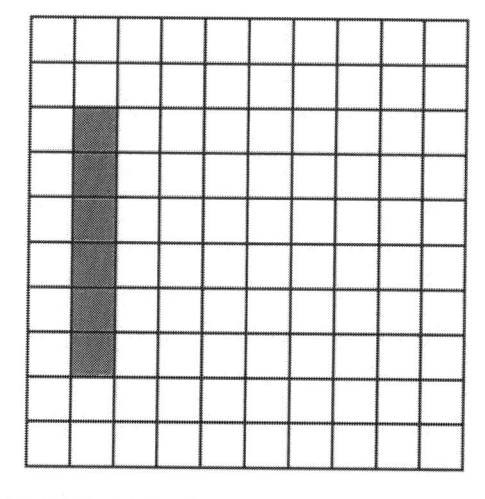

8   Sam has 16 candies. He divides them into 4 equal groups.

What fraction of the total candies is each group? _____

Joseph has 20 candies. He divides them into 4 equal groups.

What fraction of the total candies is each group? _____

Is there the same number of candies in each of Sam's groups as in each of Joseph's groups? Explain why or why not.

_____

_____

_____

9   Lennox divides a rectangle into two parts and shades one part, as shown.

Lennox states that she has shaded $\frac{1}{2}$ the shape. Explain why Lennox's statement is incorrect.

_____

_____

_____

10 Divide the rectangle below into 8 equal areas. Shade $\frac{3}{8}$ of the rectangle.

Divide the rectangle below into 4 equal areas. Shade $\frac{3}{4}$ of the rectangle.

Use the shaded models to compare the fractions $\frac{3}{8}$ and $\frac{3}{4}$.

_____

_____

_____

11 The rectangle and hexagon below are both divided into 6 equal areas.

What fraction of the rectangle is shaded? _____

What fraction of the hexagon is shaded? _____

Is the shaded area of the rectangle equal to the shaded area of the hexagon? Explain why or why not.

_____

_____

_____

Quiz 12: Composing and Decomposing Fractions

1 Which expression represents the fraction of the figure that is shaded?

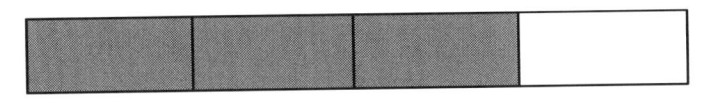

Ⓐ $\frac{1}{4} + \frac{1}{4} + \frac{1}{4}$

Ⓑ $\frac{3}{4} + \frac{3}{4} + \frac{3}{4}$

Ⓒ $\frac{1}{3} + \frac{1}{3} + \frac{1}{3}$

Ⓓ $\frac{1}{4} + \frac{2}{4} + \frac{3}{4}$

2 Darcy has completed $\frac{3}{8}$ of his science project. What fraction of the science project remains?

Ⓐ $\frac{5}{8}$ Ⓑ $\frac{1}{8}$ Ⓒ $\frac{3}{8}$ Ⓓ $\frac{7}{8}$

3 Ciera divides a piece of cardboard into 10 equal strips. She paints $\frac{1}{2}$ of the strips blue. She paints the remainder of the strips red.

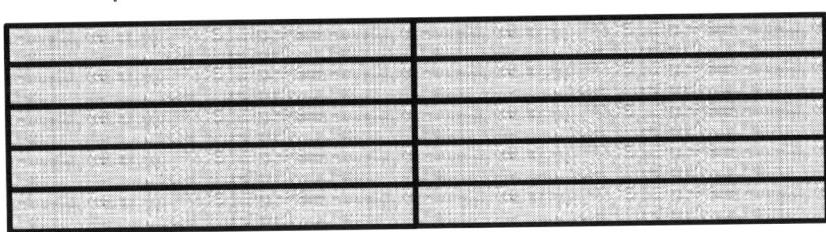

What fraction of the strips are painted red?

Ⓐ $\frac{1}{4}$ Ⓑ $\frac{9}{10}$ Ⓒ $\frac{1}{2}$ Ⓓ $\frac{1}{10}$

4 Which expressions have a sum equal to $\frac{5}{8}$? Select all the correct answers.

☐ $\frac{1}{8} + \frac{5}{8}$ ☐ $\frac{2}{8} + \frac{3}{8}$ ☐ $\frac{1}{8} + \frac{4}{8}$

☐ $\frac{7}{8} + \frac{2}{8}$ ☐ $\frac{2}{4} + \frac{3}{4}$ ☐ $\frac{5}{4} + \frac{1}{4}$

5 Complete the missing fraction in each sum.

$\frac{3}{6} + \boxed{} = \frac{5}{6}$ $\qquad$ $\frac{4}{8} + \boxed{} = \frac{5}{8}$ $\qquad$ $\frac{1}{3} + \boxed{} = \frac{3}{3}$

$\frac{1}{6} + \boxed{} = \frac{2}{6}$ $\qquad$ $\frac{2}{10} + \boxed{} = \frac{9}{10}$ $\qquad$ $\frac{2}{5} + \boxed{} = \frac{4}{5}$

6 Complete the missing fraction in each difference.

$\frac{5}{6} - \boxed{} = \frac{2}{6}$ $\qquad$ $\frac{7}{10} - \boxed{} = \frac{3}{10}$ $\qquad$ $\frac{3}{4} - \boxed{} = \frac{1}{4}$

$\frac{4}{5} - \boxed{} = \frac{3}{5}$ $\qquad$ $\frac{6}{8} - \boxed{} = \frac{2}{8}$ $\qquad$ $\frac{9}{10} - \boxed{} = \frac{1}{10}$

7 Shade the diagrams below to show how many eighths are in one quarter. Complete the equation to show how many eighths are in one quarter.

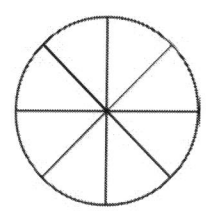

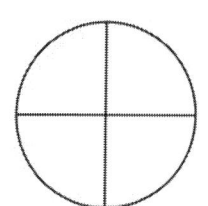

Equation $\boxed{} + \boxed{} = \frac{1}{4}$

Shade the diagrams below to show how many sixths are in one third. Then write an equation to show how many sixths are in one third.

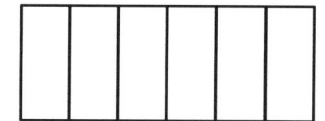

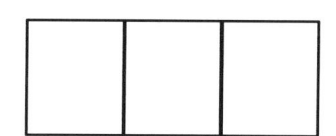

Equation

Student Quiz Book, STAAR Mathematics, Grade 3

8 Shade the first fraction model below to show the fraction that makes the sum equal to 1. Then complete the missing fraction in the equation.

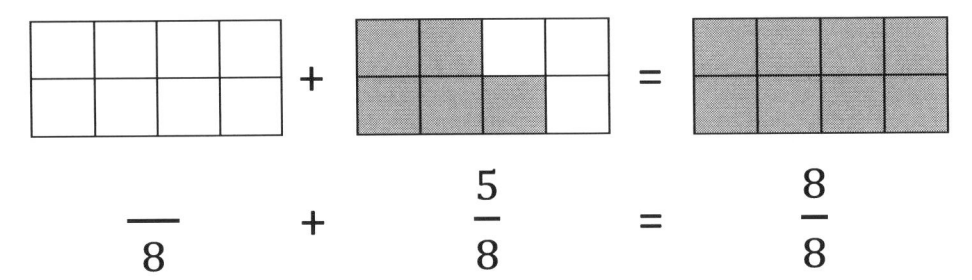

$$\frac{}{8} + \frac{5}{8} = \frac{8}{8}$$

9 Shade the diagrams below to show two equal fractions that add to 1. Then write an equation to show the sum of the fractions.

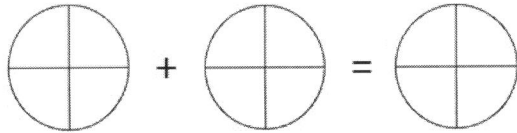

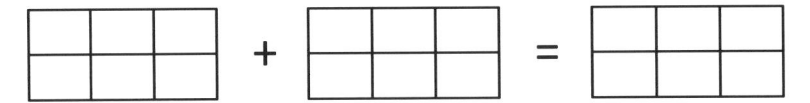

Equation

Shade the diagrams below to show four equal fractions that add to 1. Then write an equation to show the sum of the fractions.

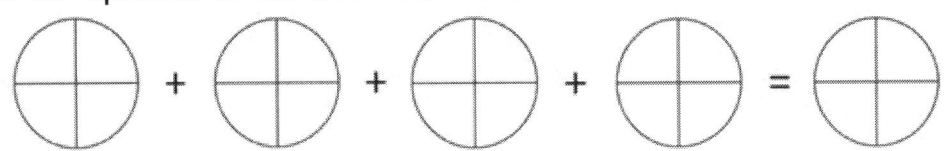

Equation

10 Shade the diagrams below to show two equal fractions that add to 1. Then write an equation to show the sum of the fractions.

Equation

Shade the diagrams below to show three equal fractions that add to 1. Then write an equation to show the sum of the fractions.

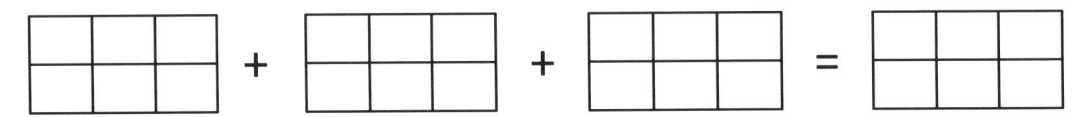

Equation

11 Jessica ordered 1 whole pizza. Jessica ate $\frac{2}{10}$ of the pizza, Jessica's sister ate $\frac{1}{10}$ of the pizza, and Jessica's father ate $\frac{3}{10}$ of the pizza. What fraction of the pizza remains? Use the diagram below to help you find the answer.

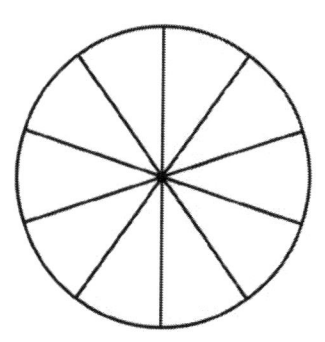

Answer _____ of the pizza remains

12 What is the value of $\frac{1}{8} + \frac{1}{8} + \frac{3}{8}$? Use the diagram below to help you find the answer.

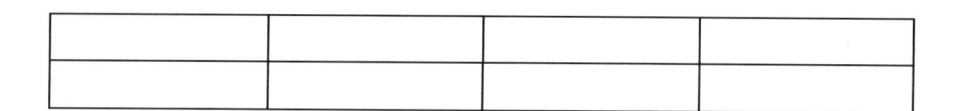

Answer _____

13 Wade ran laps of the school's running track. Each lap was $\frac{1}{3}$ of a mile. How many laps would Wade need to complete to run a total of 1 mile? Show your work or explain how you found your answer.

Answer _____ laps

Quiz 13: Using Fractions to Solve Problems

1 The diagram below represents the lengths of yards and feet.

1 foot	1 foot	1 foot

1 yard

Based on the diagram, what fraction of 1 yard is 1 foot? _____

2 Josh buys a packet of pencils. The pencils in the packet are shown below.

What fraction of the packet is each pencil? _____

He gives 2 pencils to his friend. What fraction of the pencils does he give to his friend? _____

He divides the remaining pencils into equal halves. How many pencils are in each half? _____

3 How many $\frac{1}{4}$ cup serves of juice can be made from 2 cups of juice?

Answer _____ serves

4 The diagram represents a parking lot that is $\frac{1}{4}$ full. Each rectangle represents one parking space. How many more cars need to park for it to be $\frac{1}{2}$ full?

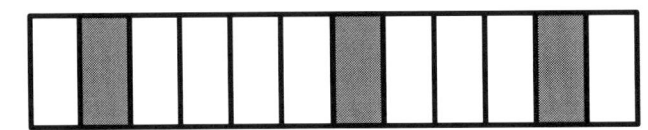

Answer _____ cars

5 The 6 guests at a party each ate 1 equal slice of cake. In all, the guests ate 1 whole cake. Complete the diagram to show one way the cake could have been divided.

6 Alex made the graph below to show how long he spent studying each subject one week.

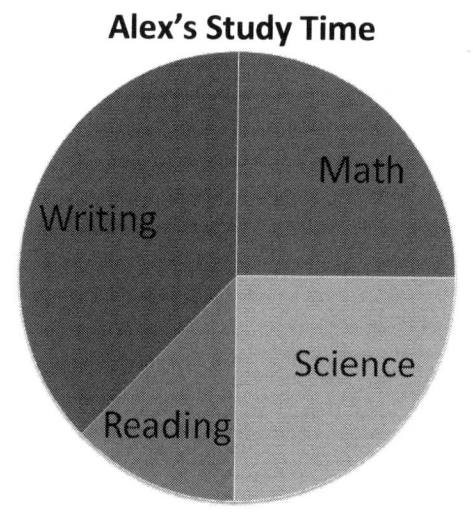

Alex's Study Time

Which subject did Alex study for $\frac{1}{8}$ of his study time? _____

What fraction of his study time was spent studying math? _____

Alex studied science for 30 minutes. How long did he study math, reading, and writing for? Show your work or explain how you found your answer.

Math _____ minutes **Reading** _____ minutes **Writing** _____ minutes

7 A group of students divided a mural into equal parts. The diagram below shows who painted each part of the mural.

Leo	Leo	Jane	Jane	Jane	Jane
Leo	Abby	Abby	Lisa	Ryan	Ryan

Which student painted $\frac{1}{3}$ of the mural? _____

What fraction of the whole mural did Abby paint? _____

What fraction of the whole mural did Lisa and Ryan paint in all? _____

What fraction of the whole mural did Jane and Ryan paint in all? _____

What fraction more of the mural did Jane paint than Ryan? Show or explain how you found your answer.

Answer _____

If equal parts of the mural were painted by 6 students, what fraction would each students paint? Show or explain how you found your answer.

Answer _____

8   Trey made the chart below to show how many three-point shots he made and missing during the first half of the basketball season.

Shots Made	Shots Missed
✓ ✓ ✓ ✓	✗ ✗ ✗ ✗ ✗ ✗ ✗ ✗

What fraction of his total shots did Trey make? Show or explain how you found your answer.

Answer _____

In the second half of the season, Trey had 12 attempts. He ends the year with $\frac{1}{2}$ his total shots made and $\frac{1}{2}$ his total shots missed. How many shots did he make and how many did he miss in the second half of the season? Show or explain how you found your answer.

Answer _____ shots made, _____ shots missed

Quiz 14: Understanding Equivalent Fractions

1 A number line is shown below.

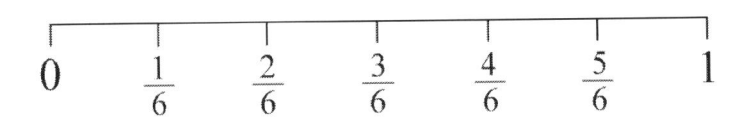

$$0 \quad \frac{1}{6} \quad \frac{2}{6} \quad \frac{3}{6} \quad \frac{4}{6} \quad \frac{5}{6} \quad 1$$

Which fraction on the number line is equivalent to $\frac{1}{3}$? _____

Which fraction on the number line is equivalent to $\frac{2}{3}$? _____

Which fraction on the number line is equivalent to $\frac{1}{2}$? _____

2 Shade the model below to show the fraction $\frac{4}{6}$.

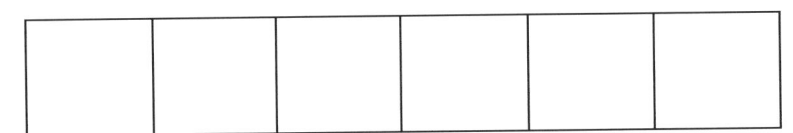

Shade the model below to show a fraction equivalent to $\frac{4}{6}$.

What fraction is shaded above? _____

3 Circle all the fractions listed below that are equivalent.

$$\frac{2}{4} \quad \frac{1}{3} \quad \frac{3}{8} \quad \frac{5}{6} \quad \frac{4}{8} \quad \frac{5}{8} \quad \frac{2}{3} \quad \frac{3}{6} \quad \frac{1}{2}$$

4 Shade half of each model below. Then use the model to complete the fractions equivalent to $\frac{1}{2}$.

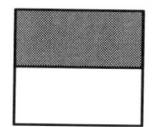

$\frac{1}{2}$ $\frac{}{4}$ $\frac{}{6}$ $\frac{}{8}$

5 Shade the diagrams below to show the fraction $\frac{2}{3}$ and two fractions equivalent to $\frac{2}{3}$. Then write the equivalent fraction under each diagram.

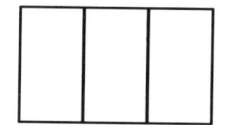

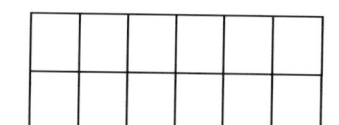

$\frac{2}{3}$

6 Shade the diagrams below to show the fraction $\frac{1}{4}$ and a fraction equivalent to $\frac{1}{4}$. Then write the equivalent fraction under the second diagram.

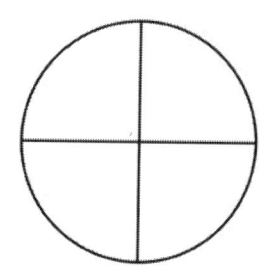

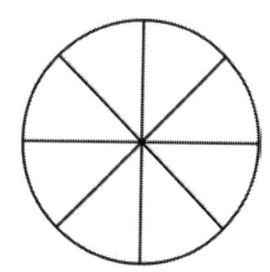

$\frac{1}{4}$

7 Aaron has quarters and dimes. Aaron's coins are shown below.

Complete the two fractions that show the fraction of coins that are quarters.

$$\frac{\square}{8} = \frac{\square}{4}$$

8 The number lines below have four points plotted.

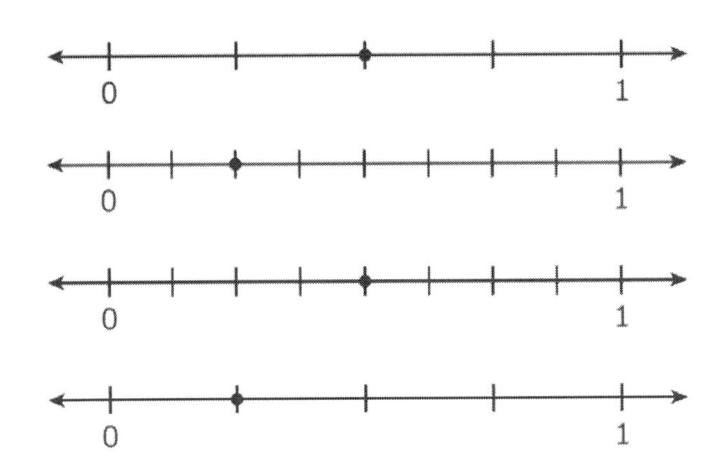

Write the two pairs of equivalent fractions on the lines below.

Answer ____ and ____ , ____ and ____

Use the number lines to list a fraction that is equivalent to $\frac{3}{4}$.

Answer ____

9 Shade the diagrams below to show the fractions $\frac{1}{2}$, $\frac{2}{4}$, and $\frac{4}{8}$.

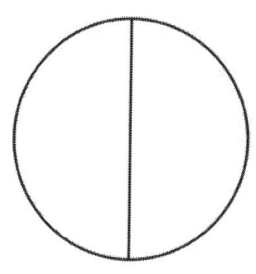

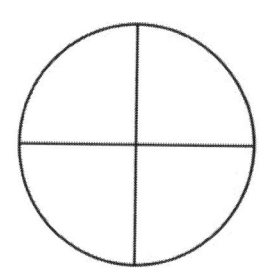

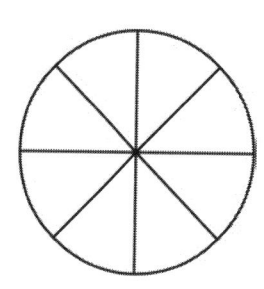

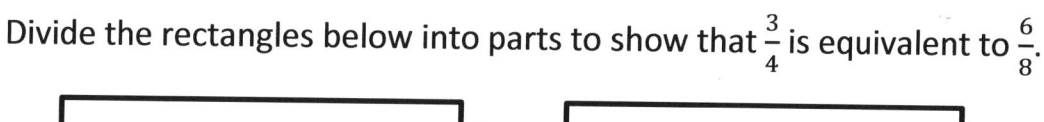

Explain how the diagrams show that the fractions are equivalent.

_____

_____

_____

_____

10 Divide the rectangles below into parts to show that $\frac{3}{4}$ is equivalent to $\frac{6}{8}$.

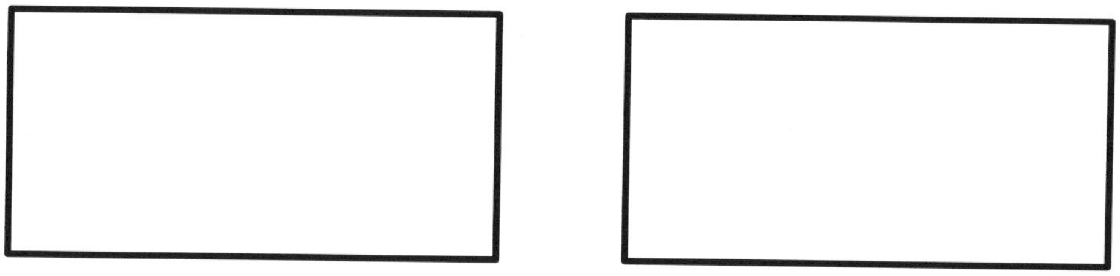

Explain how the diagrams show that the fractions are equivalent.

_____

_____

_____

_____

Quiz 15: Representing Equivalent Fractions

1 Which fraction is equivalent to $\frac{4}{6}$?

Ⓐ $\frac{2}{3}$ Ⓑ $\frac{1}{6}$ Ⓒ $\frac{1}{5}$ Ⓓ $\frac{1}{3}$

2 Which fraction is equivalent to the shaded area of the rectangle?

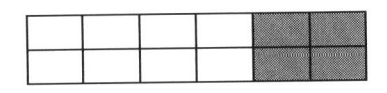

Ⓐ $\frac{4}{6}$ Ⓑ $\frac{2}{10}$ Ⓒ $\frac{2}{5}$ Ⓓ $\frac{1}{3}$

3 Doreen states that $\frac{6}{9}$ of the stars are shaded. Based on the diagram, what fraction of the stars are shaded?

Ⓐ $\frac{1}{6}$ Ⓑ $\frac{2}{3}$ Ⓒ $\frac{6}{3}$ Ⓓ $\frac{1}{2}$

4 Which fractions are equivalent to the shaded area of the circle? Select all the correct answers.

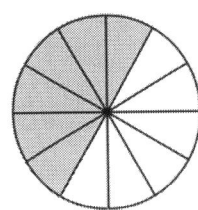

☐ $\frac{2}{6}$ ☐ $\frac{3}{6}$ ☐ $\frac{1}{3}$ ☐ $\frac{6}{6}$

☐ $\frac{1}{2}$ ☐ $\frac{3}{4}$ ☐ $\frac{1}{6}$ ☐ $\frac{2}{4}$

5 Which fraction can be placed in the empty box to make the statement below true?

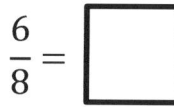

$$\frac{6}{8} = \boxed{}$$

Ⓐ $\frac{2}{6}$ Ⓑ $\frac{3}{4}$ Ⓒ $\frac{2}{3}$ Ⓓ $\frac{3}{8}$

6 Which model is shaded to show a fraction equivalent to $\frac{2}{3}$?

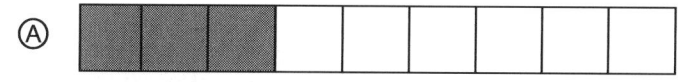

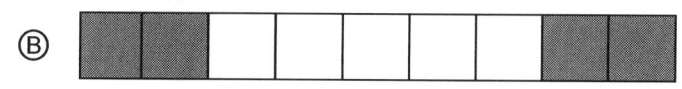

7 Four fractions are shown below. Complete the fractions so that all four fractions are equivalent.

$$\frac{1}{} \qquad \frac{}{4} \qquad \frac{}{6} \qquad \frac{}{8}$$

8 A recipe uses $\frac{1}{4}$ teaspoon of vanilla. Complete the fractions below to show two fractions equivalent to $\frac{1}{4}$.

$$\frac{\boxed{}}{8} \text{ and } \frac{4}{\boxed{}}$$

Student Quiz Book, STAAR Mathematics, Grade 3

9 Jackson bought 4 chocolate cakes and 8 vanilla cakes.

Complete the fractions that show the fraction of cakes that are chocolate.

$$\frac{\Box}{12} = \frac{\Box}{6} = \frac{\Box}{3}$$

10 Shade each figure below to show a fraction equivalent to $\frac{2}{8}$.

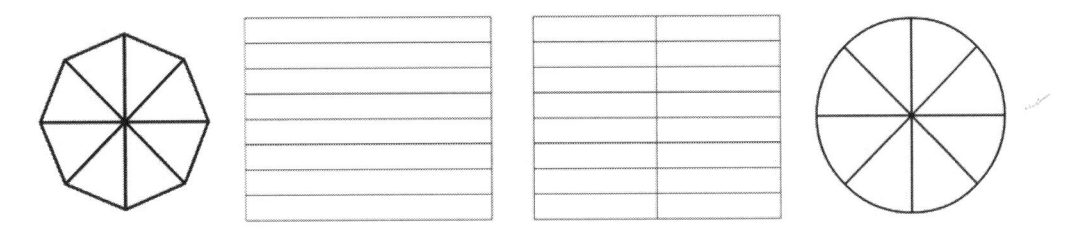

What fraction of each model is shaded? Write the fraction in lowest form.

Answer _____

11 Shade the fractions $\frac{1}{2}$ and $\frac{3}{6}$ on the fraction models below.

Shade the fraction model below to show another fraction equivalent to $\frac{1}{2}$ and $\frac{3}{6}$. Write the fraction on the line below.

What fraction did you shade? _____

12 Candice planted 15 plants in her garden. She planted 10 mint plants and 5 parsley plants, as represented below.

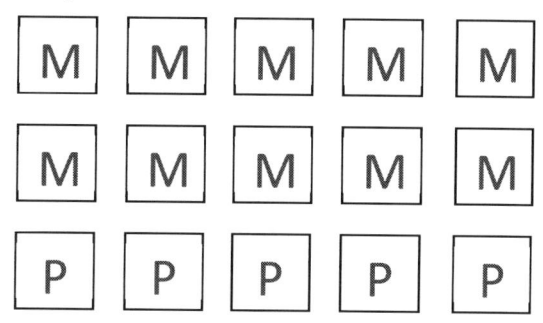

M	M	M	M	M
M	M	M	M	M
P	P	P	P	P

Complete the fractions to show the fraction of total plants that are mint and the fraction of total plants that are parsley in lowest terms.

Mint $\frac{10}{15} = \frac{}{}$ Parsley $\frac{5}{15} = \frac{}{}$

Candice wants to plant more parsley plants so that they make up $\frac{1}{2}$ the total plants. How many more parsley plants does she need? Show or explain how you found your answer.

Answer _____ plants

13 Quentin bought the bananas and oranges shown below.

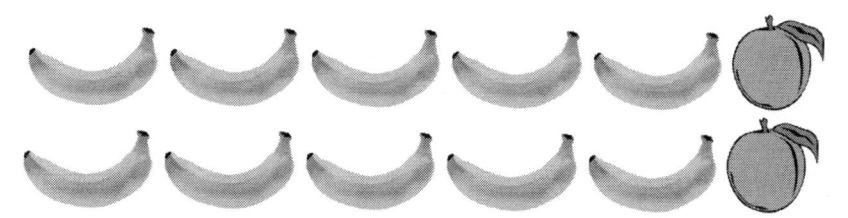

What fraction of the fruits he bought were oranges? Write your answer in lowest terms. Show or explain how you found your answer.

Answer _____

Quiz 16: Comparing Fractions

1 Which fraction below is the greatest?

Ⓐ $\frac{4}{8}$ Ⓑ $\frac{1}{4}$ Ⓒ $\frac{4}{4}$ Ⓓ $\frac{8}{4}$

2 Which set of squares has more than $\frac{3}{4}$ of the squares shaded?

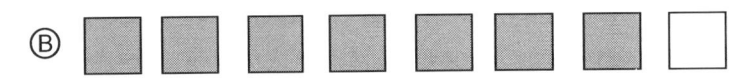

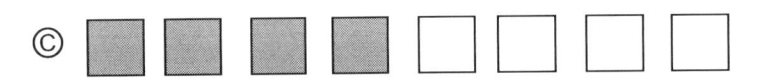

Ⓐ ▨▨▨☐☐☐☐☐

Ⓑ ▨▨▨▨▨▨▨☐

Ⓒ ▨▨▨☐☐☐☐

Ⓓ ▨▨▨▨▨☐☐☐

3 The shaded models below represent two fractions.

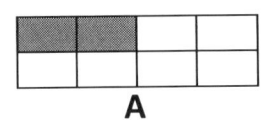

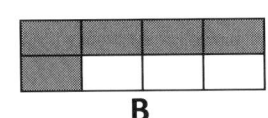

A   B

What is the difference of fraction B and fraction A?

Ⓐ $\frac{5}{8}$ Ⓑ $\frac{3}{8}$ Ⓒ $\frac{1}{3}$ Ⓓ $\frac{2}{5}$

4 Place the fractions below in order from smallest to greatest. Write the numbers 1, 2, 3, and 4 on the lines to show the order.

___ $\frac{1}{4}$

___ $\frac{1}{8}$

___ $\frac{3}{4}$

___ $\frac{7}{8}$

5 Which fractions can be placed in the empty box to make the statement below true? Select all the correct answers.

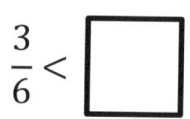

$$\frac{3}{6} < \square$$

☐ $\frac{2}{6}$ ☐ $\frac{5}{6}$ ☐ $\frac{1}{3}$ ☐ $\frac{6}{6}$

☐ $\frac{1}{2}$ ☐ $\frac{2}{3}$ ☐ $\frac{1}{6}$ ☐ $\frac{4}{6}$

6 The shapes below are labeled A through G.

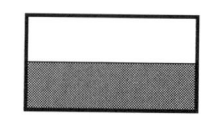

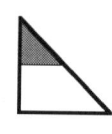

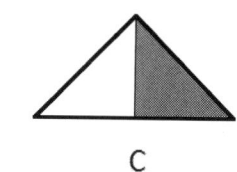

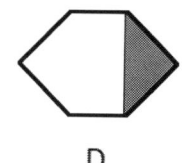

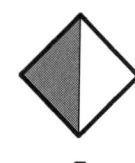

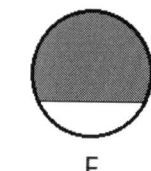

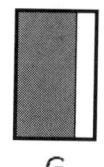

A   B   C   D   E   F   G

Which shapes have exactly $\frac{1}{2}$ the shape shaded? _____

Which shapes have less than $\frac{1}{2}$ the shape shaded? _____

Which shapes have more than $\frac{1}{2}$ the shape shaded? _____

7 Divide the rectangle below into equal areas and shade $\frac{1}{3}$ of the rectangle.

Divide the rectangle below into equal areas and shade $\frac{1}{6}$ of the rectangle.

Use the shaded models to circle the correct statement below.

$\frac{1}{3} < \frac{1}{6}$ $\frac{1}{3} > \frac{1}{6}$ $\frac{1}{3} = \frac{1}{6}$

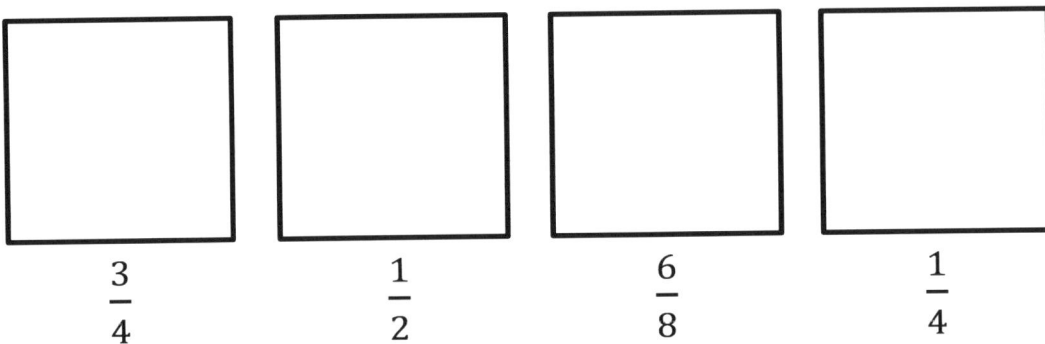

8 Divide each square below into parts and shade the fraction listed under each.

$\dfrac{3}{4}$ $\dfrac{1}{2}$ $\dfrac{6}{8}$ $\dfrac{1}{4}$

Complete the statements below by writing the correct fractions.

The fraction —— is equivalent to the fraction ——.

The fraction —— is twice the size of the fraction ——.

The sum of the fractions $\dfrac{3}{4}$ and —— is equal to 1.

The fraction $\dfrac{3}{4}$ is 3 times the size of the fraction ——.

9 Divide the two rectangles into equal parts and shade the fractions $\dfrac{2}{3}$ and $\dfrac{5}{6}$.

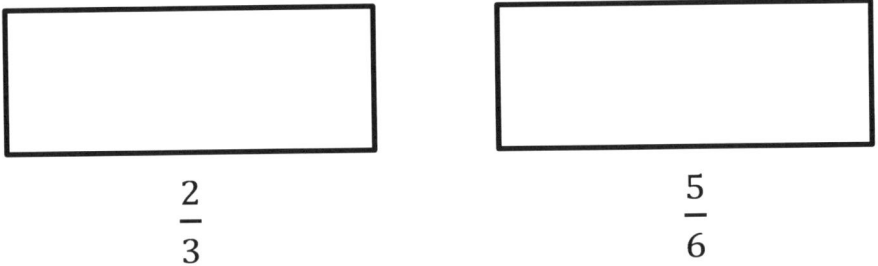

$\dfrac{2}{3}$ $\dfrac{5}{6}$

Write a statement that compares the two fractions.

_____

_____

Student Quiz Book, STAAR Mathematics, Grade 3

10 Shade the models below to show $\frac{7}{10}$ and $\frac{4}{5}$.

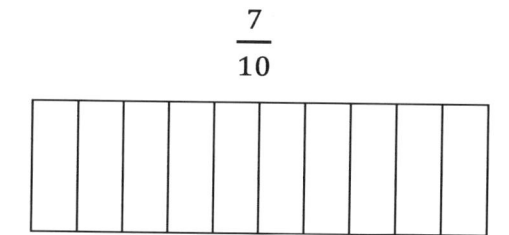

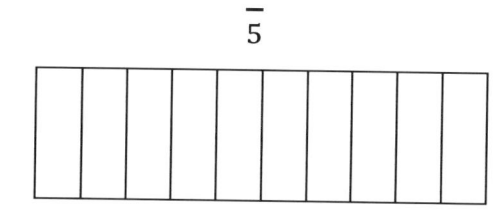

$$\frac{7}{10} \qquad\qquad \frac{4}{5}$$

Write one of the symbols below in the number sentence to compare the fractions $\frac{7}{10}$ and $\frac{4}{5}$.

$$<, >, =$$

$$\frac{7}{10} \;\square\; \frac{4}{5}$$

On the lines below, explain how the models helped you find the answer.

_____

_____

_____

11 Write a number sentence that compares the two fractions shown below. Use <, >, or = in the number sentence.

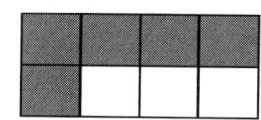

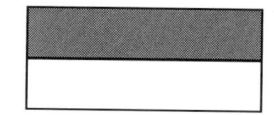

Quizzes 17 to 30

Computing with Whole Numbers

Directions

Read each question carefully. For each multiple-choice question, fill in the circle for the correct answer. For other types of questions, follow the directions given in the question.

You may use a ruler to help you answer questions. You should answer the questions without using a calculator.

MATHEMATICS SKILLS LIST
For Parents, Teachers, and Tutors

Quizzes 17 through 30 cover these skills from the Texas Essential Knowledge and Skills (TEKS).

Number and Operations

The student applies mathematical process standards to develop and use strategies and methods for whole number computations in order to solve problems with efficiency and accuracy.

The student is expected to be able to complete the following tasks.

- Solve with fluency one-step and two-step problems involving addition and subtraction within 1,000 using strategies based on place value, properties of operations, and the relationship between addition and subtraction.

- Round to the nearest 10 or 100 or use compatible numbers to estimate solutions to addition and subtraction problems.

- Determine the value of a collection of coins and bills.

- Determine the total number of objects when equally sized groups of objects are combined or arranged in arrays up to 10 by 10.

- Represent multiplication facts by using a variety of approaches such as repeated addition, equal-sized groups, arrays, area models, equal jumps on a number line, and skip counting.

- Recall facts to multiply up to 10 by 10 with automaticity and recall the corresponding division facts.

- Use strategies and algorithms, including the standard algorithm, to multiply a two-digit number by a one-digit number.

- Determine the number of objects in each group when a set of objects is partitioned into equal shares or a set of objects is shared equally.

- Determine if a number is even or odd using divisibility rules.

- Determine a quotient using the relationship between multiplication and division.

- Solve one-step and two-step problems involving multiplication and division within 100 using strategies based on objects; pictorial models, including arrays, area models, and equal groups; properties of operations; or recall of facts.

Quiz 17: Adding Whole Numbers

1. Juan read 42 pages of a book on Monday. He read another 39 pages of the book on Tuesday. How many pages did he read in all?

   Ⓐ 70   Ⓑ 71   Ⓒ 80   Ⓓ 81

2. Mr. Wilkins drove 162 miles on Monday. Then he drove 138 miles on Tuesday. How many miles did he drive in all?

   Ⓐ 200 miles   Ⓑ 300 miles   Ⓒ 310 miles   Ⓓ 290 miles

3. Sienna's school has 348 third grade students, 312 fourth grade students, and 306 fifth grade students. How many students are there in all?

   Ⓐ 954   Ⓑ 956   Ⓒ 964   Ⓓ 966

4. Complete the addition problems below.

   626 + 153   145 + 234   357 + 349   405 + 205

   750 + 164   723 + 107   447 + 462   215 + 385

   425 + 153   508 + 262   626 + 183   250 + 350

   206 + 204   492 + 208   525 + 315   708 + 152

5. Which expressions have a sum of 100? Select all the correct answers.

☐ 73 + 37 ☐ 3 + 82 + 15

☐ 18 + 84 ☐ 62 + 28 + 10

☐ 52 + 48 ☐ 75 + 25 + 25

6. Which sum has the greatest value? Select the one correct answer.

☐ 158 + 292 ☐ 130 + 295 ☐ 305 + 88

☐ 244 + 213 ☐ 212 + 218 ☐ 327 + 41

7. For each expression, complete the missing number to show two expressions with the same value.

(46 + 19) + 12   (12 + ____) + 46   (46 + ____) + 19
(33 + 89) + 66   (33 + ____) + 89   (66 + ____) + 33
(67 + 55) + 23   (____ + 67) + 55   (____ + 23) + 67
(71 + 27) + 44   (27 + 44) + ____   (44 + 71) + ____

8. For each addition equation, complete the two subtraction equations that could be used to check the answer.

35 + 44 = 79   ____ − ____ = ____   ____ − ____ = ____

77 + 52 = 129   ____ − ____ = ____   ____ − ____ = ____

24 + 89 = 113   ____ − ____ = ____   ____ − ____ = ____

152 + 141 = 293   ____ − ____ = ____   ____ − ____ = ____

305 + 285 = 590   ____ − ____ = ____   ____ − ____ = ____

641 + 111 = 752   ____ − ____ = ____   ____ − ____ = ____

9 For each addition problem below, complete the calculation in steps. In the first step, add the tens. In the second step, add the ones. In the third step, add the sum of the tens and the ones. The first one has been completed.

Problem	Step 1: Add the Tens	Step 2: Add the Ones	Step 3: Add the Two Sums
42 + 85	40 + 80 = 120	2 + 5 = 7	120 + 7 = 127
63 + 19	___ + ___ = ___	___ + ___ = ___	___ + ___ = ___
27 + 48	___ + ___ = ___	___ + ___ = ___	___ + ___ = ___
31 + 26	___ + ___ = ___	___ + ___ = ___	___ + ___ = ___
75 + 17	___ + ___ = ___	___ + ___ = ___	___ + ___ = ___
58 + 38	___ + ___ = ___	___ + ___ = ___	___ + ___ = ___

10 Dan is training for a bike race. He rode 18 miles on Monday, 19 miles on Tuesday, and 12 miles on Wednesday. How far did he ride in all?

Show your work.

Answer _____ miles

11 A zoo had 586 visitors on Saturday and 421 visitors on Sunday. How many visitors did the zoo have on the weekend?

Show your work.

Answer _____ visitors

12 Sam has 111 stamps in her collection. Courtney has 182 more stamps in her collection than Sam. How many stamps does Courtney have?

Show your work.

Answer _____ stamps

How many stamps do Sam and Courtney have together?

Show your work.

Answer _____ stamps

13 Janet wants to find the sum of the three numbers below. Janet first adds the numbers 138 and 262. Then she adds 85 to the result. Complete the equations to show the two steps.

Sum of 138, 85, 262   138 + 262 = _____   _____ + 85 = _____

Explain why the calculation is easier if 138 and 262 are added first.

_____

_____

14 For each set of numbers below, choose the two numbers to add first. Then add the third number to the result to show the total sum.

Sum of 65, 47, 35   ____ + ____ = ____   ____ + ____ = ____

Sum of 29, 71, 34   ____ + ____ = ____   ____ + ____ = ____

Sum of 88, 67, 32   ____ + ____ = ____   ____ + ____ = ____

Sum of 57, 26, 44   ____ + ____ = ____   ____ + ____ = ____

Quiz 18: Subtracting Whole Numbers

1 Heath scored 87 on a reading test. Rima scored 18 points less than Heath. How many points did Rima score?

Ⓐ 61   Ⓑ 69   Ⓒ 71   Ⓓ 79

2 Jackson had $96 in savings. He spent $18 on a present for his brother. How much money does Jackson have left?

Ⓐ $74   Ⓑ $78   Ⓒ $84   Ⓓ $88

3 Mr. Piper has to drive a total of 582 miles. He drove 291 miles on the first day. How far does Mr. Piper have left to drive?

Ⓐ 211 miles   Ⓑ 291 miles   Ⓒ 311 miles   Ⓓ 391 miles

4 Complete the subtraction problems below.

589 − 47	380 − 55	218 − 39	743 − 88
852 − 321	468 − 109	905 − 175	557 − 519
608 − 205	755 − 355	608 − 253	584 − 106
835 − 204	465 − 305	912 − 509	667 − 390

5 Which expressions have a difference of 4? Select all the correct answers.

☐ 108 – 102   ☐ 355 – 301   ☐ 100 – 64 – 32

☐ 289 – 285   ☐ 88 – 42 – 42   ☐ 845 – 800 – 45

6 Which difference is equal to 30? Select the one correct answer.

☐ 689 – 389   ☐ 689 – 359   ☐ 689 – 356

☐ 689 – 659   ☐ 689 – 686   ☐ 689 – 656

7 Which number is 40 less than 589? _____

Which number is 200 less than 589? _____

Which number is 240 less than 589? _____

8 For each expression, complete the missing numbers to show an expression with the same value.

(88 – 15) – 22   (88 – ____) – ____

(175 – 39) – 67   (175 – ____) – ____

(412 – 58) – 73   (412 – ____) – ____

9 For each subtraction equation, complete an addition equation that could be used to check the answer.

159 – 86 = 73   ____ + ____ = ____

365 – 99 = 266   ____ + ____ = ____

274 – 178 = 96   ____ + ____ = ____

867 – 745 = 122   ____ + ____ = ____

907 – 138 = 769   ____ + ____ = ____

750 – 425 = 325   ____ + ____ = ____

10 Alvin is 136 centimeters tall. Sara is 16 centimeters shorter than Alvin. How tall is Sara?

Show your work.

Answer _____ centimeters

11 The normal price of a computer is $790. During a sale, the computer is $150 less than the normal price. What is the sale price of the computer?

Show your work.

Answer $_____

12 At Emiko's school, there are 247 students in third grade. There are 29 fewer students in fourth grade. How many students are in fourth grade?

Show your work.

Answer _____ students

13 Carol had $500 to spend on office furniture. She bought a new desk for $259 and a new bookcase for $188. How much does Carol have left?

Show your work.

Answer $_____

14 Juan had $128 in his savings account. He spent $6 every week for 4 weeks. How much money would be in his savings account after 4 weeks?

Show your work.

Answer $_____

15 A school cafeteria offered four Italian meal choices. The table below shows the number of meals served of each type.

Meal	Number Served
Pasta	151
Pizza	167
Salad	213
Risotto	117

How many more salad meals were served than risotto meals?

Show your work.

Answer _____ meals

The school hoped to serve a total of 1,000 meals. How many more meals needed to be served to reach this goal?

Show your work.

Answer _____ meals

Quiz 19: Solving Word Problems Using Addition and Subtraction

1 Porter has 945 sheep in three fields. There are 185 sheep in the first field and 428 sheep in the second field. How many sheep are in the third field?

Ⓐ 332   Ⓑ 517   Ⓒ 613   Ⓓ 702

2 Leon had $138 in savings. He spent $27 at the bookstore. Then he was given $15 by his grandmother. How much money does Leon have now?

Ⓐ $106   Ⓑ $126   Ⓒ $150   Ⓓ $180

3 Audrey states that if she sells 68 pretzels, there will be 14 pretzels left. Which number sentence can be used to find the total number of pretzels she has?

Ⓐ 68 + ___ = 14   Ⓑ 14 + ___ = 68   Ⓒ 68 − ___ = 14   Ⓓ ___ − 68 = 14

4 Which expressions can be used to find the sum of 106 and 35? Select all the correct answers.

☐ (100 + 300) + (6 + 5)   ☐ 100 + (60 + 30) + 5   ☐ 100 + 30 + (6 + 5)

☐ (10 + 30) + (6 + 5)   ☐ (100 + 35) + 6   ☐ (100 + 5) + 30

5 Place the expressions below in order from smallest to greatest.
Write the numbers 1, 2, 3, and 4 on the lines to show the order.

___ 584 + 36   ___ 584 + 63   ___ 584 − 36   ___ 584 − 63

6 A school printed 1,000 comics. Teachers were given 20 comics, students were given 840 comics, and 40 comics were given to the library. Complete the expressions to show two ways to find how many comics were left.

Expression _____ − _____ − _____ − _____ = _____

Expression _____ − (_____ + _____ + _____) = _____

7   The table shows the sales a drink stand made one day.

Size	Apple Juice	Lemonade
Small	36	39
Medium	49	68
Large	57	71

How many drinks were sold in all?

Show your work.

Answer _____ drinks

How many more lemonades were sold than apple juices?

Show your work.

Answer _____ drinks

8   Belinda needs to finish reading a book with 150 pages.

- She read 26 pages on Monday.
- She read 42 pages on Tuesday.
- She read 34 pages on Wednesday.

How many more pages does she need to read to finish the book?

Show your work.

Answer _____ pages

9   The table shows how many books a store sold each day of the week.

Day	Number of Book Sales
Monday	166
Tuesday	121
Wednesday	134
Thursday	139
Friday	145
Saturday	268
Sunday	212

On which two days did the store have a total of 260 sales?

_____ and _____

On which two days did the store have a total of 300 sales?

_____ and _____

How many sales did the store have on Saturday and Sunday?

_____ sales

How many more sales did the store have on Friday than on Thursday?

_____ sales

What is the difference in sales between the day with the most sales and the day with the least sales?

_____ sales

Complete the addition equation to show that the store had twice as many sales on Saturday as on Wednesday.

_____ + _____ = _____

10 Lana buys a box of 100 beads. She uses the beads to make jewelry.

- She uses 18 beads to make each bracelet.
- She uses 24 beads to make each necklace.
- She uses 8 beads to make each anklet.

She makes 2 bracelets, 1 necklace, and 1 anklet. How many beads does she use?

Show your work.

Answer _____ beads

How many beads from the box of 100 are left over?

Show your work.

Answer _____ beads

Describe two different sets of items she could make to use all the remaining beads.

Show your work.

Answer _____ or _____

She buys another box of 100 beads. She makes 4 items and has exactly 4 beads left over. Which items did she make?

Show your work.

Answer _____

Quiz 20: Solving Two-Step Word Problems

1 Jen had 42 dimes and Meg had 18 dimes. They used all their dimes to buy hair clips for 5 dimes each. How many hair clips did Jen and Meg buy?

  Ⓐ 12 Ⓑ 14 Ⓒ 65 Ⓓ 70

2 Devlin earns $7 for each hour he works. He worked for 6 hours, and was also given tips of $35. How much did Devlin earn in all?

  Ⓐ $42 Ⓑ $48 Ⓒ $71 Ⓓ $77

3 A store had 42 muffins at the start of the day and 8 muffins left unsold at the end of the day. Each muffin sold for $2. How much money was made from the sale of the muffins that day?

  Ⓐ $36 Ⓑ $58 Ⓒ $68 Ⓓ $100

4 Sam bought 6 packets of 10 pens. He divided the pens into 4 equal groups. How many pens were in each group?

  Ⓐ 4 Ⓑ 12 Ⓒ 15 Ⓓ 20

5 The table shows how many cans students collected for a recycling drive.

	Denzel	Hudson	Colin	Garth	Sanjay	Wes
Number of Cans	44	14	18	62	26	32

Which two students collected the same total amount of cans as Garth? _____ and _____

Which two students collected the same total amount of cans as Hudson and Garth combined? _____ and _____

The goal of the recycling drive was to collect 200 cans. How many more cans need to be collected to reach the goal? _____

6 A chef buys 4 boxes of apples. Each box has 3 layers of apples, and there are 20 apples in each layer. How many apples did the chef buy?

Show your work.

Answer _____ apples

7 Bradford had $35 in savings. He then saved $8 each week for 6 weeks. How much money did Bradford have at the end of 6 weeks?

Show your work.

Answer $_____

8 A chef has 12 apple pies. Each apple pie has 8 serves. The chef serves 54 pieces of apple pie. How many pieces of apple pie are left over?

Show your work.

Answer _____ pieces of pie

9 Jeremy is making 6 photo frames. He needs 10 nails for each photo frame. He buys the nails in packs of 15. How many packs of nails does he need?

Show your work.

Answer _____ packs of nails

10 Maurice has $40 in savings. He plans to save $6 each week. How many weeks will it take for Maurice to have a total of over $80? Use pictures, words, or math to explain the work needed to find the answer.

Answer _____ weeks

11 Jo read that a kitten's weight increases by about 30 grams each day for the first 10 days. When Jo's cat had a kitten, it weighed 110 grams. How much would Jo expect the kitten to weigh after 10 days of growth? Use pictures, words, or math to explain the work needed to find the answer.

Answer _____ grams

12 Andrew buys 6 cartons of water, with 8 bottles of water in each carton. If he drinks 3 bottles of water each day, how long will all the water last? Use pictures, words, or math to explain the work needed to find the answer.

Answer _____ days

13 The sign below shows the price of fruits at a store.

Bananas	Oranges	Apples	Pears
4 for $3	10 for $4	4 for $2	6 for $3

Ben spends $12 on oranges. How many oranges did he buy?

Show your work.

Answer _____ oranges

Kim buys 8 bananas, 12 apples, and 30 pears. What is the total cost?

Show your work.

Answer $_____

Sadie buys pears. She gives the cashier $20 and receives $8 change. How many pears did she buy?

Show your work.

Answer _____ pears

Harriet buys oranges and pears. She spends $14 and receives 32 pieces of fruit. How many oranges and pears did she buy?

Show your work.

Answer _____ oranges and _____ pears

Quiz 21: Using Estimation and Rounding

1 Which is the best way to estimate the sum of 87 and 58?

Ⓐ 80 + 50   Ⓑ 90 + 50   Ⓒ 80 + 60   Ⓓ 90 + 60

2 Which is the best way to estimate the difference of 562 and 84?

Ⓐ 560 − 80   Ⓑ 560 − 90   Ⓒ 570 − 80   Ⓓ 570 − 90

3 The table shows how many cans each class collected for a food drive.

Class	Number of Cans
Miss Peterson	87
Mr. Yuri	54
Mrs. Duncan	75

Which is the best estimate of the total number of cans collected?

Ⓐ 80 + 50 + 70 = 200   Ⓑ 80 + 50 + 80 = 210

Ⓒ 90 + 50 + 80 = 220   Ⓓ 90 + 60 + 80 = 230

4 A school has 237 third grade students, 369 fourth grade students, and 325 fifth grade students. Which number sentence shows the best way to estimate the total number of students?

Ⓐ 200 + 300 + 300 = 800   Ⓑ 200 + 400 + 400 = 1,000

Ⓒ 200 + 400 + 300 = 900   Ⓓ 300 + 400 + 400 = 1,100

5 Tara sells 42 cupcakes for $3 each. Which is the best estimate of the total amount she made?

Ⓐ $40   Ⓑ $120   Ⓒ $150   Ⓓ $200

6 Trey has 58 game tokens to divide evenly between 8 friends. What is the greatest number of game tokens he could give to each friend?

Ⓐ 6   Ⓑ 7   Ⓒ 8   Ⓓ 9

7   Round the two-digit number up and down to find two numbers the product will be between. Then complete the sentence. The first one has been completed for you.

63 × 7   60 × 7 = 420   70 × 7 = 490

The product of 63 and 7 will be between 420 and 490.

71 × 3   ____ × 3 = ____   ____ × 3 = ____

The product of 71 and 3 will be between _____ and _____.

26 × 5   ____ × 5 = ____   ____ × 5 = ____

The product of 26 and 5 will be between _____ and _____.

87 × 6   ____ × 6 = ____   ____ × 6 = ____

The product of 87 and 6 will be between _____ and _____.

8   The school library has 1,412 fiction books, 1,845 non-fiction books, and 1,183 children's books. Answer each question by rounding each number to the nearest hundred and then completing the calculation.

About how many more non-fiction books are there than children's books?

_____ − _____ = _____

Answer _____ books

About how many more non-fiction books are there than fiction books?

_____ − _____ = _____

Answer _____ books

About how many books are there in all?

_____ + _____ + _____ = _____

Answer _____ books

9. Mr. Oliver has $1000 to spend on office equipment. The list below shows what he plans to buy.

- 1 printer that costs $275.
- 1 scanner that costs $218.
- 1 laptop that costs $369.

Round the cost of each item to the nearest ten.

Printer $_____   Scanner $_____   Laptop $_____

Use the rounded amounts to find about how much money Mr. Oliver will have left if he buys the three items.

Show your work.

Answer $_____

10. A car traveled 189 miles in 3 hours. About how many miles did the car travel each hour?

Show your work.

Answer _____ miles

11. A theater has 497 seats. People are sitting in 352 of the seats. About how many seats are empty?

Show your work.

Answer _____ seats

12 The table below shows how many visitors a zoo had on three days.

Day	Number of People
Friday	237
Saturday	258
Sunday	198

About how many visitors did the zoo have over the three days? Round each number to the nearest ten to find the answer.

Show your work.

Answer _____ visitors

Each visitor bought a $20 ticket to visit the zoo. On which day did the zoo make closest to $4,000 in ticket sales? Show your work or explain how you found the answer.

Answer _____

13 Ricky saved $8 each week for 32 weeks. Would he have saved just under $240 or just over $240? Explain your answer.

14 Darius says that the product of 4 and 9 must be less than 40. Explain why Darius is correct.

Quiz 22: Finding the Value of Money

1. What is the total value of the coins shown below?

   Ⓐ $0.05   Ⓑ $0.25   Ⓒ $0.50   Ⓓ $1.25

2. Erin bought lunch. She was given the change shown below. How much change was Erin given?

   Ⓐ 40 cents   Ⓑ 41 cents   Ⓒ 46 cents   Ⓓ 66 cents

3. Eva saved the money shown below. How much money did Eva save?

   Ⓐ $1.20   Ⓑ $1.25   Ⓒ $5.20   Ⓓ $5.25

4. Ling has a penny, a dime, and a quarter. How much money does Ling have?

   Answer $_____

5 What is the value of the coins shown below?

Answer _____ cents

6 David bought a drink. He paid for the drink with a one dollar bill, a quarter, and two nickels. How much was the drink?

Ⓐ $1.25 Ⓑ $1.30 Ⓒ $1.35 Ⓓ $1.45

7 Jo swapped all the coins below for nickels of the same total value.

How many nickels should he have received? _____ nickels

8 Dana is saving to buy a book that costs $12. The money she has saved so far is shown below.

How much money has Dana saved? $_____

How much more does Dana need to save to have $12? $_____

Quiz 23: Representing Multiplication

1 Which expression is represented by the model below?

Ⓐ 3 × 3 Ⓑ 3 × 15 Ⓒ 5 × 3 Ⓓ 10 × 2

2 A classroom has the student desks organized as shown below.

Which expression shows how to find the number of student desks?

Ⓐ 4 × 4 Ⓑ 8 × 2 Ⓒ 8 × 8 Ⓓ 8 × 4

3 Sierra organizes 40 coins into equal rows. Which of these could describe the rows? Select all the possible answers.

☐ 20 rows of 20 coins each

☐ 8 rows of 5 coins each

☐ 40 rows of 10 coins each

☐ 4 rows of 4 coins each

☐ 6 rows of 7 coins each

☐ 10 rows of 4 coins each

4   Rebecca buys 8 packets of pencils. There are 8 pencils in each packet. How many pencils does she buy in all? Write your answer on the line below.

Answer _____ pencils

5   Write and solve a multiplication expression to answer each question.

Sam plants 6 rows of 5 flowers each. How many flowers did he plant?

_____ × _____ = _____

There are 9 piles of 3 books each. How many books are there in all?

_____ × _____ = _____

Tai folds 8 napkins each minute. How many can he fold in 10 minutes?

_____ × _____ = _____

Donnie buys 6 tickets for $7 each. How many dollars does he spend in all?

_____ × _____ = _____

There are 8 potatoes in each bag. How many potatoes are in 5 bags?

_____ × _____ = _____

6   There are 48 students at a music camp. They need to be divided into groups with an equal number of students in each group. Complete the table to describe four different ways the students could be divided.

Number of Groups	Number of Students in Each Group

7 Jessica was asked to write a description of a situation where the total number of items is represented by the expression below.

    7 × 24

Jessica started her description, as shown below. Complete the description.

There were 7 boxes of water on a truck. _____

_____

_____

8 Davis has 3 basketball lessons a week. Write a description of a problem Davis could solve with the expression below.

    3 × 60

_____

_____

_____

9 A store sells notepads for $3 each. Write a description of a problem that could be solved with the expression below.

    3 × 15

_____

_____

_____

10 Avril uses 6 beads to make a bracelet, as shown below.

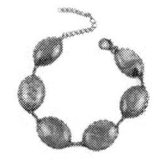

Complete the table to show the number of beads needed to make each number of bracelets.

Number of Bracelets	Expression	Total Number of Beads
1	1 × 6	6
2		
3		
4		
5		

11 In the space below, draw one way 16 coins can be organized into equal rows. Then complete the equation to show the total number of coins.

Equation _____ × _____ = _____

12 Otis buys 3 sheets of stickers. Each sheet has 6 rows of 4 stickers each. Write an equation to find the total number of stickers. Then write the number of stickers on the blank line.

Equation

Answer _____ stickers

Quiz 24: Using Multiplication Facts

1 What is the value of the expression 6 × 4?

   Ⓐ 18   Ⓑ 24   Ⓒ 28   Ⓓ 32

2 Joe says that if he runs 5 miles twice a week, he will run a total of 7 miles. Which of these describes Joe's statement?

   Ⓐ He is correct because the sum of 5 and 2 is 7.

   Ⓑ He is correct because 7 is 2 more than 5.

   Ⓒ He is incorrect because the product of 5 and 2 is 10.

   Ⓓ He is incorrect because 7 times 5 is equal to 35.

3 Which of these could be used to find the number of muffins that can be baked in the muffin tin below?

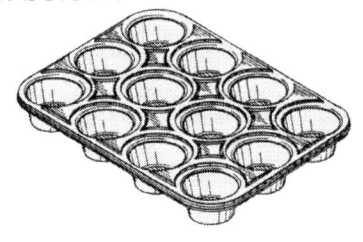

   Ⓐ the product of 3 and 4
   Ⓑ the product of 4 and 6
   Ⓒ the product of 6 and 6
   Ⓓ the product of 12 and 12

4 Select all the equations that are correct when the number 6 is placed on the blank line.

   ☐ 36 ÷ ___ = 4   ☐ 10 × ___ = 60

   ☐ 42 ÷ ___ = 7   ☐ 30 × 5 = ___

   ☐ 48 ÷ 8 = ___   ☐ ___ × 9 = 52

5 Find the value of the missing number in each statement. Write the correct number on the blank line. Then write a division equation to show that the number is correct. The first one has been completed for you.

6 equals __24__ divided by 4 $24 \div 4 = 6$

8 equals ____ divided by 2   ____ $\div$ ____ = ____

7 equals ____ divided by 9   ____ $\div$ ____ = ____

5 equals ____ divided by 4   ____ $\div$ ____ = ____

9 equals ____ divided by 3   ____ $\div$ ____ = ____

6 Sawyer sells some baseball cards for $3 each. Which of these could be the total amount he makes?

Ⓐ $14   Ⓑ $15   Ⓒ $16   Ⓓ $17

7 Kelly makes a tower by placing layers of blocks on top of each other. Each layer has 4 blocks, as shown below.

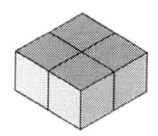

Which of these could be the total number of blocks in Kelly's tower? Circle all the possible answers.

14   18   20   22   24   26   28   30   32   34

Explain why the numbers you did not circle are not possible answers.

_____

_____

_____

Quiz 25: Solving Word Problems Using Multiplication

1 Juan and Lisa have the same number of dimes. Juan sorted his dimes into 6 piles with 5 dimes in each pile. Lisa sorted her dimes into 3 equal piles. How many dimes were in each of Lisa's piles?

Ⓐ 9   Ⓑ 10   Ⓒ 15   Ⓓ 30

2 Mrs. Donovan worked for 8 hours a day for 4 days of the week. She earned $10 for each hour she worked. How much did Mrs. Donovan earn in all?

Ⓐ $80   Ⓑ $120   Ⓒ $320   Ⓓ $400

3 A stores sells small milkshakes for $2 each, medium milkshakes for $3 each, and large milkshakes for $5 each. Write 1, 2, 3, and 4 on the lines to place the orders from lowest cost to highest cost.

_____ 4 small milkshakes and 2 medium milkshakes

_____ 3 large milkshakes

_____ 2 small milkshakes and 3 medium milkshakes

_____ 4 medium milkshakes

4 Zac is organizing 36 chairs for a school play. Which of these are ways he could place all 36 chairs? Select all the possible answers.

☐ 4 rows of 9 chairs

☐ 5 rows of 7 chairs

☐ 8 rows of 4 chairs

☐ 6 rows of 6 chairs

☐ 3 rows of 10 chairs

☐ 6 rows of 3 chairs

5   Flour is sold in bags of 4 pounds each. A diner orders several bags of flour. Which of these could be the total number of pounds of flour? Circle all the possible answers.

   20   26   30   36   42   44   52

   How many pounds of flour would be in an order of 10 bags? _____ pounds

6   The diagram below shows how tables and chairs are set up to seat all the guests at a wedding.

   Complete the sentence to describe how the tables are set up.

   There are ____ tables and each table seats ____ people.

   How many people can be seated at the wedding?

   Show your work.

   Answer _____ people

   The wedding planner decides there should be only 6 people at each table. How many tables would be needed to seat all the people?

   Show your work.

   Answer _____ tables

7 The list shows how long four team members practice baseball each week.

    Milton practices for 20 minutes 7 times a week.
    Rod practices for 30 minutes 5 times a week.
    Paolo practices for 60 minutes 2 times a week.
    Trey practices for 50 minutes 4 times a week.

Which team member practices for the least amount of time? _____

Which team member practices for the most amount of time? _____

8 Eggs are sold in cartons of 6 eggs each. Each carton costs $3. Complete the table to show how many eggs are in each number of cartons and the cost of each number of cartons.

Number of Cartons of Eggs	Total Number of Eggs	Total Cost (in dollars)
4		
6		
8		
10		

9 Hailey plants 3 rows of roses with 8 roses in each row. How many roses does she plant in all? Write your answer below.

Answer _____ roses

10 Lester buys 6 tickets to a play for $7 each. What is the total cost of the tickets? Write your answer below.

Answer $_____

11 Stefan made a path by laying down planks of wood, as shown below.

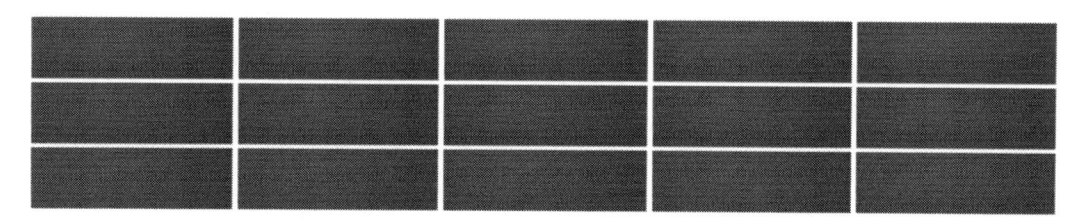

How many planks of wood did he use?

Show your work.

Answer _____ planks of wood

Each plank of wood was 4 feet long. How long was the path?

Show your work.

Answer _____ feet

12 Rex is planting lettuces in his garden. He has 28 lettuces to plant. He plants the lettuces in 6 rows with an equal number of lettuces in each row. What is the most number of lettuces he can plant in each of the 6 rows? Use words or pictures to show how you found your answer.

Answer _____ lettuces

Quiz 26: Representing Division

1 Which equation is represented by the model below?

Ⓐ 24 ÷ 8 = 3   Ⓑ 8 ÷ 4 = 2   Ⓒ 21 ÷ 7 = 3   Ⓓ 72 ÷ 3 = 24

2 There are 12 sunflowers in a bunch.

The sunflowers are divided evenly between 3 vases. Which equation can be used to find how many sunflowers are in each vase?

Ⓐ 12 ÷ 6 = 2   Ⓑ 12 × 3 = 36   Ⓒ 12 ÷ 3 = 4   Ⓓ 36 ÷ 3 = 12

3 Select all the situations that can be represented by 30 ÷ 3.

☐ A teacher sorts 30 students into 3 equal groups.

☐ A class of 30 students gets 3 new students.

☐ A classroom has 30 desks organized into 3 equal rows.

☐ A group of 30 students give a talk for 3 minutes each.

☐ A test has 30 questions worth 3 points each.

☐ A classroom with 30 desks has 3 empty desks.

☐ There are 3 school buses and 30 students on each bus.

4 Write and solve a division expression to answer each question.

Mia sorts 30 blocks into 6 equal piles. How many blocks are in each pile?

_____ ÷ _____ = _____

A coach puts 28 boys in 4 equal teams. How many boys are in each team?

_____ ÷ _____ = _____

Joel earns $9 per hour. How many hours does he work to make $72?

_____ ÷ _____ = _____

Muffins sell for $4 each. How many muffins need to be sold to make $32?

_____ ÷ _____ = _____

5 Mr. Denton is ordering pizzas for a party. Each pizza has 8 slices.

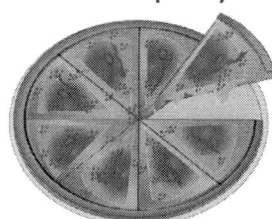

Complete the equation to show how to find the number of pizzas he will need to order to have 40 slices.

_____ ÷ _____ = _____

6 Hal has 80 photos. He places them in equal groups and has no photos left over. Circle the three other numbers below that could be the number of groups he sorted the photos into.

(2)   3   4   5   6   7   8   9

Write numbers on the lines to find the number of photos in each group.

80 ÷ _2_ = _40_   80 ÷ ____ = ____

80 ÷ ____ = ____   80 ÷ ____ = ____

7 Carrie was asked to write a description of a situation where the number of items is represented by the expression below.

$24 \div 6$

Carrie started her description, as shown below. Complete the description.

There are 24 students in a class. _____

_____

_____

8 Morgan has 36 baseball cards. Write a description of a problem Morgan could solve with the expression below.

$36 \div 4$

_____

_____

_____

9 Anna has 50 candies in a bag. Write a description of a problem Anna could solve with the expression below.

$50 \div 10$

_____

_____

_____

10 Leon has 20 apples. Draw circles around the apples to place them in 5 equal groups.

How many apples are in each group? _____ apples

11 Lenny has 12 quarters. He sorts them into groups of 4. Draw a diagram to show how many groups of quarters he will have. Then complete the equation to show how to find how many groups he will have.

Equation _____ ÷ _____ = _____

12 Marina has 18 tomatoes and 3 bags. She places an equal number of tomatoes in each bag.

Write an equation to show how many tomatoes she places in each bag. Then write the number of tomatoes in each bag on the blank line.

Equation

Answer _____ tomatoes

Quiz 27: Using Division Facts

1 What is the value of the expression 63 ÷ 9?

Ⓐ 6 Ⓑ 7 Ⓒ 8 Ⓓ 9

2 Jeremy says that if he places 12 coins in rows of 4, there will be 8 rows. Which of these describes Jeremy's statement?

Ⓐ He is correct because 4 less than 12 is equal to 8.

Ⓑ He is correct because the sum of 8 and 4 is 12.

Ⓒ He is incorrect because the product of 12 and 4 is 48.

Ⓓ He is incorrect because 12 divided by 4 is equal to 3.

3 Which of these describes a situation where there will be 6 students in each group?

Ⓐ 48 students divided into 8 equal groups

Ⓑ 56 students divided into 7 equal groups

Ⓒ 63 students divided into 7 equal groups

Ⓓ 72 students divided into 8 equal groups

4 Select all the equations that are correct when the number 3 is placed on the blank line.

☐ 25 ÷ ___ = 5

☐ 18 ÷ ___ = 9

☐ 21 ÷ ___ = 7

☐ 3 ÷ 1 = ___

☐ 15 ÷ 5 = ___

☐ 10 × ___ = 30

☐ 8 × 5 = ___

☐ ___ × 4 = 24

☐ ___ × 9 = 27

☐ 7 × ___ = 42

5 Find the value of the missing number in each statement. Write the correct number on the blank line. Then write a multiplication equation to show that the number is correct. The first one has been completed for you.

35 equals __5__ multiplied by 7 $5 \times 7 = 35$

64 equals ____ multiplied by 8   ____ × ____ = ____

36 equals ____ multiplied by 4   ____ × ____ = ____

14 equals ____ multiplied by 2   ____ × ____ = ____

48 equals ____ multiplied by 6   ____ × ____ = ____

6 Complete the table by writing a division equation that shows that the number is a factor. The first one has been completed for you.

Number	Factor	Equation
40	5	$40 \div 8 = 5$
32	8	
70	10	
18	6	
56	7	
27	3	

7 A coach wants to divide 30 players into 8 equal teams. Explain why this is not possible. Then tell a way he could divide the players into equal teams.

_____

_____

Answer _____ teams of _____ players each

Quiz 28: Solving Word Problems Using Division

1 Li put 54 pens into 9 equal groups. How many pens were in each group?

  Ⓐ 5 Ⓑ 6 Ⓒ 7 Ⓓ 8

2 A farmer packed 72 bottles of orange juice into packs of 8 bottles each. How many packs were there?

  Ⓐ 6 Ⓑ 7 Ⓒ 8 Ⓓ 9

3 Which of these would have 4 students in each team? Select all the correct answers.

  ☐ 28 students divided into 7 equal teams

  ☐ 36 students divided into 6 equal teams

  ☐ 40 students divided into 8 equal teams

  ☐ 24 students divided into 6 equal teams

  ☐ 32 students divided into 8 equal teams

  ☐ 44 students divided into 4 equal teams

4 A baker had 80 pounds of flour. He placed equal amounts into bags. He filled 10 bags. How many pounds were in each bag?

  Answer _____ pounds

5 A pet store has 48 fish. They want to put 4 fish in each fish tank. How many fish tanks would be needed?

  Answer _____ fish tanks

6 Students at a bake sale divided cakes into 8 pieces and sold each piece for $2. If the total sales were $80, how many complete cakes did they sell?

Show your work.

Answer _____ cakes

7 Jay bought 8 pens for $3 each. Leanne bought 6 notebooks. The price of each notebook was the same. Leanne spent the same total amount as Jay.

How much was each notebook?

Show your work.

Answer $_____

8 Mr. Anderson bought 12 children's ticket to a show for $4 each. Mrs. Chavez bought 8 adult tickets for the same total amount. How much was each adult ticket?

Show your work.

Answer $_____

9 Four classes at a school all have the desks arranged in equal rows. The table shows how the desks are arranged in each class. Complete the missing numbers in the table.

Class	Total Number of Desks	Number of Rows of Desks	Number of Desks in each Row
Mrs. Jenson	30	5	
Mr. Hoy	28		7
Miss Parker		4	8
Mr. Lewis	27		9

10 The table below shows how many cups of juice are filled for different numbers of cartons of juice.

Cartons of Juice	Cups of Juice
3	12
5	20
6	?
?	28
?	32
9	36

How many cups of juice are filled from 6 cartons of juice? _____ cups

How many cartons of juice will be needed to serve 28 cups? _____ cartons

How many cartons of juice will be needed to serve 32 cups? _____ cartons

Cups of juice are sold for $2 each. How many cups of juice need to be sold to make $80? _____ cups

11 Al made the diagram below to show how he will stack cans in equal rows.

Complete the equation and sentence to tell how all the cans are stacked.

___ ÷ ___ = ___   There are ___ cans in ___ rows of ___ cans each.

Complete the equation to represent how the cans could be stacked in 3 rows. Then complete the sentence.

___ ÷ ___ = ___   There are ___ cans in 3 rows of ___ cans each.

12 Students are making shapes by placing square tiles on a board. Tori used 64 tiles, Amelia used 54 tiles, Dina used 49 tiles, and Ivy used 50 tiles.

Who could have made a rectangle that was 5 tiles long? How many tiles high would the shape be? Show or explain how you found your answer.

Student _____   **Height** _____ tiles

Who could have made a rectangle that was 9 tiles long? How many tiles high would the shape be? Show or explain how you found your answer.

Student _____   **Height** _____ tiles

Which two students could have made square shapes? Show or explain how you found your answer.

Students _____ and _____

Quiz 29: Identifying Even and Odd Numbers

1 Which number below is an even number?

Ⓐ 93   Ⓑ 95   Ⓒ 96   Ⓓ 99

2 Gina states that the number 124 is an even number. Which statement best explains how you can tell that Gina is correct?

Ⓐ The number 124 cannot be evenly divided by 10.

Ⓑ The number 124 can be evenly divided by 2.

Ⓒ The number 124 is a three-digit number.

Ⓓ The number 124 is greater than 100.

3 Look at the number sentence below.

$$1031 \div 2 = 515 \text{ remainder } 1$$

What does the number sentence show about the number 1,031?

Ⓐ It is an even number because it can be divided by 2.

Ⓑ It is an odd number because it has a remainder when it is divided by 2.

Ⓒ It is an even number because 515 + 1 gives an even number.

Ⓓ It is an odd number because 515 is an odd number.

4 Circle all the numbers listed below that are odd numbers.

17	20	26	29	34
41	42	45	48	49
56	67	80	91	96

5   Carter has the pennies shown below.

    List three ways he could divide them into two groups with an even number of pennies in each group.

    One group of _____ pennies and one group of _____ pennies.

    One group of _____ pennies and one group of _____ pennies.

    One group of _____ pennies and one group of _____ pennies.

6   The table below lists how many students were at a baseball training session on five different days.

Day	Monday	Tuesday	Friday	Saturday	Sunday
Students	49	53	62	71	78

    On which days could the students be divided into two groups with an equal number of students in each group?

    Answer _____ and _____

7   Charlene has 83 snow globes in her collection. Could she divide them into two equal groups? Explain how you know.

    _____

    _____

    _____

Quiz 30: Using Properties of Numbers to Multiply and Divide

1 Which number sentence can be used to find the value of 63 ÷ 9?

Ⓐ 9 × ___ = 63   Ⓑ 9 + ___ = 63   Ⓒ 9 × 63 = ___   Ⓓ 9 + 63 = ___

2 Which number sentence can be used to check the value of 7 × 3 = 21?

Ⓐ 21 ÷ 7 = ___   Ⓑ 21 + 7 = ___   Ⓒ 21 × 3 = ___   Ⓓ 21 − 7 = ___

3 For each multiplication equation, complete two division equations that could be used to check the answer.

6 × 4 = 24	___ ÷ ___ = ___	___ ÷ ___ = ___
7 × 6 = 42	___ ÷ ___ = ___	___ ÷ ___ = ___
3 × 9 = 27	___ ÷ ___ = ___	___ ÷ ___ = ___
8 × 4 = 32	___ ÷ ___ = ___	___ ÷ ___ = ___
5 × 7 = 35	___ ÷ ___ = ___	___ ÷ ___ = ___
9 × 8 = 72	___ ÷ ___ = ___	___ ÷ ___ = ___

4 For each division equation, complete two multiplication equations that could be used to check the answer.

36 ÷ 4 = 9	___ × ___ = ___	___ × ___ = ___
20 ÷ 4 = 5	___ × ___ = ___	___ × ___ = ___
18 ÷ 2 = 9	___ × ___ = ___	___ × ___ = ___
48 ÷ 8 = 6	___ × ___ = ___	___ × ___ = ___
30 ÷ 6 = 5	___ × ___ = ___	___ × ___ = ___
28 ÷ 4 = 7	___ × ___ = ___	___ × ___ = ___

5 Complete the missing values in the equations below.

4 × 6 = ____ × 4	7 × 1 = ____ × 7	5 × ____ = 6 × 5
8 × 9 = ____ × 8	5 × 4 = ____ × 5	2 × ____ = 8 × 2
3 × 5 = ____ × 3	9 × 3 = ____ × 9	1 × ____ = 7 × 1

6 Complete the table to show the two steps in finding the value of each expression. The first one has been completed for you.

Expression	Step 1	Step 2
(3 × 4) × 10	12 × 10	120
(3 × 2) × 8		
(2 × 4) × 9		
(14 ÷ 7) × 6		
(36 ÷ 6) × 4		
(45 ÷ 5) × 7		

7 Complete the missing values to create an equivalent expression. Then find the value of the expression.

4 × (6 + 2) = (____ × ____) + (____ × ____)

Answer _____

115

8 Select all the expressions that are equal to 81.

☐ 9 × (4 + 5) ☐ (9 × 3) + (9 × 6)

☐ (8 + 1) × 7 ☐ (5 × 4) + (6 × 3)

☐ 3 × 6 × 9 ☐ (1 × 9) + (9 × 9)

9 Which of these shows a correct way to find 60 ÷ 2 ÷ 6?

Ⓐ 60 ÷ (6 − 2) = 60 ÷ 4 = 15   Ⓑ 60 ÷ 2 = 30, 30 × 6 = 180

Ⓒ 60 ÷ 6 = 10, 10 ÷ 2 = 5   Ⓓ (60 − 6) ÷ 2 = 54 ÷ 2 = 27

10 Complete the number sentences by writing the missing number in each blank space. Then complete the calculation.

14 × 2 = (10 × 2) + (___ × 2)   18 × 4 = (10 × 4) + (___ × 4)

= _____ + _____   = _____ + _____

= _____   = _____

25 × 6 = (20 × 6) + (5 × ___)   36 × 3 = (30 × 3) + (6 × ___)

= _____ + _____   = _____ + _____

= _____   = _____

15 × 3 = (___ × 3) + (___ × 3)   43 × 5 = (___ × 5) + (___ × 5)

= _____ + _____   = _____ + _____

= _____   = _____

28 × 7 = (___ × ___) + (___ × ___)   52 × 7 = (___ × ___) + (___ × ___)

= _____ + _____   = _____ + _____

= _____   = _____

11 Complete the number sentences below to show three different ways to complete the calculation in two steps.

$$2 \times 5 \times 6$$

_____ × _____ = 10, then _____ × _____ = _____

_____ × _____ = 12, then _____ × _____ = _____

_____ × _____ = 30, then _____ × _____ = _____

12 Coins are placed in 2 rows of 16 coins each. Greg divided the coins into two groups to calculate the total number of coins, as shown below.

Complete the expression to show how to find how many coins there are. Write the answer on the line.

(2 × _____) + (2 × _____)

Answer _____ coins

Draw rectangles to divide the coins into two equal groups. Then complete the expression to show how to find how many coins there are. Write the answer on the line.

(_____ × _____) + (_____ × _____)

Answer _____ coins

Quizzes 31 to 39

Analyzing and Creating Patterns and Relationships

Directions

Read each question carefully. For each multiple-choice question, fill in the circle for the correct answer. For other types of questions, follow the directions given in the question.

You may use a ruler to help you answer questions. You should answer the questions without using a calculator.

MATHEMATICS SKILLS LIST
For Parents, Teachers, and Tutors

Quizzes 31 through 39 cover these skills from the Texas Essential Knowledge and Skills (TEKS).

Algebraic Reasoning

The student applies mathematical process standards to analyze and create patterns and relationships.

The student is expected to be able to complete the following tasks.

- Represent one- and two-step problems involving addition and subtraction of whole numbers to 1,000 using pictorial models, number lines, and equations.

- Represent and solve one- and two-step multiplication and division problems within 100 using arrays, strip diagrams, and equations.

- Describe a multiplication expression as a comparison such as 3 x 24 represents 3 times as much as 24.

- Determine the unknown whole number in a multiplication or division equation relating three whole numbers when the unknown is either a missing factor or product.

- Represent real-world relationships using number pairs in a table and verbal descriptions.

Quiz 31: Representing Word Problems with Equations

1   Emilio organized 32 marbles into 4 equal piles. Which number sentence could be used to find the number of marbles in each pile?

   Ⓐ $4 \div \_\_\_ = 32$ Ⓑ $4 \times \_\_\_ = 32$

   Ⓒ $\_\_\_ + 4 = 32$ Ⓓ $\_\_\_ - 4 = 32$

2   Max had 15 baseball cards. He bought 6 baseball cards. Then he lost 2 baseball cards. Which expression can be used to find the number of baseball cards Max has now?

   Ⓐ $15 + 6 + 2$ Ⓑ $15 + 6 - 2$

   Ⓒ $15 - 6 + 2$ Ⓓ $15 - 6 - 2$

3   During a sale, each television is on sale for $150 less than the normal price. Adam buys a television during the sale for $845. Which equation can be used to find the normal price of the television, p?

   Ⓐ $p + 150 = 845$ Ⓑ $p - 150 = 845$

   Ⓒ $845 - p = 150$ Ⓓ $150 + p = 845$

4   Julie had $10. She bought a drink for $2. She spent the rest of the money buying sandwiches for $4 each. Which equation can be used to find how many sandwiches she bought, s?

   Ⓐ $10 + 2 = s \div 4$ Ⓑ $10 + 2 = 4 \times s$

   Ⓒ $10 - 2 = s \div 4$ Ⓓ $10 - 2 = 4 \times s$

5   Ursula sells T-shirts for $8 each. She made $72 selling T-shirts. Which number sentences could be used to find how many T-shirts she sold, n? Select all the correct answers.

   ☐ $72 \div n = 8$ ☐ $72 \div 8 = n$

   ☐ $8 \times n = 72$ ☐ $n \times 8 = 72$

   ☐ $8 \div n = 72$ ☐ $8 \times 72 = n$

6 A store sells milkshakes for $4 each. Match the problem with the expression that can be used to solve it. Draw lines to show the matches.

Bill buys 5 milkshakes. What is the total cost?   20 ÷ 4 = 5

How much change should you get if you pay for 1 milkshake with a $5 bill?   5 + 4 = 9

Erin has $20. How many milkshakes can Erin buy?   5 × 4 = 20

Lloyd buys 1 milkshake and a cookie for $5. What is the total amount Lloyd spent?   5 − 4 = 1

7 Write an equation to match each statement. Then find the missing number. The first one has been completed for you.

Statement	Equation	Missing Number
6 more than a number is equal to 14	___ + 6 = 14	8
a number times 5 is equal to 45		
12 less than a number is equal to 20		
20 divided by a number is equal to 4		
the sum of a number and 13 is equal to 30		
a number divided by 10 is equal to 5		
a number less 4 is equal to 24		
the product of a number and 7 is 28		

8 Jarred organized chairs into 6 rows of 9 chairs each and had 2 chairs left over. Write the correct symbols in the expression to show how to find the total number of chairs, c.

$$6 \,\square\, 9 \,\square\, 2 = c$$

9 Nerida has 62 pennies. She finds another 48 pennies. She uses the pennies to buy a pencil case for 85 pennies. Complete the equation to show how many pennies she has left, p. Then solve the equation to find the answer.

_____ + _____ − _____ = p

Answer _____ pennies

10 Samuel plans to study for 120 minutes. He wants to study math for 60 minutes, history for 20 minutes, and science for the rest of the time. Complete the equation to show how many minutes, m, he can study science for. Then solve the equation to find the answer.

_____ + _____ + m = _____

Answer _____ minutes

11 Kylar has to learn a total of 80 French words for a test. He has already learned 30 words. He wants to learn 5 new words every day. Complete the equation to show how many more days, d, he needs to study to learn the 80 words. Then solve the equation to find the answer.

(_____ − _____) ÷ _____ = d

Answer _____ days

12 Stefan is driving 380 miles to visit his uncle. He drove 170 miles before stopping for breakfast, and then another 140 miles before stopping for lunch. Write an equation to show how to find the number of miles he has left to drive, *m*. Then solve the equation to find the answer.

Answer _____ miles

13 Connor needs 36 white tiles and 28 black tiles to cover his back porch. The tiles are sold in boxes of 4. Write an equation to show how to find the number of boxes of tiles he needs to buy, *b*. Then solve the equation to find the answer.

Answer _____ boxes of tiles

14 Zeke plays basketball. Write an equation to represent each problem. Use *x* as the missing value. Then solve the equation to find the answer.

Zeke's team scored 86 points. Zeke scored 22 of those points. How many points did the other players score?

Equation   **Answer** _____ points

Zeke has 3 practices of equal length and practices for a total of 120 minutes. How long is each practice session?

Equation   **Answer** _____ minutes

Zeke had 12 free throw attempts and made 9 of them. How many free throws did he miss?

Equation   **Answer** _____ free throws

Zeke's team scored 86 points, and won the game by 9 points. What was the other team's score?

Equation   **Answer** _____ points

Quiz 32: Representing Word Problems with Diagrams

1 Which expression is represented on the diagram below?

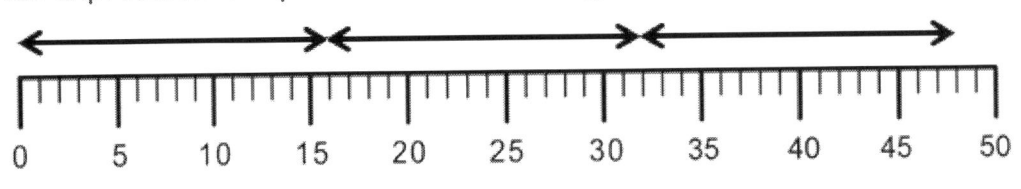

Ⓐ 16 + 16 + 16 Ⓑ 48 ÷ 2 ÷ 2 Ⓒ 24 + 24 Ⓓ 8 × 6

2 Use the number line below to represent 8 × 6.

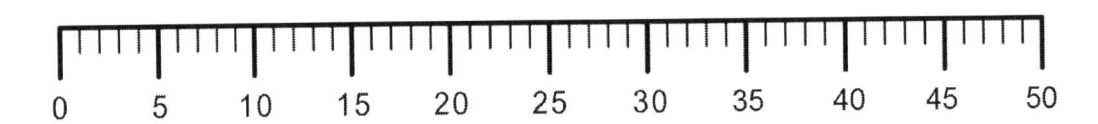

What is the value of 8 × 6? _____

3 Use the number line below to show that 15 can be evenly divided into 90. Then use the number line you completed to write the missing number in the equation.

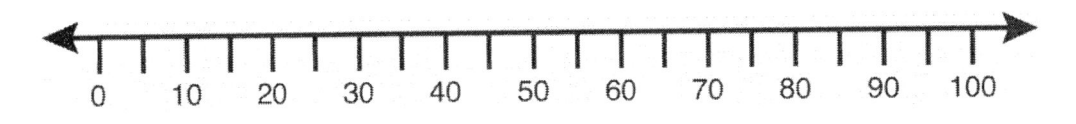

15 × _____ = 90

Use the number line below to find another pair of numbers that complete the equation below.

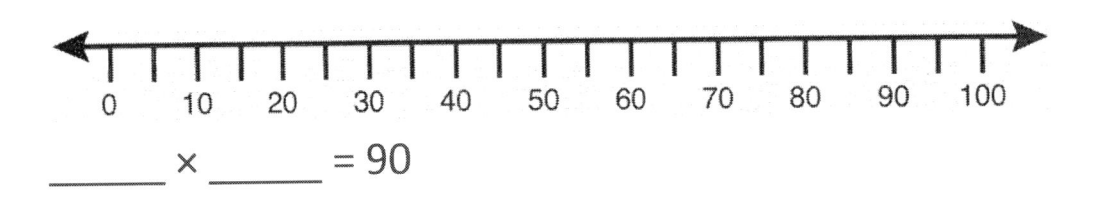

_____ × _____ = 90

4 Andre practiced basketball for 15 minutes in the morning and 55 minutes in the afternoon. How long did he practice for in all? Show how to find the answer on the number line below. Then write the answer on the line.

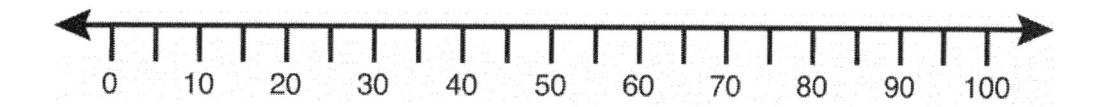

Answer _____ minutes

5 Delvina has $20 in savings. She needs 4 times as much to buy a camera. How much does she need to buy the camera? Show how to find the answer on the number line below. Then write the answer on the line.

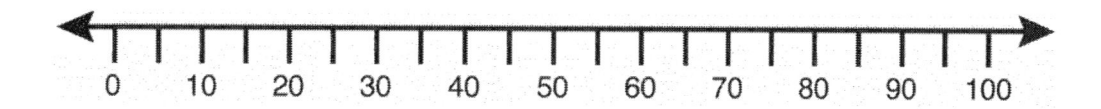

Answer $_____

6 What is the value of the expression below?

15 + 35 + 20

Show how to find the answer on the number line below. Then write the answer on the line.

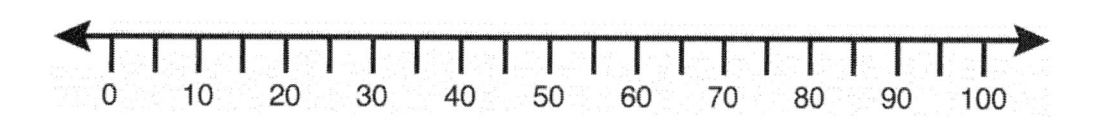

Answer _____

7 Kim is buying notebooks for $3 each. She drew the diagram below to show how many notebooks she can buy for $12.

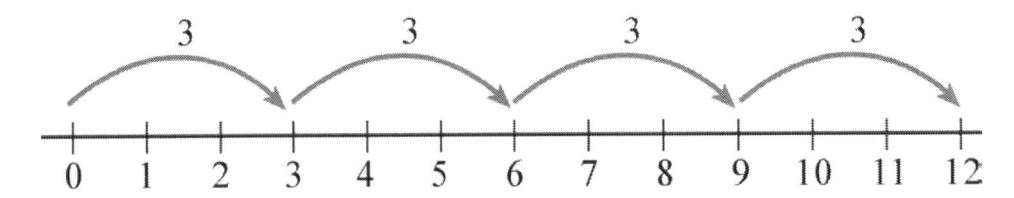

How many notebooks can she buy? _____ notebooks

Explain how the diagram helped you find the answer.

_____

_____

_____

8 Stuart makes the first layer of a wall by placing 6 bricks in a row. He uses another 6 bricks to make the second row. He keeps adding layers of 6 bricks until the wall is complete.

Which of these could be the total number of bricks in the wall? Circle all the possible answers.

22   24   32   36   40   44   48   52   58   64

Explain why the numbers you did not circle are not possible answers.

_____

_____

_____

9 Hannah shaded the grid to show two ways 45 squares can be arranged into a rectangle. Use the diagram to write four different division equations using whole numbers.

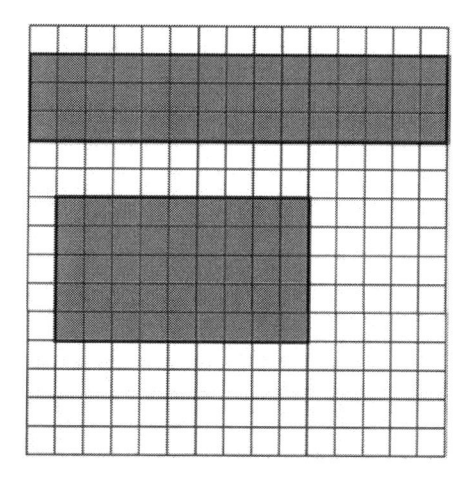

45 ÷ _____ = _____   45 ÷ _____ = _____

45 ÷ _____ = _____   45 ÷ _____ = _____

10 Kelly drew a 13 by 6 rectangle on a grid and shaded each row of the rectangle. Use the diagram to complete the equations below.

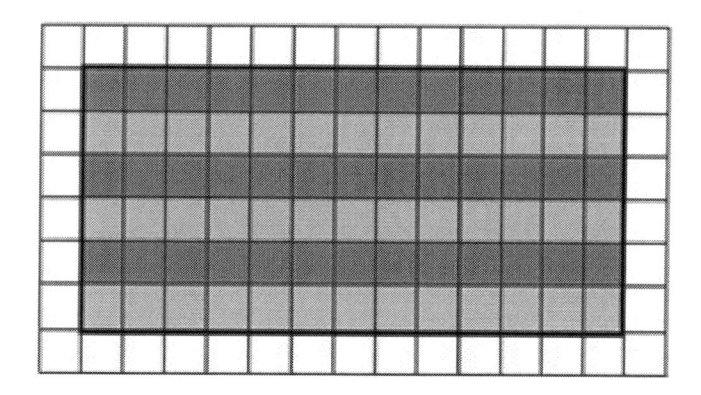

13 × 1 = _____   13 × 2 = _____   13 × 3 = _____

13 × 4 = _____   13 × 5 = _____   13 × 6 = _____

Quiz 33: Representing Multiplication and Division with Arrays

1 Which number sentence represents the array shown below?

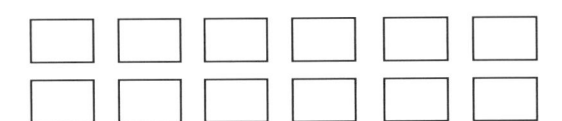

Ⓐ $6 + 2 = 8$ Ⓑ $6 \times 6 = 36$ Ⓒ $6 \times 2 = 12$ Ⓓ $20 - 8 = 12$

2 A 9 by 4 array is shown below.

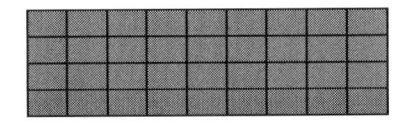

What is the product of 9 and 4?

Ⓐ 13 Ⓑ 26 Ⓒ 36 Ⓓ 54

3 An array for the number 28 is shown below.

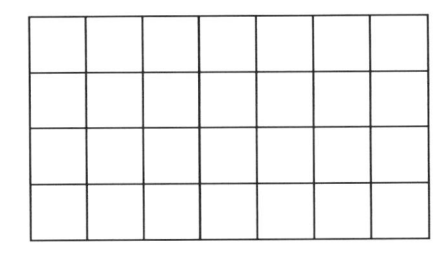

Which number is a factor of 28?

Ⓐ 3 Ⓑ 5 Ⓒ 7 Ⓓ 11

4 Which number sentence could be solved using the array below?

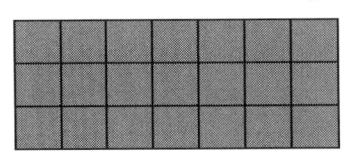

Ⓐ $21 \div \_\_ = 7$ Ⓑ $70 \div \_\_ = 7$ Ⓒ $18 \div \_\_ = 3$ Ⓓ $30 \div \_\_ = 3$

5   Write a multiplication equation that represents each array shown below.

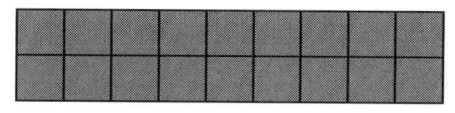

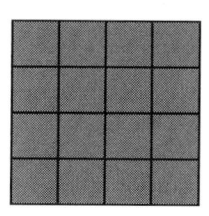

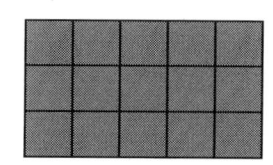

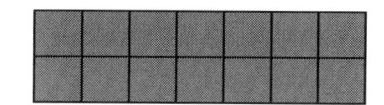

_____ × _____ = _____

_____ × _____ = _____

_____ × _____ = _____

_____ × _____ = _____

6   Joe has 12 apples. He eats 2 apples every day.

How many days would it take Joe to eat all the apples? _____ days

7   Andy had 12 books. She divided the books into 3 equal stacks. Draw an array that represents how many books are in each stack.

How many books are in each stack? _____ books

Quiz 34: Representing Multiplication and Division with Equations

1 Carter organized 36 apples into 4 equal piles. Which number sentence could be used to find the number of apples in each pile?

Ⓐ 4 ÷ ___ = 36

Ⓑ 4 × ___ = 36

Ⓒ 36 × 4 = ___

Ⓓ ___ ÷ 4 = 36

2 Each milk carton below contains 8 fluid ounces of milk.

Which number sentence could be used to find how many fluid ounces of milk there are in all?

Ⓐ 4 ÷ ___ = 8

Ⓑ 4 × ___ = 8

Ⓒ 8 × 4 = ___

Ⓓ 8 ÷ ___ = 4

3 Mr. Baxter earns $9 for each hour he works. He earned $72 for one day's work. Which number sentences could be used to find how many hours he worked that day? Select all the correct answers.

☐ 72 ÷ ___ = 9

☐ 72 ÷ 9 = ___

☐ 9 × ___ = 72

☐ ___ × 9 = 72

☐ 9 ÷ ___ = 72

☐ 9 × 72 = ___

4 Maria sold 8 cupcakes for an equal amount and made a total of $24. Which of these describes how much she sold each cupcake for?

Ⓐ $3 each, because 24 ÷ 8 = 3

Ⓑ $16 each, because 24 − 8 = 16

Ⓒ $32 each, because 24 + 8 = 32

Ⓓ $192 each, because 24 × 8 = 192

5 Write an equation to match each statement. Then find the missing number. The first one has been completed for you.

Statement	Equation	Missing Number
3 times a number is equal to 18	3 × ___ = 18	6
30 divided by a number is equal to 10		
a number times 6 is equal to 42		
twice a number is equal to 12		
a number divided by 5 is equal to 7		

6 Write multiplication expressions to complete the list of all the factors pairs for each number.

Number	Factor Pairs
12	1 × 12 ___ × ___ ___ × ___
16	1 × 16 ___ × ___ ___ × ___
18	1 × 18 ___ × ___ ___ × ___
20	1 × 20 ___ × ___ ___ × ___
24	1 × 24 ___ × ___ ___ × ___ ___ × ___
30	1 × 30 ___ × ___ ___ × ___ ___ × ___
40	1 × 40 ___ × ___ ___ × ___ ___ × ___

7   Darren had 56 photos to place in an album. He placed 8 photos on each page. Complete the equation to show how to find the number of pages of the album Darren filled. Then write the answer below.

56 ÷ _____ = _____

Answer _____ pages

Darren wants to add 4 star stickers to each page with photos on it. Complete the equation to find how many star stickers Darren will need. Then write the answer below.

_____ × 4 = _____

Answer _____ stickers

8   Lila baked 72 muffins for a bake sale. She packed them into bags of 8 muffins each. Complete the equation to show how to find how many bags of muffins Lila had. Then write the answer below.

_____ ÷ _____ = _____

Answer _____ bags

Lila sold the bags of muffins for $4 each and sold all the bags. Complete the equation to show how much Lila made, in dollars. Then write the answer below.

_____ × _____ = _____

Answer $_____

9 Becca is organizing tables for a party. She has 28 people to seat and she wants to seat 4 people at each table. Write an equation to show how to find the number of tables that Becca will need. Then write the answer below.

Answer _____ tables

Becca wants to put a vase of flowers on each table, with 3 sunflowers in each vase. Write an equation to show how to find the number of sunflowers needed. Then write the answer below.

Answer _____ sunflowers

10 Mr. Palmer is organizing students into groups to complete a science project. He puts 27 students into groups of 3 students each. Write an equation to show how to find the number of groups. Then write the answer below.

Answer _____ groups

Each group of students is given 5 leaves. Write an equation to show how to find the number of leaves in all. Then write the answer below.

Answer _____ leaves

Quiz 35: Understanding Multiplication as a Comparison

1 Which situation can be represented by the equation 9 × 6 = 54?

Ⓐ Ally saved $9 one week and $6 the next week.

Ⓑ Ally had $54 in savings left after spending $9.

Ⓒ Ally saved $9 each week for 6 weeks.

Ⓓ Ally spent $54 each month for 6 months.

2 Which of these is represented by the model below?

Ⓐ 20 is 4 times as many as 5

Ⓑ 40 is 2 times as many as 20

Ⓒ 5 is 4 times greater than 20

Ⓓ 4 is 20 times greater than 5

3 Dan and Leah placed coins in piles. Every pile had the same number of coins in it. Dan's piles are shown below.

Leah has 3 times as many piles as Dan. How many coins does Leah have?

Ⓐ 12 Ⓑ 24 Ⓒ 42 Ⓓ 72

4 Kimi found that her dog's mass was 4 times as much as her cat's mass. If her cat's mass was 8 kilograms, what was her dog's mass?

Ⓐ 2 kg Ⓑ 12 kg Ⓒ 32 kg Ⓓ 48 kg

5. Complete each statement with two numbers that make the statement true. Then complete the equation to represent the statement.

14 is ____ times as many as ____   14 = ____ × ____

21 is ____ times as many as ____   21 = ____ × ____

35 is ____ times as many as ____   35 = ____ × ____

49 is ____ times as many as ____   49 = ____ × ____

55 is ____ times as many as ____   55 = ____ × ____

6. The table below shows how far students live from school.

Student	Wesley	Flynn	Gino	Thomas	Corey
Distance (miles)	2	6	18	30	?

Complete each statement below with the correct number.

Flynn lives ____ times as far from school as Wesley.

Gino lives ____ times as far from school as Wesley.

Thomas lives ____ times as far from school as Wesley.

Gino lives ____ times as far from school as Flynn.

Thomas lives ____ times as far from school as Flynn.

Corey lives 7 times as far from school as Flynn. How far does Corey live from school? ____ miles

7 Decide if each problem can be solved with addition or with multiplication. Circle the correct word to show your choice. Then write an expression that can be used to solve the problem. Write your answer on the line.

Hannah is 14. Oliver is 3 years older than Hannah. How old is Oliver?

        addition   multiplication

Expression _____   **Answer** _____ years old

A pound of peaches costs 5 times as much as a pound of apples. A pound of apples costs $3. How much does a pound of peaches cost?

        addition   multiplication

Expression _____   **Answer** $_____

A new building has 5 times as many floors as the old building. The old building had 6 floors. How many floors does the new building have?

        addition   multiplication

Expression _____   **Answer** _____ floors

Fiona's new school has 15 more fourth grade students than her last school. Her last school had 80 fourth grade students. How many fourth grade students does her new school have?

        addition   multiplication

Expression _____   **Answer** _____ students

A store sold 18 cameras on Thursday and 4 times as many on Friday. How many cameras were sold on Friday?

        addition   multiplication

Expression _____   **Answer** _____ cameras

Quiz 36: Finding Missing Numbers in Equations

1 In which of these does the number 4 make the equation true?

Ⓐ 24 ÷ □ = 6   Ⓑ □ ÷ 6 = 24

Ⓒ 24 × 6 = □   Ⓓ □ × 24 = 6

2 Which number makes the number sentence below true?

□ ÷ 3 = 6

Ⓐ 9   Ⓑ 12   Ⓒ 18   Ⓓ 24

3 Which number makes the number sentence below true?

□ × 96 = 6

Ⓐ 12   Ⓑ 14   Ⓒ 16   Ⓓ 18

4 In which number sentence does the number 7 make the equation true?

Ⓐ 24 ÷ □ = 6   Ⓑ 36 ÷ □ = 6

Ⓒ 42 ÷ □ = 6   Ⓓ 48 ÷ □ = 6

5 Which number makes the number sentence below true?

36 ÷ □ = 9

Answer _____

6 Which number makes the number sentence below true?

5 × □ = 95

Answer _____

7 Complete each number sentence by writing the missing number on the blank line.

7 × 3 = _____ 3 × 3 = _____ 1 × 4 = _____

6 × 4 = _____ 5 × 6 = _____ 8 × 5 = _____

2 × 8 = _____ 8 × 7 = _____ 3 × 8 = _____

9 × 9 = _____ 6 × 7 = _____ 7 × 5 = _____

4 × 7 = _____ 9 × 4 = _____ 2 × 6 = _____

8 Complete each number sentence by writing the missing number on the blank line.

2 × _____ = 18 4 × _____ = 24 7 × _____ = 70

_____ × 7 = 21 _____ × 8 = 40 _____ × 6 = 36

4 × _____ = 36 9 × _____ = 9 7 × _____ = 56

_____ × 5 = 50 _____ × 6 = 48 _____ × 4 = 20

9 Complete each number sentence by writing the missing 1-digit numbers on the blank lines.

____ × ____ = 14 ____ × ____ = 35 ____ × ____ = 64

____ × ____ = 27 ____ × ____ = 48 ____ × ____ = 54

____ × ____ = 32 ____ × ____ = 63 ____ × ____ = 25

10 Complete each number sentence by writing the missing number on the blank line.

$12 \div 2 =$ _____ $63 \div 9 =$ _____ $25 \div 5 =$ _____

$24 \div 3 =$ _____ $56 \div 8 =$ _____ $18 \div 6 =$ _____

$35 \div 5 =$ _____ $60 \div 6 =$ _____ $36 \div 4 =$ _____

$70 \div 7 =$ _____ $9 \div 1 =$ _____ $49 \div 7 =$ _____

$36 \div 6 =$ _____ $32 \div 4 =$ _____ $72 \div 8 =$ _____

11 Complete each number sentence by writing the missing number on the blank line.

$8 \div$ _____ $= 2$ $27 \div$ _____ $= 9$ $16 \div$ _____ $= 4$

$20 \div$ _____ $= 5$ $90 \div$ _____ $= 10$ $18 \div$ _____ $= 2$

$54 \div$ _____ $= 6$ $42 \div$ _____ $= 7$ $64 \div$ _____ $= 8$

$63 \div$ _____ $= 3$ $81 \div$ _____ $= 9$ $125 \div$ _____ $= 5$

12 Complete each number sentence by writing the missing number on the blank line.

_____ $\div 7 = 3$ _____ $\div 2 = 8$ _____ $\div 5 = 8$

_____ $\div 6 = 5$ _____ $\div 9 = 5$ _____ $\div 8 = 6$

_____ $\div 3 = 10$ _____ $\div 1 = 4$ _____ $\div 9 = 9$

Quiz 37: Understanding Patterns

1 Which number comes next in the pattern below?

2, 5, 8, 11, 14, ...

Ⓐ 16 Ⓑ 17 Ⓒ 20 Ⓓ 25

2 If *n* is a number in the pattern, which rule can be used to find the next number in the pattern?

4, 6, 8, 10, 12, 14, 16, ...

Ⓐ $n + 2$ Ⓑ $n - 2$ Ⓒ $n + 4$ Ⓓ $n - 4$

3 A florist makes bunches of flowers by placing 4 flowers together and tying them with 1 piece of ribbon. Which expression can be used to find the number of flowers used if 8 pieces of ribbon are used?

Ⓐ 8 ÷ 4 Ⓑ 8 + 4 Ⓒ 8 × 4 Ⓓ 8 - 4

4 The table below shows the relationship between the number of tables set in a restaurant and the number of napkins used.

Number of Tables	3	6	9	12	15
Number of Napkins	24	48		96	120

Based on the pattern, which number sentence can be used to find the number of napkins needed to set 9 tables?

Ⓐ 96 ÷ 2 Ⓑ 9 × 24 Ⓒ 42 × 2 Ⓓ 9 × 8

5 Brook is 14 years old. Chad has the same birth date, but is 7 years younger. When Brook is 18 years old, how old will Chad be?

Ⓐ 9 years old Ⓑ 11 years old Ⓒ 15 years old Ⓓ 21 years old

6 Jasper has 14 baseball cards. He buys more baseball cards in packets of 4 baseball cards each. Complete the pattern that shows how many baseball cards Jasper could have.

14, _____, _____, _____, _____, _____, _____

7 The first six numbers in a pattern are shown below. Which statement is true about every number in the pattern?

5, 10, 15, 20, 25, 30, ...

Ⓐ It is divisible by 5.　　　　Ⓑ It is a multiple of 10.

Ⓒ It is an odd number.　　　Ⓓ It is an even number.

8 Fill in the blanks to describe each pattern below.

Pattern	Description
2, 5, 8, 11, 14, 17, ...	The pattern starts at ____. Each number is ____ more than the one before it.
3, 6, 12, 24, 48, ...	The pattern starts at ____. Each number is ____ times more than the one before it.
40, 36, 32, 28, 24, ...	The pattern starts at ____. Each number is ____ less than the one before it.
1, 6, 11, 16, 21, 26, ...	The pattern starts at ____. Each number is ____ more than the one before it.
100, 89, 78, 67, 56, ...	The pattern starts at ____. Each number is ____ less than the one before it.
1, 4, 16, 64, 256, ...	The pattern starts at ____. Each number is ____ times more than the one before it.

9. For each pattern, write an expression that can be used to find the next number in the pattern. Use *n* to represent the last number in the pattern. Then complete the missing numbers.

Pattern	Expression
6, 9, 12, 15, 18, 21, ____, ____	*n* + 3
6, 10, 14, 18, 22, ____, ____	
48, 42, 36, 30, 24, ____, ____	
64, 32, 16, 8, ____, ____	
1, 2, 4, 8, 16, ____, ____	

10. Sort the patterns described below into those that will have only odd numbers, those that will have only even numbers, and those that will have both. List the letters in the table to show your answers.

- A   starts at 5, adds 4 to each number
- B   starts at 80, subtracts 3 from each number
- C   starts at 2, each number is twice the one before it
- D   starts at 5, adds 7 to each number
- E   starts at 35, each number is 6 less than the one before it
- F   starts at 16, adds 9 to each number
- G   starts at 1, each number is 3 times the one before it
- H   starts at 10, each number is 8 more than the one before it
- I   starts at 3, each number is twice the one before it
- J   starts at 4, multiplies each number by 10

Patterns with Only Odd Numbers	Patterns with Only Even Numbers	Patterns with Odd and Even Numbers

11 A bakery sells its rolls in bags of 8 for $3 each bag. Complete the table.

Number of Bags of Rolls	Total Number of Rolls	Total Cost ($)
2		
3		
4		
5		
6		

Explain why the total number of rolls will always be even.

_____

_____

Explain why the total cost is not always even.

_____

_____

12 Apple trees were planted in rows. Each row had the same number of apple trees. Complete the missing numbers in the table below.

Number of Rows	4	5	6	7	8	9	10
Number of Trees	24	30	36				

Explain why the total number of apple trees will always be a multiple of 6.

_____

_____

Quiz 38: Representing Real-World Relationships

1 Josh buys bagels in packets of 4. If Josh counts the bagels in groups of 4, which number could he count?

Ⓐ 6　　　　Ⓑ 10　　　　Ⓒ 15　　　　Ⓓ 16

2 Martin buys screws in packets of 8.

If Martin counts the screws in groups of 8, which number could he **NOT** count?

Ⓐ 16　　　　Ⓑ 24　　　　Ⓒ 32　　　　Ⓓ 36

3 There are 12 roses in a bunch. Leanne counts the roses in groups of 12.

Which number would Leanne count?

Ⓐ 25　　　　Ⓑ 30　　　　Ⓒ 36　　　　Ⓓ 50

4 Terri has tokens for arcade games.

If Terri counts her tokens in groups of 6, which list shows only numbers she would count?

Ⓐ 12, 16, 20　　Ⓑ 12, 18, 24　　Ⓒ 6, 10, 12　　Ⓓ 6, 12, 20

5 Jennifer sells cupcakes for $3 each. Complete the list below to show how much she would make for selling 1, 2, 3, 4 or 5 cupcakes.

$3, _____, _____, _____, _____

6 A farmer sells eggs in cartons of 6 eggs each.

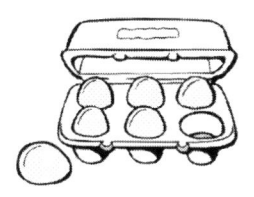

A bakery placed an order for several cartons of 6 eggs. Which of these could be the total number of eggs ordered?

Ⓐ 48   Ⓑ 50   Ⓒ 52   Ⓓ 56

7 Leticia used muffin tins like the one below to bake batches of muffins for a bake sale. The muffin tin was full for each batch.

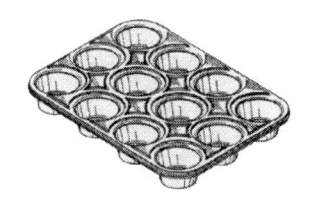

Which of these could be the total number of muffins she baked? Select all the possible answers.

☐ 18   ☐ 24   ☐ 30   ☐ 42

☐ 48   ☐ 52   ☐ 60   ☐ 84

8 A pet store feeds each fish 5 food pellets per day. Which expression could be used to find how many pellets would be needed to feed 20 fish?

Ⓐ 20 × 5   Ⓑ 20 ÷ 5   Ⓒ 20 + 5   Ⓓ 20 − 5

9 Belle is putting baseball cards in an album. She can fit 8 baseball cards on each page. Complete the list to show how many baseball cards she can fit on 5, 6, 7, and 8 pages.

8, 16, 24, 32, _____, _____, _____, _____

10 The table below shows the total number of beads Simone uses to make different numbers of bracelets.

Number of Bracelets	Number of Beads
3	60
4	80
5	100

Which of the following describes the relationship in the table?

Ⓐ number of bracelets × 20 = total number of beads

Ⓑ number of bracelets × 60 = total number of beads

Ⓒ number of bracelets × 100 = total number of beads

Ⓓ number of bracelets × 5 = total number of beads

11 The table below shows the total number of chairs that are needed to go with different numbers of tables.

Number of Tables	Number of Chairs
4	24
6	36
10	60

Which of the following describes the relationship in the table?

Ⓐ number of tables ÷ 6 = number of chairs

Ⓑ number of tables × 6 = number of chairs

Ⓒ number of tables ÷ 4 = number of chairs

Ⓓ number of tables × 4 = number of chairs

12 Kane is cutting oranges into wedges. He cuts each orange into 6 wedges. Complete the equation with a correct symbol and number to show the relationship between the number of oranges and the number of wedges.

number of oranges ☐ ☐ = number of wedges

13 Daniel was packing 72 soda cans into boxes. He placed 6 soda cans in each box. Which equation can be used to find b, the number of boxes he used?

Ⓐ $b = 72 \div 6$ Ⓑ $b = 72 - 6$ Ⓒ $b = 72 \times 6$ Ⓓ $b = 72 + 6$

14 Jenna is placing her earrings on a stand. Each shelf of the stand can hold 8 pairs of earrings. Jenna filled 16 shelves. Which equation can be used to find e, the number of pairs of earrings that Jenna placed on the stand?

Ⓐ $e = 16 \div 8$ Ⓑ $e = 16 - 8$ Ⓒ $e = 16 \times 8$ Ⓓ $e = 16 + 8$

15 Marita is buying bags of flour. There are 4 pounds of flour in each bag. Write an equation that shows the relationship between the number of bags of flour, b, and the number of pounds of flour, p.

Equation

Use the equation to find the number of pounds of flour Marita would have if she bought 6 bags of flour.

Show your work.

Answer _____ pounds

16 Tyra wrote the equation below to show the relationship between the number of laps of a track she runs, l, and the distance she runs in meters, d.

$$d = 400 \times l$$

Describe what the equation tells about the distance of each lap of the track.

_____

_____

Quiz 39: Using Tables to Represent Relationships

1 Kendra studies math for 20 minutes every day. Complete the table to show how long she studies math for in total if she studies from 1 to 7 days.

Number of Days	Number of Minutes
1	
2	
3	
4	
5	
6	
7	

2 Andy is learning to speak French. Andy learns 5 new words every day. Complete the table to show how many news words Andy will learn when he studies for different numbers of days.

Number of Days	Total Number of Words Learned
2	
5	
10	
14	
20	
30	

3 Linda uses 3 pieces of bread to make a sandwich. Complete the table to show the relationship between the number of sandwiches and the number of pieces of bread.

Number of Sandwiches	Number of Pieces of Bread
4	
6	
10	
12	
15	
18	

4 Brenda is slicing apples into 8 slices each. Complete the table to show the relationship between the number of apples and the number of apple slices.

Number of Apples	Number of Apple Slices
3	
6	
8	
10	
15	
18	
25	

5 Oranges are sold in bags of 8. The table below shows the number of oranges in 2, 3, and 4 bags.

Number of Bags	Number of Oranges
2	16
3	24
4	32
5	

How many oranges are in 5 bags?

Ⓐ 35 Ⓑ 40 Ⓒ 42 Ⓓ 48

6 Wendy is making cupcakes. She puts the same number of candies on each cake. The table shows how many candies she uses for 5, 10, and 15 cakes.

Number of Cupcakes	Number of Candies
5	15
10	30
15	45
	75

Based on the table above, how many cupcakes could Wendy make if she has 75 candies?

Ⓐ 20 Ⓑ 25 Ⓒ 30 Ⓓ 35

7 Eastwood School is having a car wash. The table below shows how much money is made for washing 6, 10, and 12 cars.

Number of Cars Washed	Amount Made
6	$18
10	$30
12	$36
18	

How much money would the school make if they washed 18 cars?

Ⓐ $3 Ⓑ $41 Ⓒ $48 Ⓓ $54

8   Apple trees were planted in rows. Each row had the same number of trees.

Number of Rows	Number of Apple Trees
4	24
5	30
6	36
7	42

Based on the table, how many apples trees were in each row?

Answer _____ apple trees

9   Katie saw the sign below at a fruit stand.

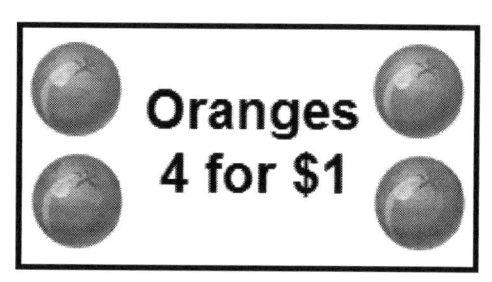

Oranges 4 for $1

Complete the table below to show how many oranges Katie would receive for different amounts of money spent.

Amount Spent ($)	Number of Oranges
2	
4	
5	
9	

How much money would Katie need to spend to buy 28 oranges? Show your work or explain how you found your answer.

Answer $_____

Quizzes 40 to 50

Understanding and Analyzing the Properties of Shapes

Directions

Read each question carefully. For each multiple-choice question, fill in the circle for the correct answer. For other types of questions, follow the directions given in the question.

You may use a ruler to help you answer questions. You should answer the questions without using a calculator.

MATHEMATICS SKILLS LIST
For Parents, Teachers, and Tutors

Quizzes 40 through 50 cover these skills from the Texas Essential Knowledge and Skills (TEKS).

Geometry and Measurement

The student applies mathematical process standards to analyze attributes of two-dimensional geometric figures to develop generalizations about their properties.

The student is expected to be able to complete the following tasks.

- Classify and sort two- and three-dimensional figures, including cones, cylinders, spheres, triangular and rectangular prisms, and cubes, based on attributes using formal geometric language.

- Use attributes to recognize rhombuses, parallelograms, trapezoids, rectangles, and squares as examples of quadrilaterals and draw examples of quadrilaterals that do not belong to any of these subcategories.

- Determine the area of rectangles with whole number side lengths in problems using multiplication related to the number of rows times the number of unit squares in each row.

- Decompose composite figures formed by rectangles into non-overlapping rectangles to determine the area of the original figure using the additive property of area.

- Decompose two congruent two-dimensional figures into parts with equal areas and express the area of each part as a unit fraction of the whole and recognize that equal shares of identical wholes need not have the same shape.

Quiz 40: Classifying Two-Dimensional Shapes

1. Which term describes the three shapes shown below?

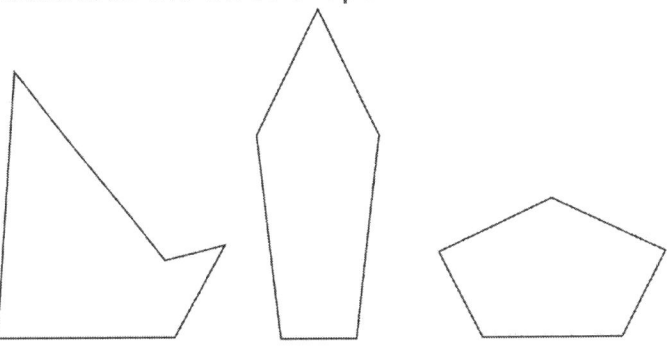

    Ⓐ octagon   Ⓑ pentagon   Ⓒ hexagon   Ⓓ quadrilateral

2. What is the shape of the outside of the nut shown below?

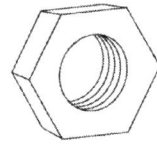

    Ⓐ hexagon   Ⓑ octagon   Ⓒ pentagon   Ⓓ square

3. Which statement is true about rhombuses and rectangles?

    Ⓐ They always have 4 equal sides.

    Ⓑ They always have 4 right angles.

    Ⓒ They always have 4 equal angles.

    Ⓓ They always have 4 sides.

4. Two shapes both have four equal sides. Which of these could the two shapes be?

    Ⓐ square and rectangle

    Ⓑ square and rhombus

    Ⓒ rhombus and rectangle

    Ⓓ square and trapezoid

5 A quadrilateral has 4 equal angles. Which question should be asked to determine if the shape is a rectangle or a square?

Ⓐ What is the measure of each angle?

Ⓑ Is the shape a parallelogram?

Ⓒ Are all the sides of the shape equal?

Ⓓ Does the shape have right angles?

6 Select all the shapes listed below that are parallelograms.

☐ square ☐ trapezoid ☐ rectangle

☐ rhombus ☐ triangle ☐ pentagon

7 Circle all the figures below that are octagons.

On the lines below, describe what characteristic all the octagons have in common.

_____

_____

8 Which two polygons make up the sides of each figure shown below? Write your answers on the lines next to each shape.

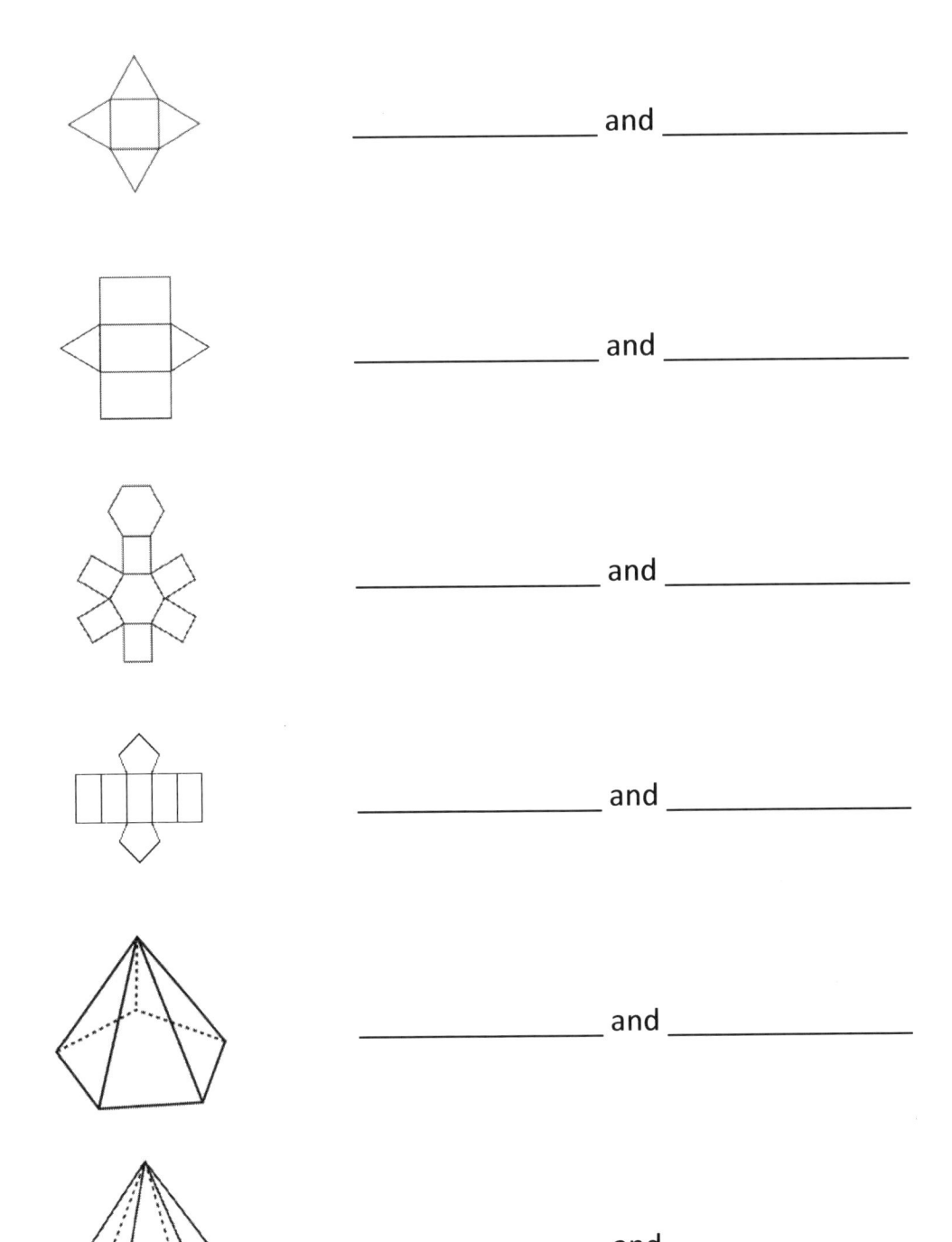

_____ and _____

_____ and _____

_____ and _____

_____ and _____

_____ and _____

_____ and _____

9   Look at the shapes below.

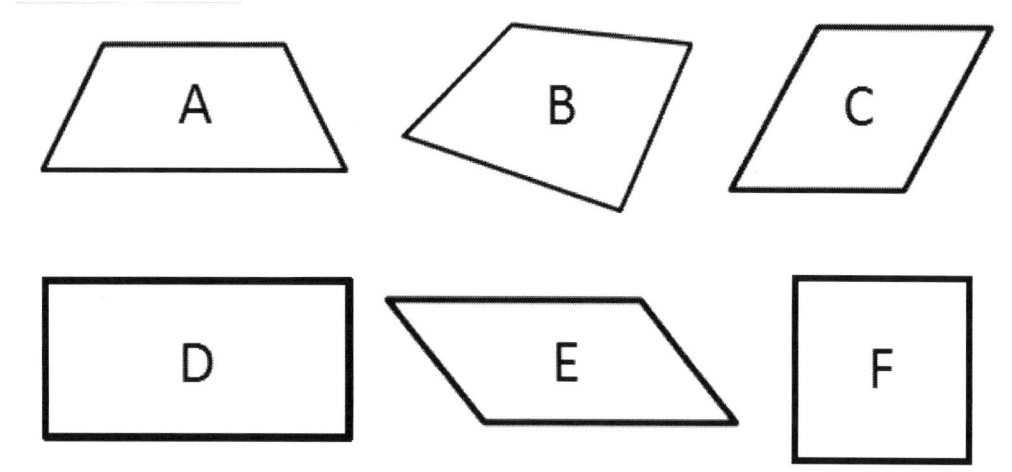

Which shape is a rhombus but not a square? _____

Describe three features that tell that the shape is a rhombus.

1. _____

2. _____

3. _____

Which shape is a trapezoid? _____

Describe two features that tell that the shape is a trapezoid.

1. _____

2. _____

Which shape is a square? _____

Describe two features that tell that the shape is a square.

1. _____

2. _____

Quiz 41: Comparing and Sorting Two-Dimensional Shapes

1 Which shape has more sides than a pentagon?

    Ⓐ triangle   Ⓑ rectangle   Ⓒ octagon   Ⓓ trapezoid

2 Order the shapes below from least to most sides. Write the numbers 1, 2, 3, and 4 on the lines to show the order.

    ___ hexagon   ___ octagon   ___ pentagon   ___ square

3 Dorian and Marco both drew octagons. Which statement must be true of the figures Dorian and Marco drew?

    Ⓐ They must be exactly the same.

    Ⓑ They must have the same number of angles.

    Ⓒ They must have the same side lengths.

    Ⓓ They must have the same angle measures.

4 Tavena sketched the four triangles shown below. Answer the questions below by writing the correct letter on each line.

Which triangle has a right angle? _____

Which triangle has exactly two equal angles? _____

Which triangle has all sides of equal length? _____

Which two triangles have no sides of equal length? _____ and _____

5   Complete the table below by describing each feature of a square and a rectangle.

Feature	Square	Rectangle
Number of Sides		
Number of Angles		
Right Angles		
Parallel Sides		
Equal Sides		

Based on the table, which feature can be used to tell a square and a rectangle apart?

_____

_____

6   Describe three ways a square is similar to a rhombus.

1. _____

2. _____

3. _____

Describe two ways a square is different from a rhombus.

1. _____

2. _____

7 Two shapes are shown below.

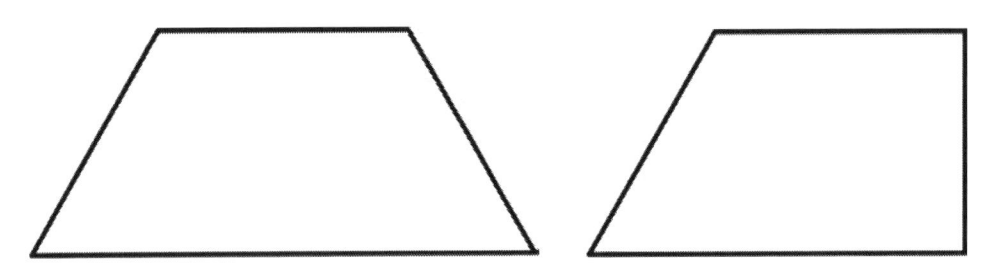

What do the two shapes have in common?

_____

_____

What makes the second shape different from the first?

_____

_____

8 For each group of shapes below, draw a fourth shape that fits in the same category in the empty circle.

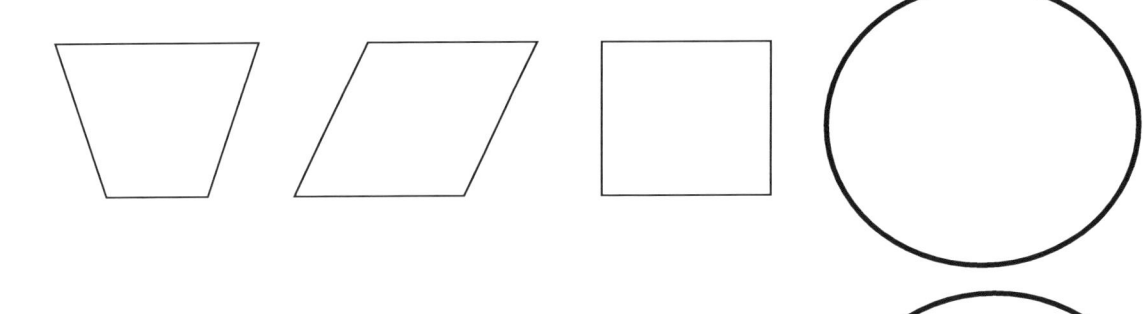

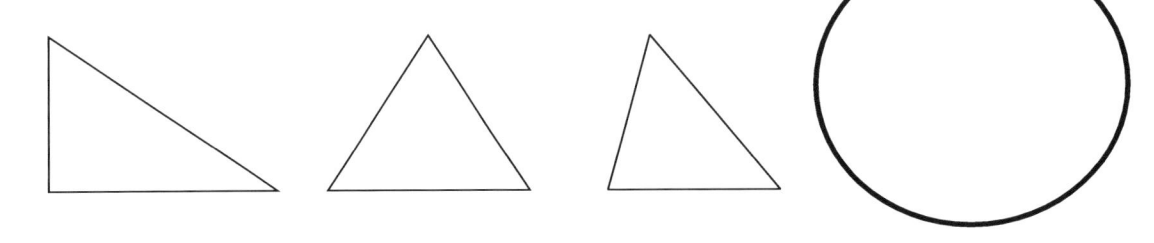

9 On each grid below, draw a polygon with the description given.

Draw a polygon with the same number of sides as a square, but no sides of equal length.	
Draw a polygon with 1 less side than an octagon.	
Draw a polygon with twice as many sides as a triangle.	
Draw a polygon with the same number of sides as the shape shown below, but no sides of equal length. 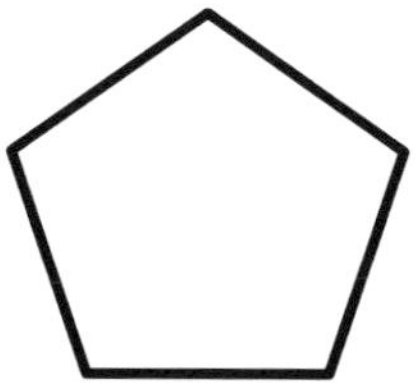	

Quiz 42: Understanding and Using the Properties of Shapes

1   A rectangle and a trapezoid are shown below.

Which of the following do these shapes always have in common?

Ⓐ number of sides   Ⓑ right angles

Ⓒ pairs of equal sides   Ⓓ side lengths

2   A rhombus is shown below.

Which sentence best explains why a rhombus is a quadrilateral?

Ⓐ It has equal sides.   Ⓑ It has parallel sides.

Ⓒ It has four sides.   Ⓓ It has no right angles.

3   What do all the shapes shown below have in common? Select all the correct answers.

☐ total number of sides   ☐ right angles

☐ length of the sides   ☐ four equal angles

☐ height of the sides   ☐ four equal sides

4   The flag of the Bahamas is shown below.

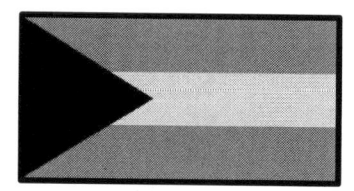

What type of quadrilateral makes up part of the flag? _____

Based on the number of sides, which other two shapes make up the flag?

_____ and _____

5   Sort the shapes shown below into pentagons and hexagons. Write the letters in the table to sort the shapes.

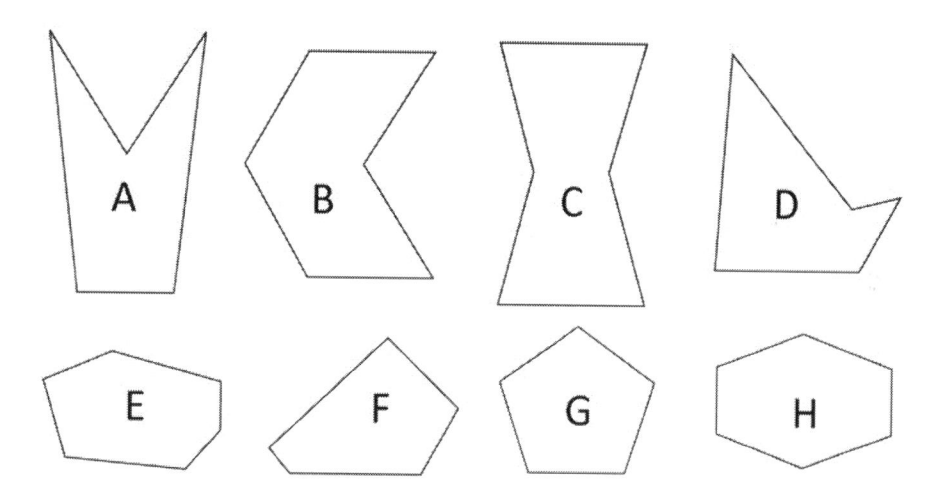

Pentagons	Hexagons

Complete the sentences to describe the pentagons and hexagons.

The pentagons all have ___ sides.

The hexagons all have ___ sides.

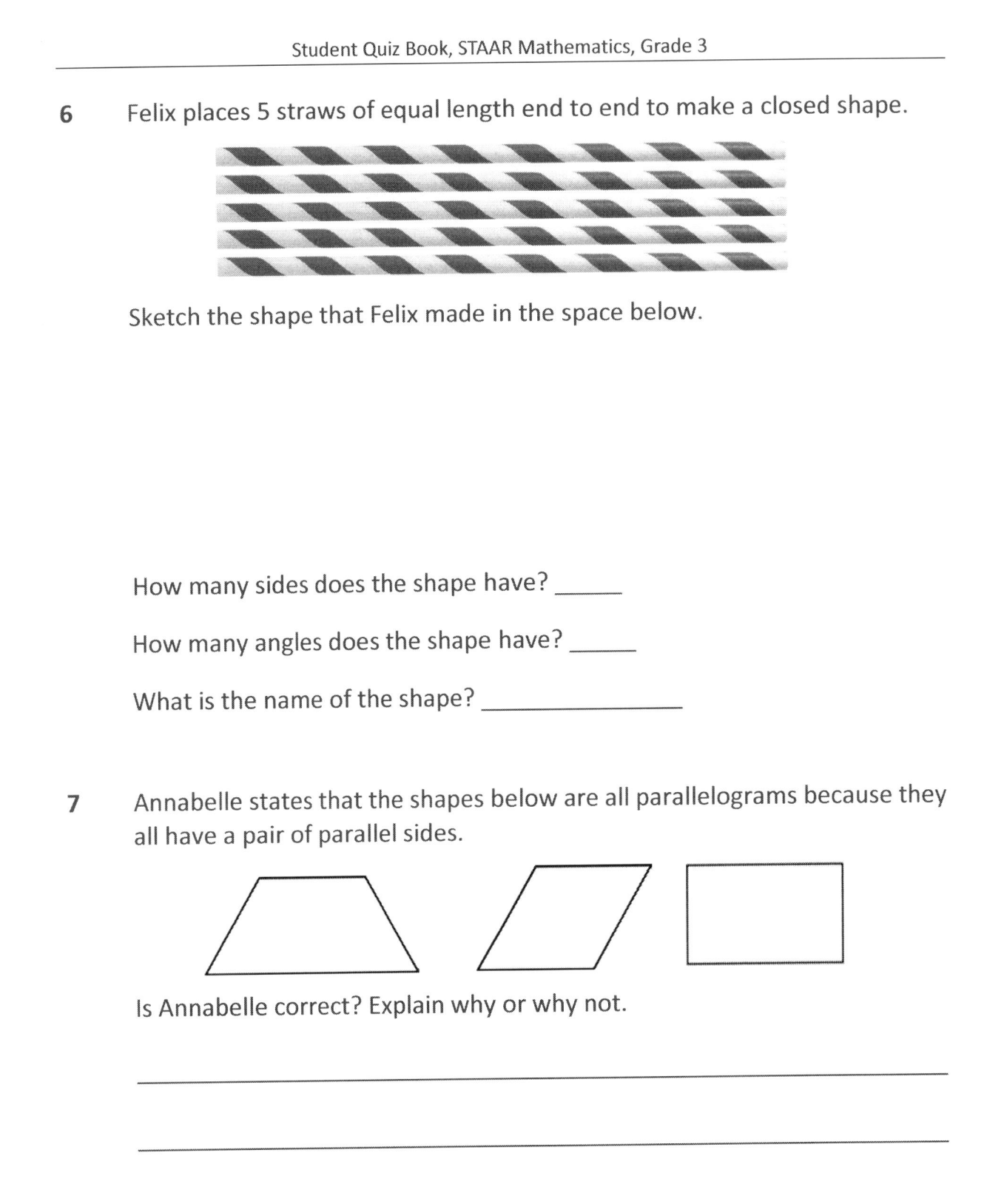

6 Felix places 5 straws of equal length end to end to make a closed shape.

Sketch the shape that Felix made in the space below.

How many sides does the shape have? _____

How many angles does the shape have? _____

What is the name of the shape? _____

7 Annabelle states that the shapes below are all parallelograms because they all have a pair of parallel sides.

Is Annabelle correct? Explain why or why not.

_____

_____

_____

_____

8 Which shapes described can have at least one right angle? Select all the correct answers.

☐ square with a side length of 4 units

☐ rhombus with 2 pairs of equal angles

☐ rectangle with a height twice its width

☐ trapezoid with parallel sides of 2 units and 5 units

Draw an example of each shape you selected with at least one right angle.

9 Jasmine drew the three shapes shown below.

What do the three shapes have in common?

_____

_____

What makes the first two shapes different from the last shape?

_____

_____

Quiz 43: Classifying Three-Dimensional Shapes

1. What is the shape of the marbles shown below?

    Ⓐ cone Ⓑ cylinder Ⓒ sphere Ⓓ pyramid

2. Which word best describes the shape of each layer of the wedding cake?

    Ⓐ cone Ⓑ cube Ⓒ cylinder Ⓓ sphere

3. What is the shape of the gift shown below?

    Ⓐ triangular prism Ⓑ square pyramid
    Ⓒ rectangular prism Ⓓ triangular pyramid

4 Which two shapes is the object below made up of? Circle the two shapes.

cone	sphere	triangular prism

cube	cylinder	rectangular prism

5 Circle the item below that is a sphere.

6 Margaret folded the net shown below to make a shape.

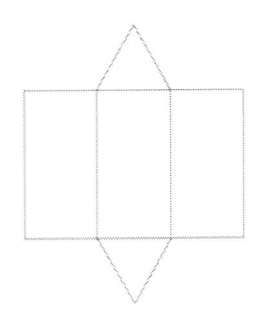

What shape did Margaret make?

Ⓐ triangular prism
Ⓑ triangular pyramid
Ⓒ rectangular prism
Ⓓ rectangular pyramid

7 Miranda has the cardboard shapes shown below. Which of these could Miranda make using all three shapes?

Ⓐ cone
Ⓑ sphere
Ⓒ rectangular prism
Ⓓ cylinder

8 A three-dimensional shape has six faces. Which question should be asked to determine if the shape is a cube or a rectangular prism?

Ⓐ Are any of the faces circles?
Ⓑ What is the total area of the faces?
Ⓒ Are all the sides of the shape squares?
Ⓓ How many edges does the shape have?

9 Circle the shape below that is a triangular prism.

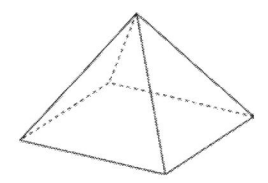

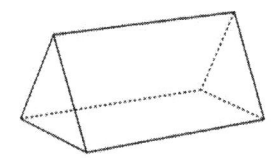

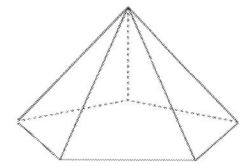

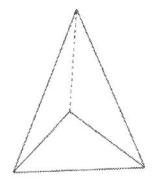

10 Aidan made party hats by folding a piece of cardboard around a point, as shown below.

What is the shape of each party hat?

Answer _____

11 Look at the letter blocks below.

What is the shape of each letter block?

Answer _____

Two letter blocks are placed side by side to form a new shape. What is the shape of the new shape?

Answer _____

Quiz 44: Comparing and Sorting Three-Dimensional Shapes

1 Which shape has more than 1 round face?

    Ⓐ cone   Ⓑ sphere   Ⓒ cylinder   Ⓓ cube

2 Erin looks at the bottom face of a solid. The bottom face is a square. Which shape could **NOT** be the shape of the solid?

    Ⓐ cylinder   Ⓑ rectangular prism

    Ⓒ square pyramid   Ⓓ cube

3 One side of a solid has the shape shown below.

Which of these could the solid be?

    Ⓐ triangular prism   Ⓑ cylinder

    Ⓒ rectangular prism   Ⓓ sphere

4 Two cans are in the shape of cylinders. Which statement must be true of the two cans?

    Ⓐ They must be exactly the same.

    Ⓑ They must have the same height.

    Ⓒ They must have the same number of faces.

    Ⓓ They must have circular faces with the same width.

5 Order the solids below from least to most faces. Write the numbers 1, 2, 3, and 4 on the lines to show the order.

    ___ cone   ___ sphere   ___ cube   ___ cylinder

6 Look at the shape shown below.

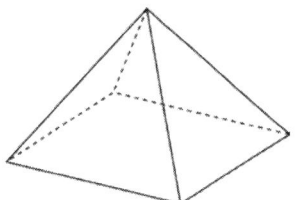

How many faces does the shape have?

Answer _____ faces

How many edges does the shape have?

Answer _____ edges

How many vertices does the shape have?

Answer _____ vertices

7 Complete the table below by describing each feature of the triangular prism and the rectangular prism below.

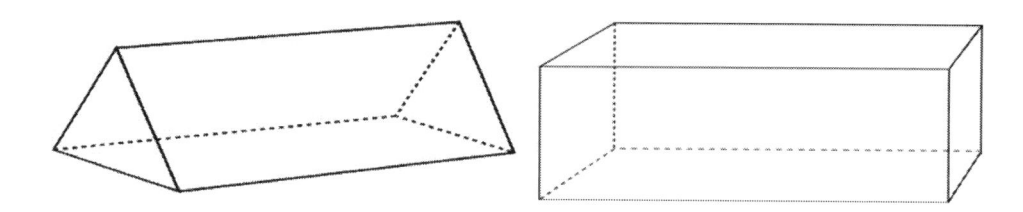

Feature	Triangular Prism	Rectangular Prism
Number of Faces		
Shape of the Faces		
Number of Edges		
Number of Vertices		

8 Alana used blocks to make the two shapes shown below.

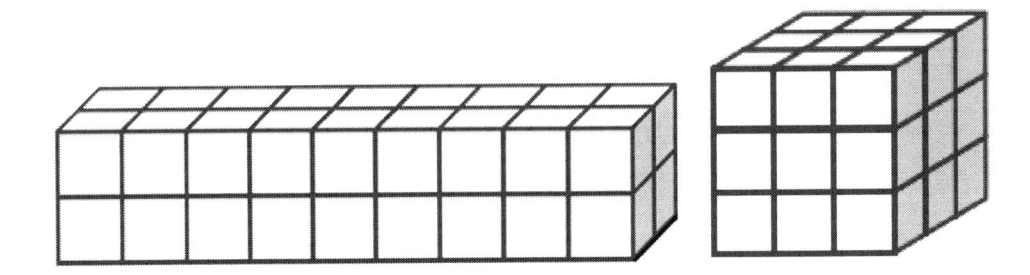

Describe two ways the two shapes are similar.

1. _____

2. _____

Describe two ways the two shapes are different.

1. _____

2. _____

9 A cylinder, a cone, and a sphere are shown below.

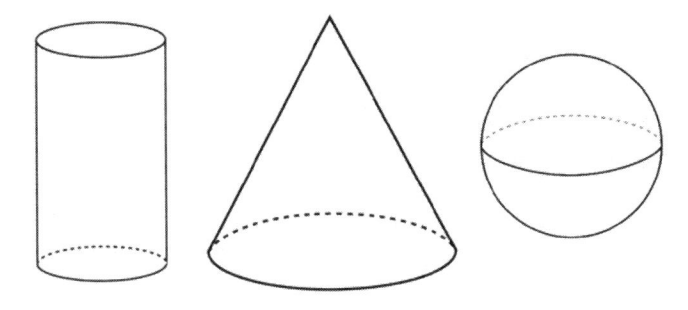

Compare the number of edges of each shape.

_____

_____

10   The diagram below shows the side view of four different solids.

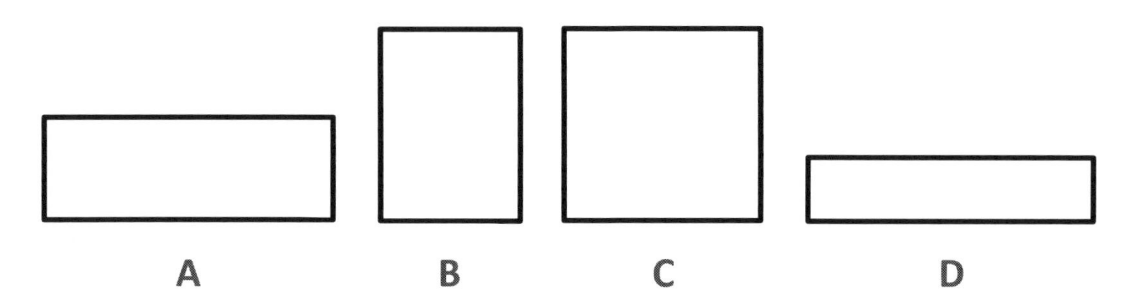

    A   B   C   D

    Which solid shown could be a cube? _____

    On the lines below, explain how you can tell.

    _____

    _____

11   Look at the figures below.

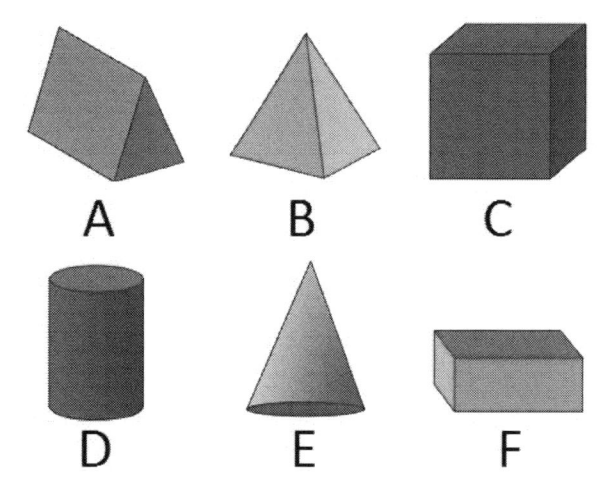

    A   B   C
    D   E   F

    Which two figures have 6 faces? _____ and _____

    Which figure has 6 vertices? _____

    Which figure has exactly 1 round face? _____

    Which figure has the most faces the same size and shape? _____

Quiz 45: Identifying and Drawing Quadrilaterals

1 Which shape below is a quadrilateral?

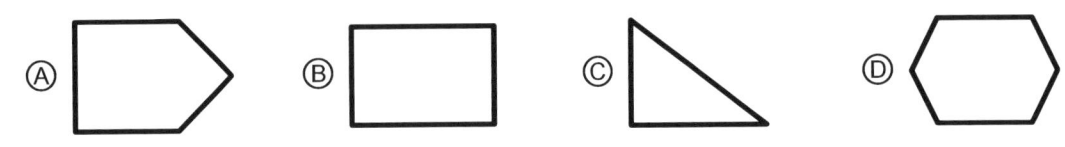

Ⓐ Ⓑ Ⓒ Ⓓ

2 Select all the shapes below that are trapezoids.

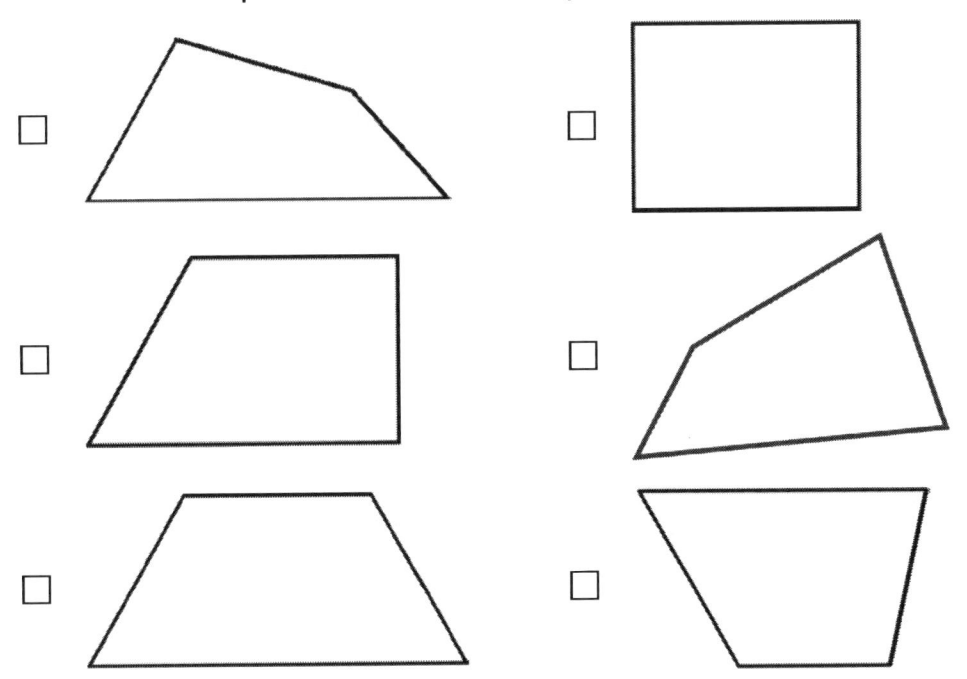

☐ ☐

☐ ☐

☐ ☐

3 Amber drew a quadrilateral by drawing four lines of equal length. Draw the two quadrilaterals she could have drawn below and name each one.

Name _____   Name _____

4 Kane placed shapes together to make images of different items. The diagrams below show the images he made. For each image, complete the sentences to describe the number of each shape used.

	He used 1 _____. He used 1 _____. He used 5 _____.
	He used 1 _____. He used 2 _____. He used 3 _____.
	He used 1 _____. He used 1 _____. He used 1 _____. He used 5 _____.
	He used 1 _____. He used 2 _____. He used 3 _____.

5   Circle all the shapes below that are quadrilaterals.

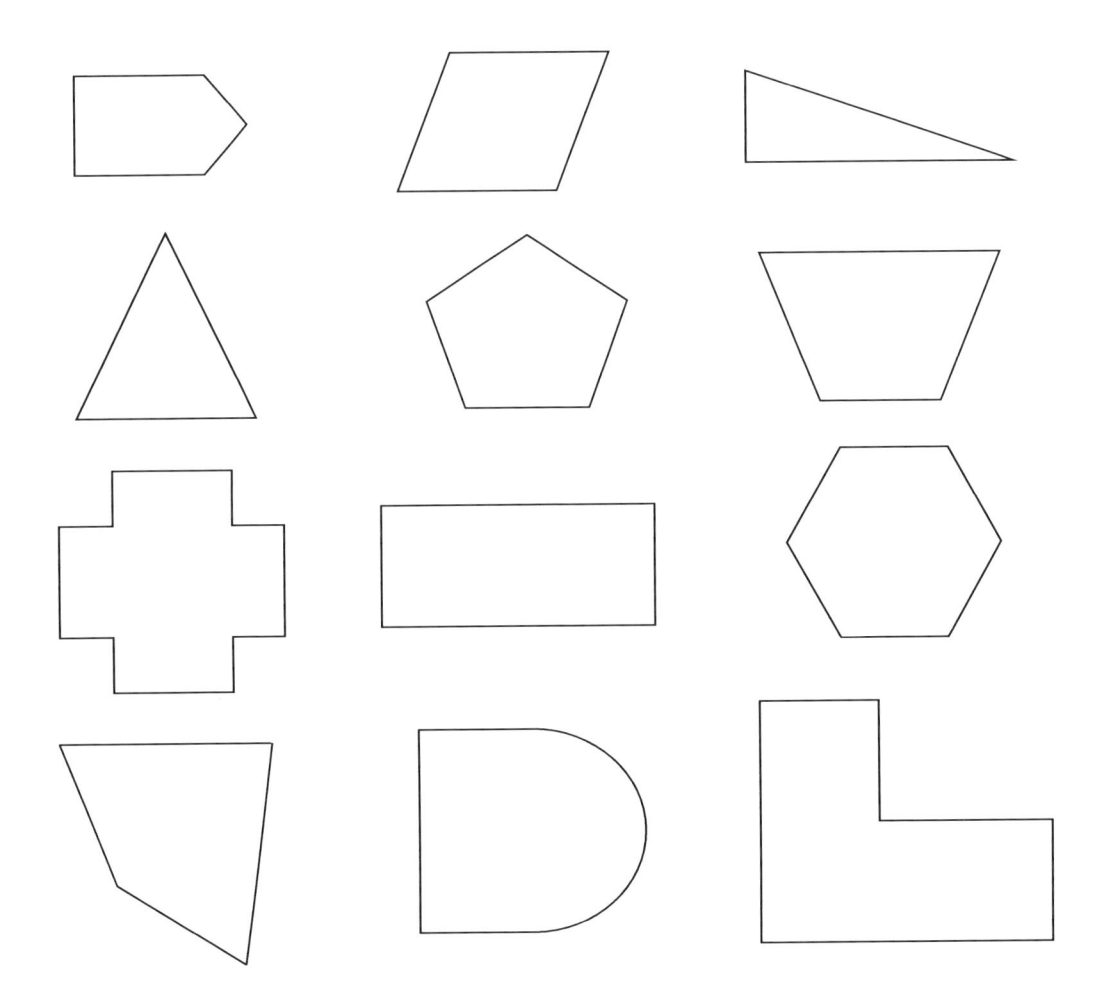

Which two quadrilaterals are also parallelograms? Name the shapes.

_____ and _____

In the space below, draw another quadrilateral that is a parallelogram and name the shape.

Name _____

6. On each grid below, draw a quadrilateral with the description given and name the shape.

Draw a parallelogram with two sides of 8 units each, and two sides of 4 units each.

Name _____

Draw a shape with one right angle and exactly two parallel sides.

Name _____

Draw a quadrilateral with four equal sides, but no right angles.

Name _____

Draw a quadrilateral with four sides of 5 units each, and four equal angles.

Name _____

Quiz 46: Finding the Area of Shapes

1. Each square on the grid below measures 1 cm by 1 cm. What is the area of the shaded figure on the grid?

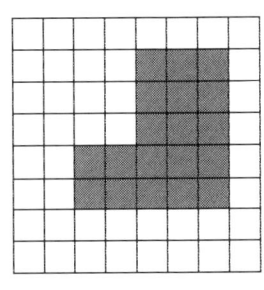

   Ⓐ 17 cm²   Ⓑ 18 cm²   Ⓒ 19 cm²   Ⓓ 20 cm²

2. Joseph made the design below on grid paper. What is the area of the shaded part of Joseph's design, in square units?

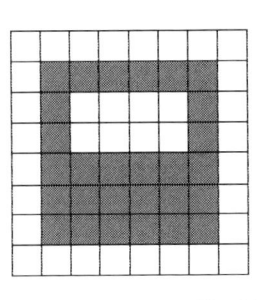

   Ⓐ 24   Ⓑ 28   Ⓒ 30   Ⓓ 36

3. Each square on the grid below measures 1 cm by 1 cm.

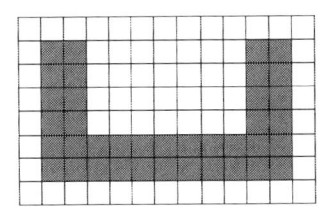

   Which expressions can be used to find the area of the shaded shape, in square centimeters? Select all the correct answers.

   ☐ 12 + 14 + 12   ☐ 8 + 14 + 8

   ☐ 12 + 22 + 8   ☐ 8 + 22 + 8

4 Find the area of each figure shown below. Write the area on the blank line.

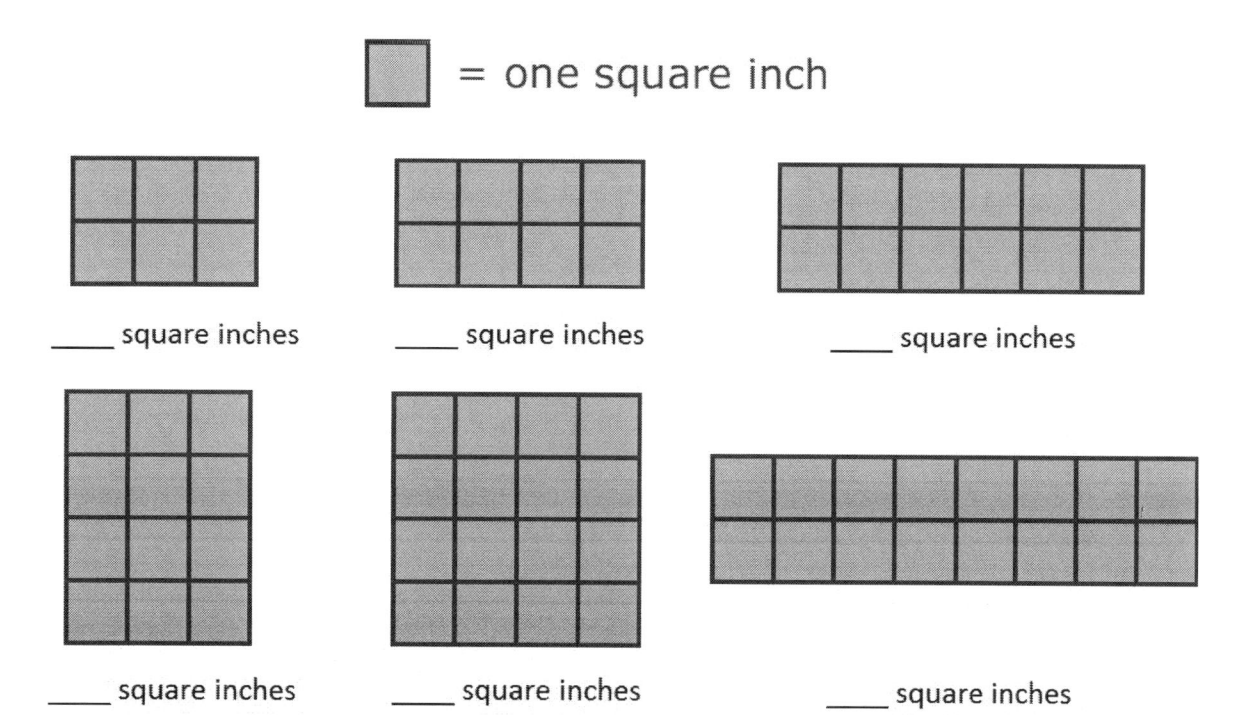

☐ = one square inch

____ square inches   ____ square inches   ____ square inches

____ square inches   ____ square inches   ____ square inches

5 The shapes below are each made out of 1 unit squares. Find the area of each shape in square units. Write each area on the line under each shape.

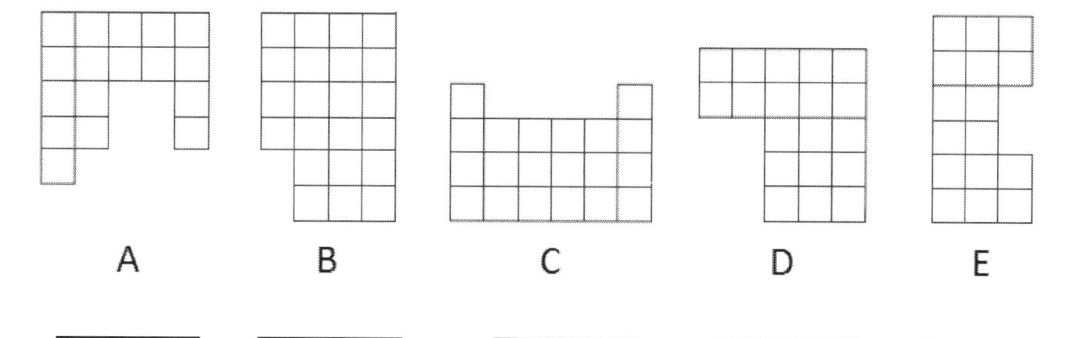

A   B   C   D   E

____   ____   ____   ____   ____

Identify the shape whose area can be found by each expression below. Write the letter for the correct shape on the blank line.

____ (6 × 3) + 1 + 1   ____ (3 × 2) + (2 × 2) + (3 × 2)

____ (4 × 6) − 2   ____ 5 + 5 + 3 + 3 + 3

6 A rectangular garden has an area of 18 square meters. The garden is 6 meters long. Draw the shape of the garden on the grid below.

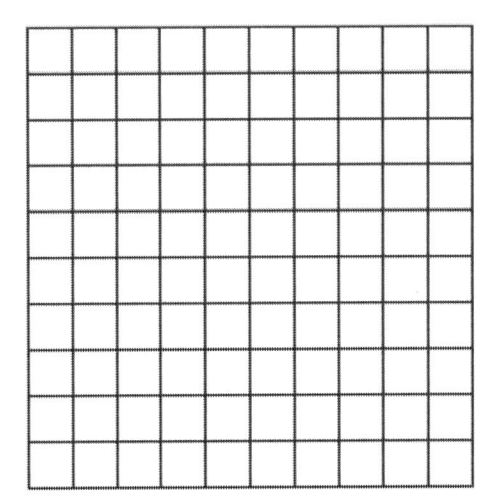

KEY
☐ = 1 square meter

Complete the number sentences below to show two ways you can tell that the area of the garden is 18 square meters.

_____ × _____ = 18   _____ + _____ + _____ = 18

7 Carly drew the shape below on a grid.

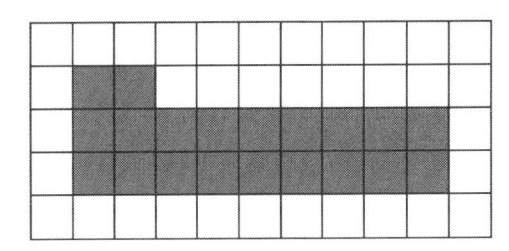

Complete the addition expression that can be used to find the area of the shape, in square units.

(3 × 2) + (_____ × _____)

Complete the subtraction expression that can be used to find the area of the shape.

(3 × 9) − (_____ × _____)

8   The shaded part of the diagram below represents the part of a park that is used for a playground. Each square represents 1 square meter.

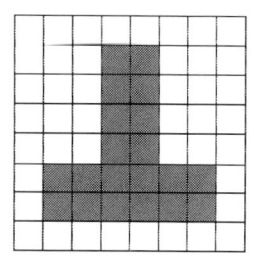

What is the area of the playground? Use words or equations to show how you found your answer.

Answer _____ square meters

What is the area of the park that is not used for a playground? Use words or equations to show how you found your answer.

Answer _____ square meters

9   Dom drew two shapes on a grid, as shown below.

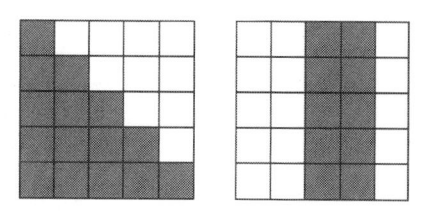

How many more square units is the first shape than the second shape? Use words or equations to show how you found your answer.

Answer _____ square units

Quiz 47: Finding the Area of Rectangles

1 A rectangular poster is 6 inches wide and 8 inches high. What is the area of the poster?

Ⓐ 14 square inches

Ⓑ 28 square inches

Ⓒ 42 square inches

Ⓓ 48 square inches

2 Kyle's bedroom floor is in the shape of a rectangle. It is 8 feet long and 9 feet wide. What is the area of Kyle's bedroom floor?

Ⓐ 17 square feet

Ⓑ 34 square feet

Ⓒ 72 square feet

Ⓓ 89 square feet

3 Which expression can be used to find the area of a rectangle with a length of 3 meters and a width of 7 meters, in square meters?

Ⓐ 3 + 7

Ⓑ 3 × 7

Ⓒ 2 × (3 + 7)

Ⓓ 3 × 3 × 3

4 What is the area of the rectangle shown below?

4 m

8 m

Answer _____ square meters

5 Em has 1-inch square stickers. She uses exactly 36 square stickers to cover the front of a book. There are no gaps and no overlaps. Which of these could be the measurements of the cover? Select all the possible answers.

☐ 4 inch by 9 inch

☐ 8 inch by 7 inch

☐ 6 inch by 6 inch

☐ 5 inch by 6 inch

☐ 12 inch by 3 inch

☐ 16 inch by 2 inch

6. The table below shows the length, width, and area of different rectangular fields. Complete the table with the missing information.

Length (meters)	Width (meters)	Area (square meters)
5	7	
10		40
	9	27
3		15
6		42
	2	40
30		90

7. The rectangle below has an area of 56 square inches.

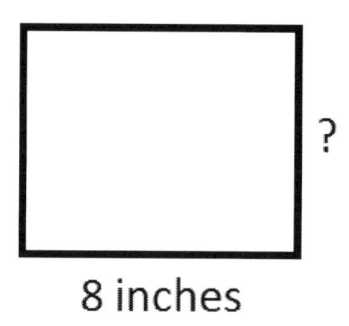

8 inches

What is the length of the missing side? Show or explain how you got your answer.

Answer _____ inches

183

8   Jackson shaded 24 squares on a grid to create a rectangle. On the grids below, shade the four possible rectangles Jackson could have shaded. Write the possible lengths and heights under each grid.

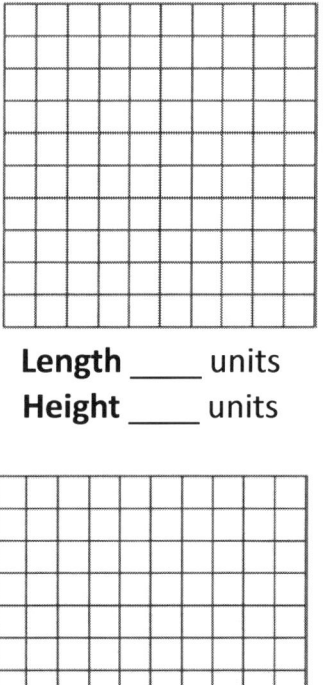

Length _____ units
Height _____ units

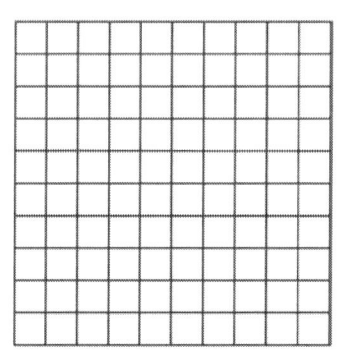

Length _____ units
Height _____ units

Length _____ units
Height _____ units

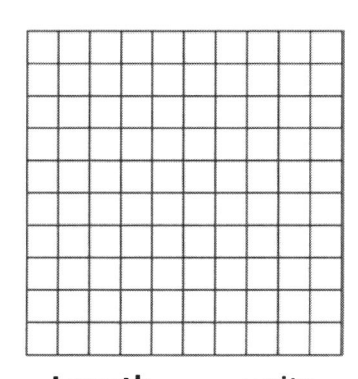

Length _____ units
Height _____ units

9   The shaded area on the grid represents a shape with an area of 12 square units. Complete the equation that shows that the area is 12 square units. Then draw a shape on the second grid with a different length but the same area. Complete the equation to show that the area is the same.

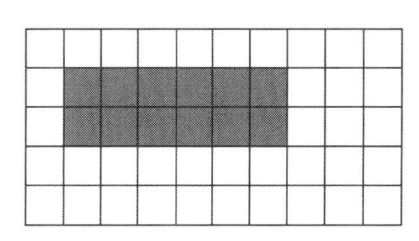

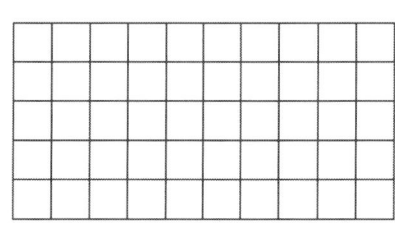

_____ × _____ = _____   _____ × _____ = _____

10 Find the area of each rectangle shown below.

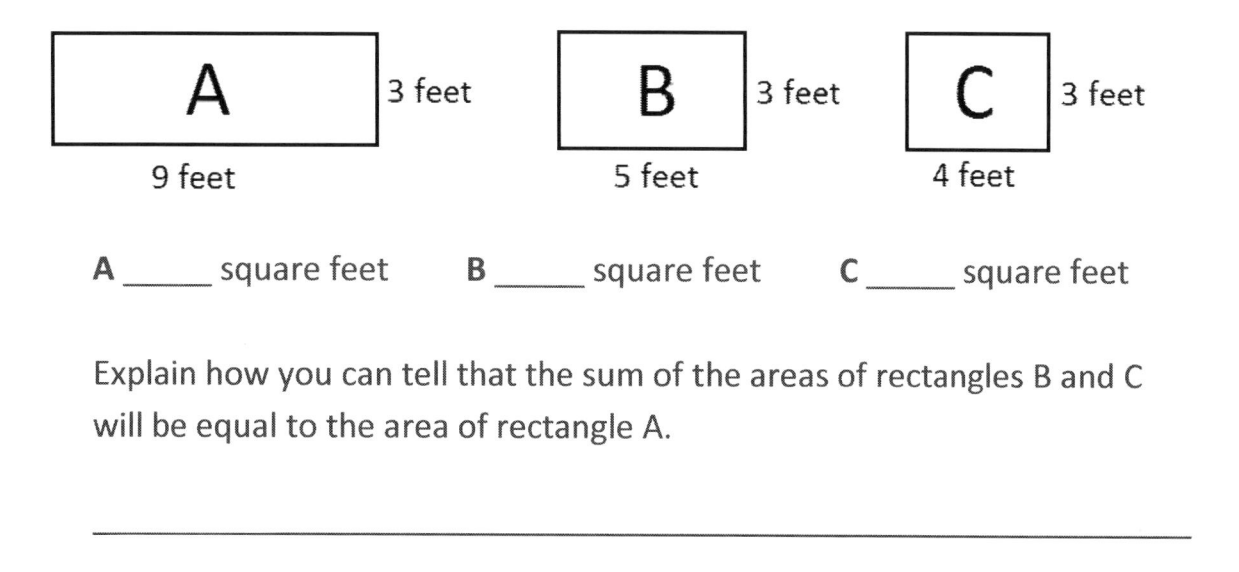

A	3 feet
9 feet	

B	3 feet
5 feet	

C	3 feet
4 feet	

A _____ square feet   B _____ square feet   C _____ square feet

Explain how you can tell that the sum of the areas of rectangles B and C will be equal to the area of rectangle A.

_____

_____

_____

11 Sofia is making a quilt out of 1-inch squares. The quilt will be 8 squares long, as shown below.

Sofia wants the quilt to have a total area of 32 square inches. How many squares wide must the quilt be? Show or explain how you got your answer.

Answer _____ squares

Quiz 48: Using Area to Solve Problems

1 Justine makes some statements about the top of a table. Which statement describes the area of the top of the table?

Ⓐ It would take 24 inches of tape to place a border around it.

Ⓑ It would take 18 square-inch tiles to cover it.

Ⓒ It is 9 inches from one side to the other.

Ⓓ It is 30 inches above the ground.

2 Which question can be answered by finding the area of the football field?

Ⓐ How many steps would need to be taken to walk around the edge of the football field once?

Ⓑ How long would it take to walk from one end of the field to the other?

Ⓒ How many 1-meter square sheets would it take to cover the football field completely?

Ⓓ How many 1-meter rulers could be laid from the left side of the field to the right?

3 Zane wants to find the area of a poster. Which two details does Zane need to find the area? Select the two correct answers.

☐ how much it cost   ☐ how wide it is

☐ how tall it is   ☐ how heavy it is

4 Skye uses 1-inch squares to make a rectangle. She uses 12 squares. Which of these can be determined from this? Select all the correct answers.

☐ the length of the rectangle   ☐ the height of the rectangle

☐ the area of the rectangle   ☐ the perimeter of the rectangle

5. The picture below shows six photo frames labeled A through F.

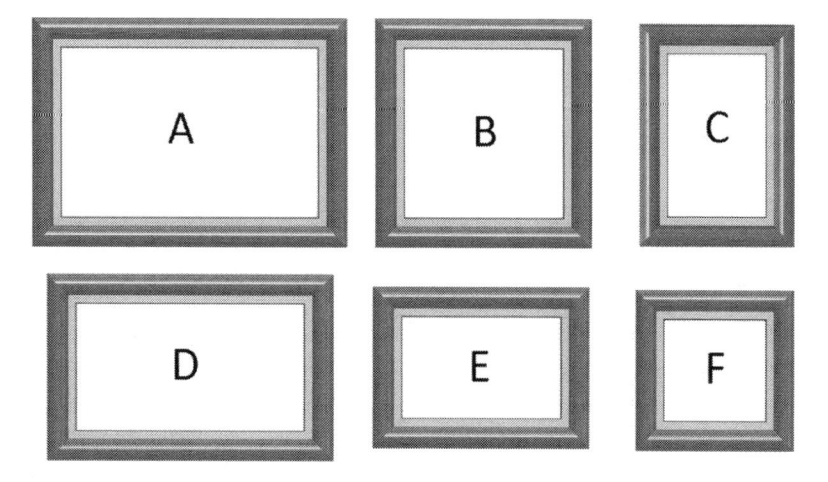

    Which frame appears to have the greatest area? _____

    Which frame appears to have the smallest area? _____

    Which two frames appear to have the same area? _____ and _____

    Explain how you could check your answers.

    _____

    _____

    _____

6. A banner is divided into 4 rows of 9 squares each. Each square has an area of 1 square foot.

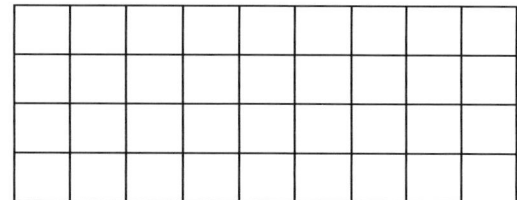

    What is the area of the banner?

    Answer _____ square feet

7 Kendra has a piece of note paper that is 6 inches long and 2 inches wide. She cut it into squares of 1 square inch each. Draw lines below to show how she cut the note paper.

How many squares did she cut the note paper into? _____

Explain what this tells you about the area of the note paper.

_____

_____

_____

8 The grids below have squares with units of 1 square centimeter (cm²). Draw a rectangle on the first grid with the length, height, and area given. Then draw rectangles on the second and third grids to match the information given, and complete the missing information.

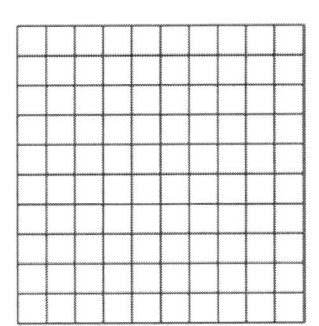

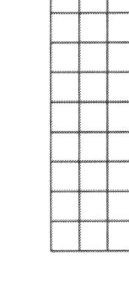

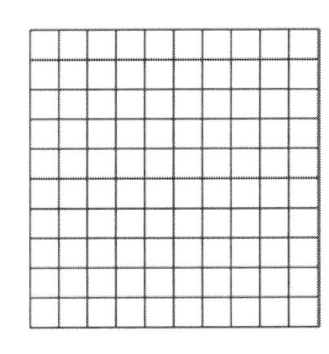

Length = 4 cm
Height = 6 cm
Area = 24 cm²

Length = 8 cm
Height = _____ cm
Area = 40 cm²

Length = _____ cm
Height = 3 cm
Area = 27 cm²

9   Two vegetable gardens are shaped like rectangles. The small garden is 6 feet long and 3 feet wide. The large garden is also 3 feet wide, but is 12 feet long.

3 ft

6 ft

3 ft

12 ft

What is the area of the small garden? _____ square feet

How can the area of the small garden be used to find the area of the large garden? Explain your answer.

_____

_____

_____

A third garden has the same area as the large garden, but is shaped like a square. What are the side lengths of the third garden?

Show your work.

Answer _____ feet

Quiz 49: Finding the Area of Composite Shapes

1 Which of these finds the area of the shape below, in square units?

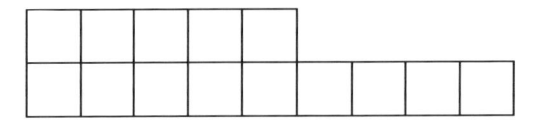

Ⓐ (2 × 2) + 4 = 8
Ⓑ (2 × 4) + 5 = 13
Ⓒ (5 × 2) + 4 = 14
Ⓓ (5 × 4) + 5 = 25

2 What is the area of the shaded figure on the grid, in square units?

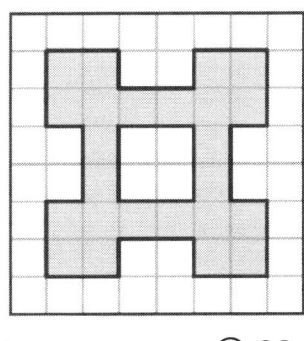

Ⓐ 20 Ⓑ 24 Ⓒ 28 Ⓓ 32

3 Allison made a shape by placing two pieces of cardboard together, as shown below.

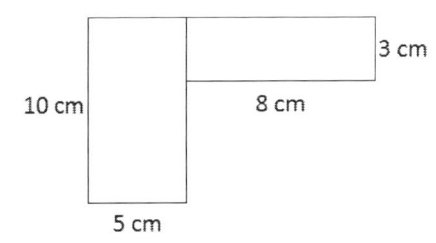

10 cm, 5 cm, 8 cm, 3 cm

She adds a third piece of cardboard to make a shape with a total area of 130 square centimeters. Which of these could be the shape of the third piece of cardboard?

Ⓐ 5 cm by 10 cm
Ⓑ 3 cm by 13 cm
Ⓒ 8 cm by 7 cm
Ⓓ 6 cm by 9 cm

4 Complete the expressions to show how to find the area of each shape, in square units.

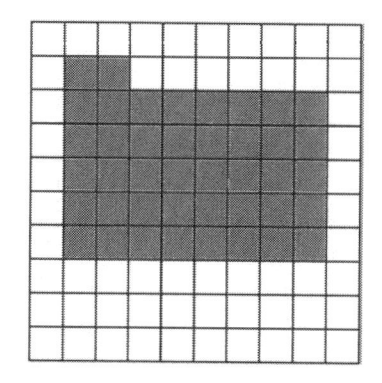

(___ × ___) + (___ × ___)   (___ × ___) + (___ × ___)

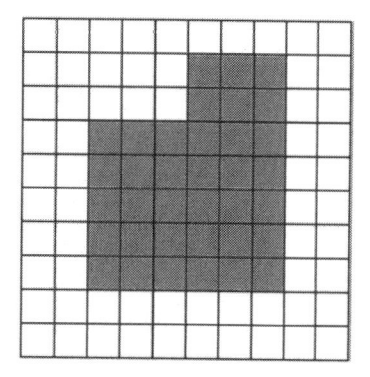

(___ × ___) + (___ × ___)   (___ × ___) + (___ × ___)

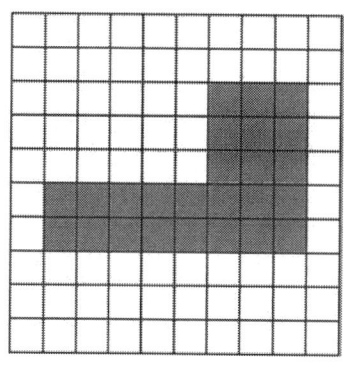

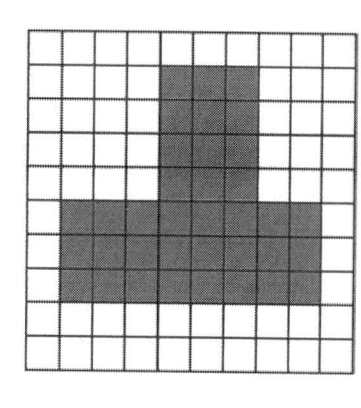

5 Draw a shape on each grid whose area can be found by the calculation shown.

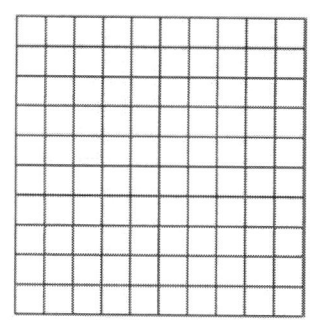

(6 × 2) + (4 × 3) = 24 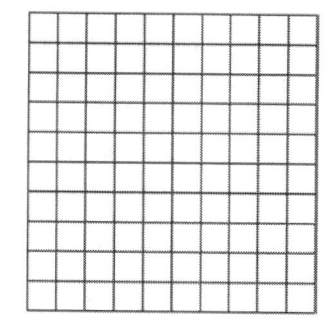   (5 × 2) + (3 × 3) = 19 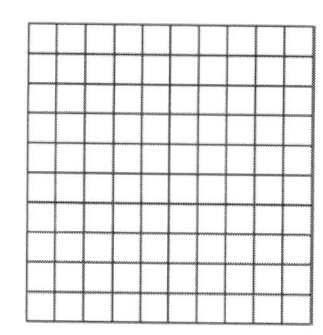   (8 × 1) + (2 × 4) = 16

6 Sally used the expression (5 × 4) + (8 × 2) to find the area of a kitchen bench, in square feet. On the grid below, draw one possible shape of the kitchen bench. Then find the area of the kitchen bench.

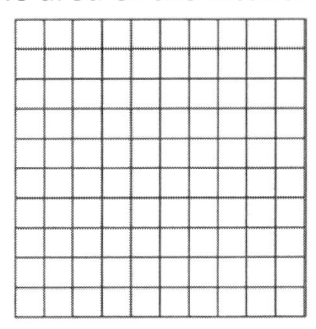

Answer _____ square feet

7 The diagram below shows the shape of George's kitchen floor.

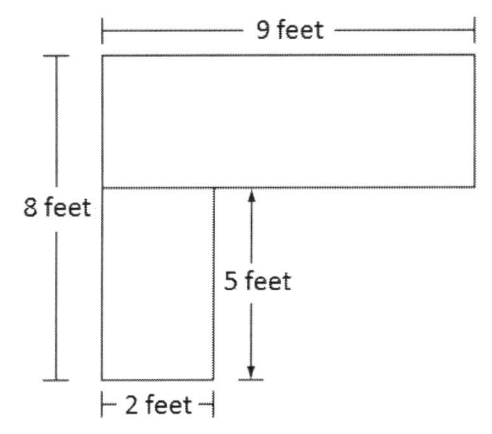

George wants to tile the kitchen floor with 1-foot square tiles. Each tile costs $3. What is the total cost of the tiles George needs?

Show your work.

Answer $_____

8 A model of the shape of a swimming pool is shown below. A fence is built around the pool 2 meters from each edge.

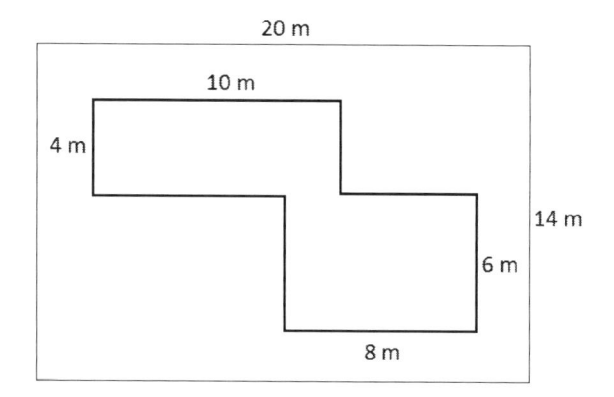

```
           20 m
     ┌─────────────┐
     │    10 m     │
     │  ┌──────┐   │
   4 m  │      │   │
     │  │      └───┤
     │  │          │ 14 m
     │  │      ┌───┤
     │  │      │ 6 m
     │  └──────┘   │
     │    8 m      │
     └─────────────┘
```

What is the area of the base of the swimming pool? Use words or equations to show how you found your answer.

Answer _____ square meters

The area around the pool inside the fence is tiled. What is the area of the tiled area? Use words or equations to show how you found your answer.

Answer _____ square meters

9 Kieran covered the top of a desk with wooden panels, as shown below.

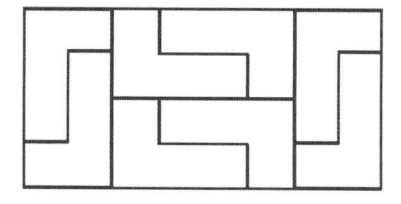

Each panel had an area of 4 square feet. What is the total area covered by the panels? Show or explain how you found your answer.

Answer _____ square feet

Quiz 50: Dividing Shapes into Parts

1 Students were asked to divide a triangle into equal halves. The diagram below shows how four students divided the shape.

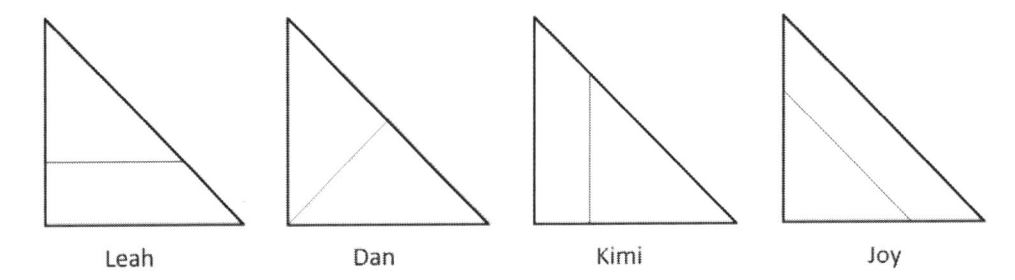

Leah   Dan   Kimi   Joy

Which student divided the triangle correctly?

Ⓐ Leah   Ⓑ Dan   Ⓒ Kimi   Ⓓ Joy

2 Which circle below is divided into parts of $\frac{1}{5}$ each?

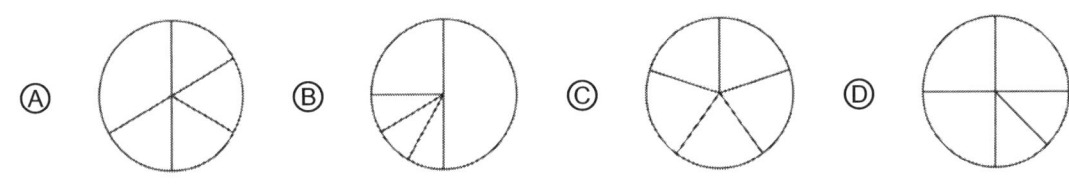

Ⓐ   Ⓑ   Ⓒ   Ⓓ

3 Which figure has $\frac{1}{4}$ shaded?

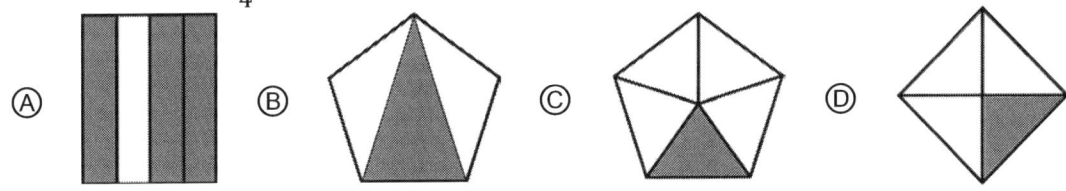

Ⓐ   Ⓑ   Ⓒ   Ⓓ

4 A pie is divided into pieces of $\frac{1}{6}$ of a pie each.

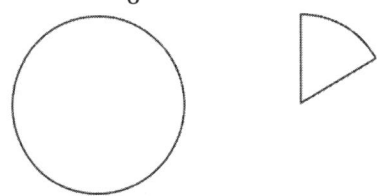

How many pieces make up a whole pie? _____ pieces

5 Divide each shape shown below into parts of equal area and shade the fraction given.

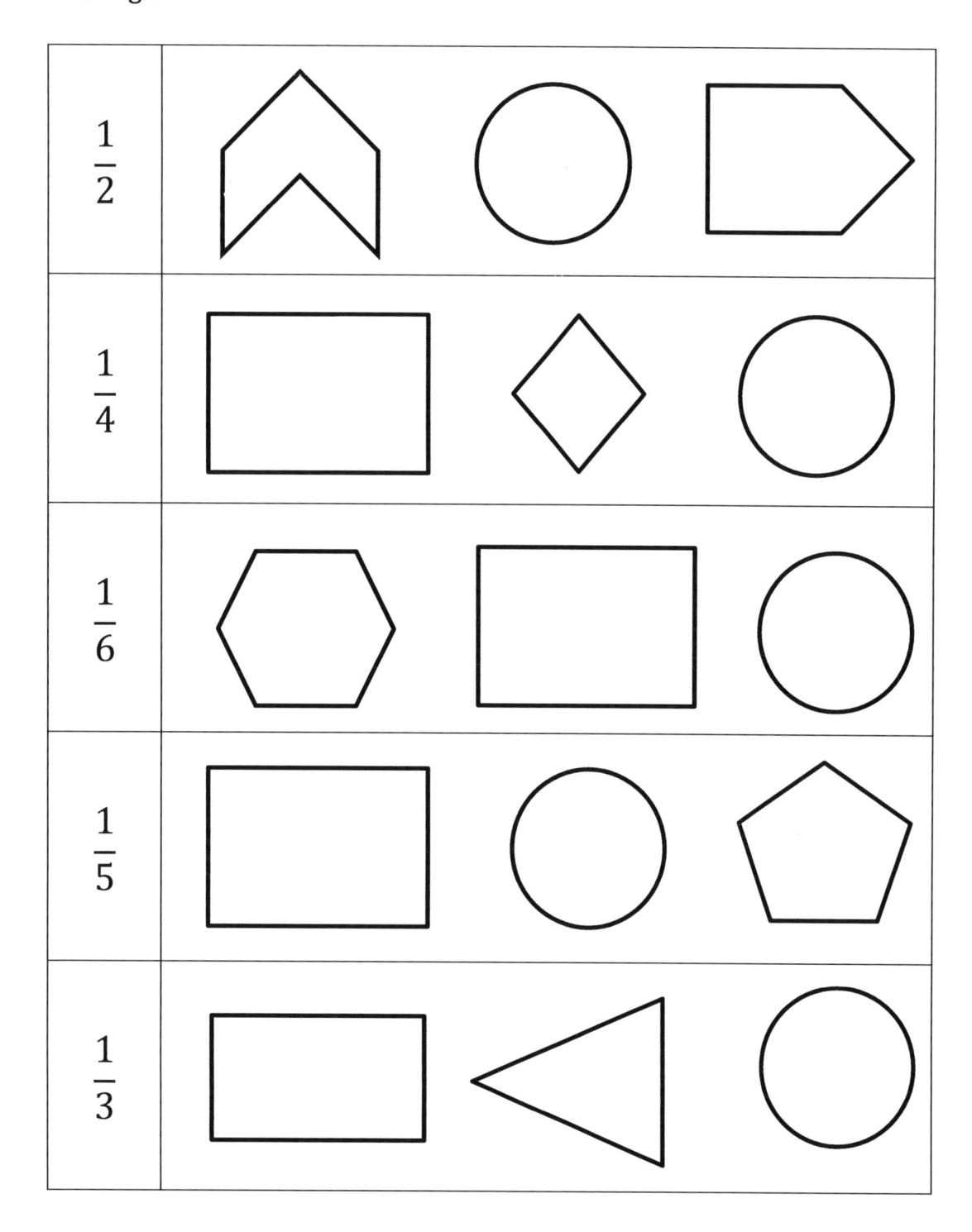

$\dfrac{1}{2}$	
$\dfrac{1}{4}$	
$\dfrac{1}{6}$	
$\dfrac{1}{5}$	
$\dfrac{1}{3}$	

6 Students were asked to shade $\frac{1}{4}$ of a square. Four answers are below.

- Jay
- Enrico
- Danny
- Kasim

Which student shaded the square correctly? _____

Complete the sentences to describe the mistake three students made.

Jay shaded ___ parts instead of ___.

Enrico divided the square into ___ parts instead of ___.

_____ did not divide the square into equal parts.

7 Students were asked to shade $\frac{1}{4}$ of a rectangle. Four answers are below.

- Dana
- Emiko
- Julie
- Tiana

Which student shaded the rectangle correctly? _____

Write a sentence to describe the mistake the other three students made.

1. _____

2. _____

3. _____

8 Which fraction is represented by each row of the fraction strip?

Answer _____

9 Kate divided the circle below into parts and stated that the circle is divided into thirds. Divide the second circle below into thirds correctly.

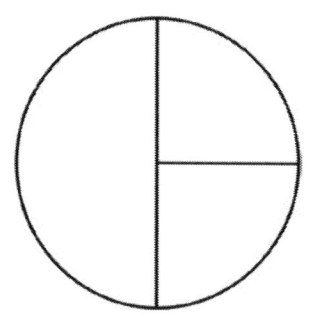

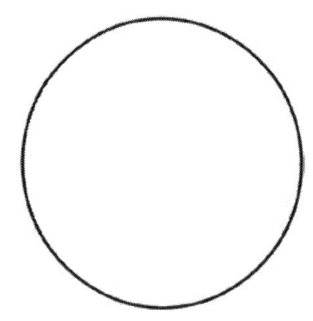

Explain why Kate's circle is not divided into thirds correctly and the circle you divided is.

_____

_____

10 The grid below shows $\frac{1}{4}$ of a rectangle. Shade the grid to show the whole rectangle.

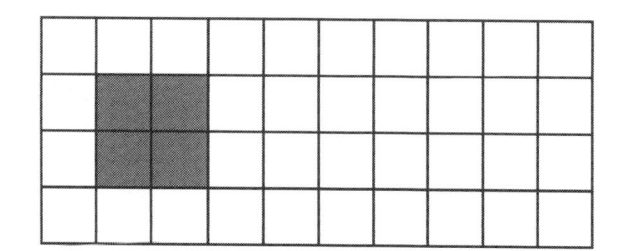

Quizzes 51 to 58

Solving Measurement Problems

Directions

Read each question carefully. For each multiple-choice question, fill in the circle for the correct answer. For other types of questions, follow the directions given in the question.

You may use a ruler to help you answer questions. You should answer the questions without using a calculator.

MATHEMATICS SKILLS LIST
For Parents, Teachers, and Tutors

Quizzes 51 through 58 cover these skills from the Texas Essential Knowledge and Skills (TEKS).

Geometry and Measurement

The student applies mathematical process standards to select appropriate units, strategies, and tools to solve problems involving customary and metric measurement.

The student is expected to be able to complete the following tasks.

- Determine the perimeter of a polygon or a missing length when given perimeter and remaining side lengths in problems.

- Determine the solutions to problems involving addition and subtraction of time intervals in minutes using pictorial models or tools such as a 15-minute event plus a 30-minute event equals 45 minutes.

- Determine when it is appropriate to use measurements of liquid volume (capacity) or weight.

- Determine liquid volume (capacity) or weight using appropriate units and tools.

Quiz 51: Understanding and Measuring Perimeter

1. Which question can be answered by finding the perimeter of a paddock?

   Ⓐ How many cows can be placed in the paddock if each cow needs a space of 100 square feet?

   Ⓑ What is the total length of fencing needed to go around all the edges of the paddock once?

   Ⓒ How many fields of 1 square yard each can the paddock be divided into?

   Ⓓ How many 1-yard rulers could be laid in a straight line from the left side of the paddock to the right?

2. A picture frame is 8 inches wide and 5 inches high. What is the perimeter of the frame?

   Ⓐ 26 inches   Ⓑ 32 inches   Ⓒ 20 inches   Ⓓ 40 inches

3. What is the perimeter of the rectangle shown below?

   2 cm
   11 cm

   Ⓐ 13 cm   Ⓑ 18 cm   Ⓒ 22 cm   Ⓓ 26 cm

4. The dimensions of different rectangles are listed below. Select all the rectangles that have the same perimeters.

   ☐ 7 cm by 3 cm   ☐ 10 cm by 2 cm   ☐ 5 cm by 12 cm

   ☐ 4 cm by 9 cm   ☐ 9 cm by 1 cm   ☐ 8 cm by 2 cm

   ☐ 15 cm by 3 cm   ☐ 4 cm by 5 cm   ☐ 6 cm by 9 cm

   ☐ 8 cm by 6 cm   ☐ 6 cm by 4 cm   ☐ 3 cm by 8 cm

5 Each grid has squares of 1 cm by 1 cm. For each shaded shape, complete the number sentence that can be used to find the perimeter of the shape. Then complete the calculation to find the perimeter.

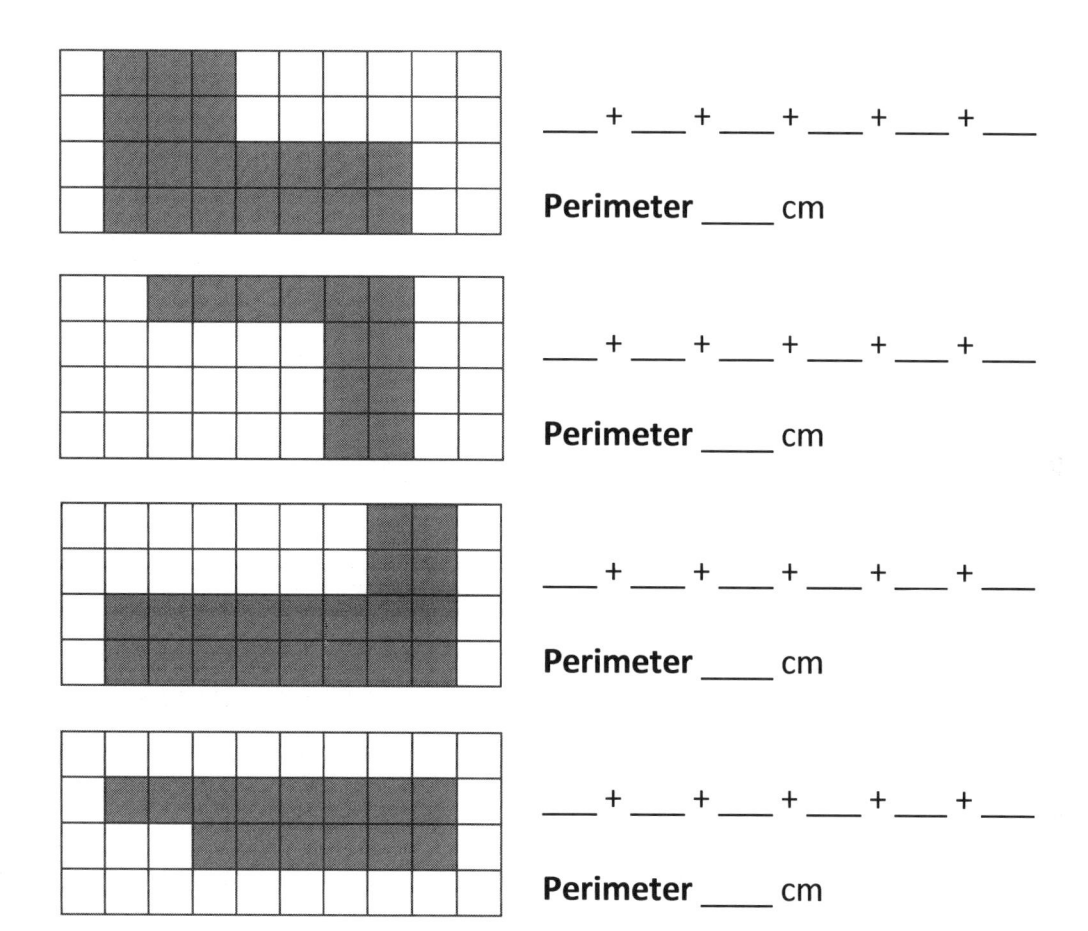

___ + ___ + ___ + ___ + ___ + ___

Perimeter ____ cm

___ + ___ + ___ + ___ + ___ + ___

Perimeter ____ cm

___ + ___ + ___ + ___ + ___ + ___

Perimeter ____ cm

___ + ___ + ___ + ___ + ___ + ___

Perimeter ____ cm

6 Frankie used 1-inch square cards to make the rectangles shown below. Complete the equations to show two different ways to find the perimeter of each rectangle, in inches.

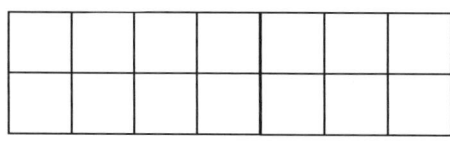

2 x (____ + ____) = ____

____ + ____ + ____ + ____ = ____

2 x (____ + ____) = ____

____ + ____ + ____ + ____ = ____

7 A block for a children's puzzle has the shape shown below.

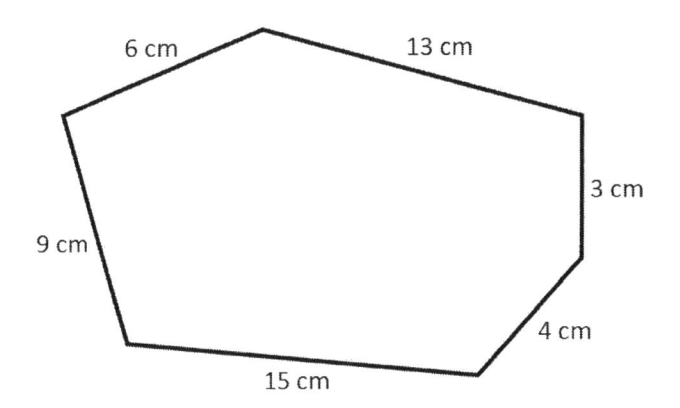

6 cm
13 cm
3 cm
9 cm
4 cm
15 cm

What is the perimeter of the block?

Show your work.

Answer _____ cm

8 Joel used cubes with side lengths of 1 inch to build a border around a garden bed, as shown below.

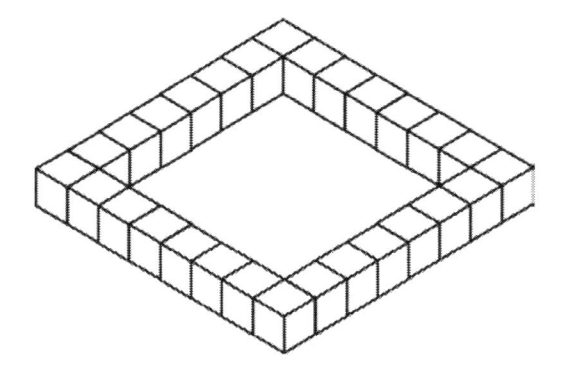

What is the perimeter of the outside of the garden bed? Show your work or explain how you found your answer.

Answer _____ inches

9 The grids below have squares with side lengths of 1 cm. Draw a rectangle on the first grid with the length and height given. Then find the perimeter of the rectangle. Draw rectangles on the second and third grids to match the information given, and complete the missing information.

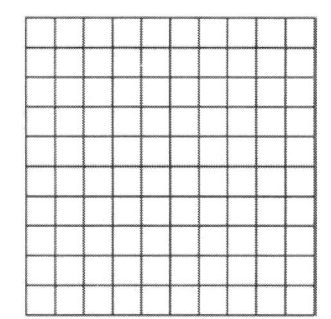

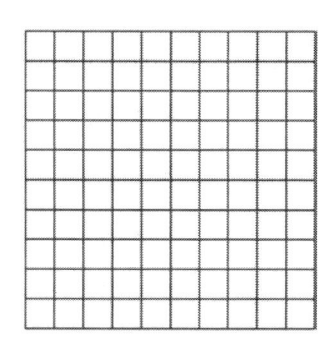

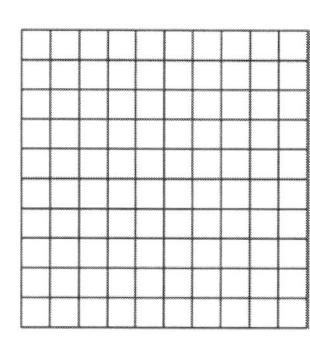

Length = 8 cm
Height = 3 cm
Perimeter = _____ cm

Length = 10 cm
Height = _____ cm
Perimeter = 32 cm

Length = _____ cm
Height = 7 cm
Perimeter = 26 cm

10 Lexie wants to cut out a rectangular note card. She wants the card to have a perimeter of 24 cm. Draw two possible dimensions of Lexie's card on the 1-centimeter grids below. Then write equations to show that the perimeter of each is 24 cm.

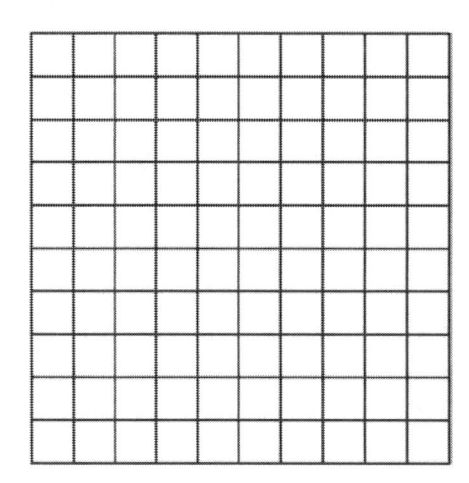

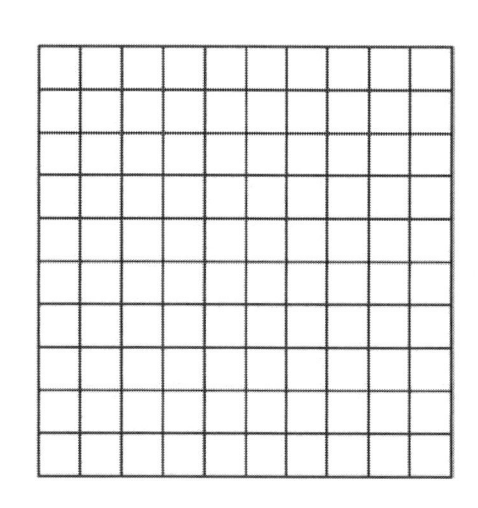

Equation

Equation

Quiz 52: Solving Problems Involving Perimeter

1 The rectangle below has a perimeter of 28 cm.

[Rectangle with 4 cm height and ? cm length]

What is the length of the rectangle?

Ⓐ 7 cm Ⓑ 10 cm Ⓒ 12 cm Ⓓ 20 cm

2 Priya has 40 feet of logs she can place around the four sides of a rectangular garden bed. She wants the garden bed to be 8 feet long. How wide should the garden be to use all the logs?

Ⓐ 5 feet Ⓑ 6 feet Ⓒ 12 feet Ⓓ 16 feet

3 Max and his classmates are making signs to hang around the school gym. Max makes a sign with the shape shown below.

[Triangle with sides 6 in., 24 in., 24 in.]

Cal makes a hexagon-shaped sign with 6 equal sides. If Max and Cal have signs with the same perimeter, how long is each side of Cal's sign?

Ⓐ 5 inches Ⓑ 6 inches Ⓒ 8 inches Ⓓ 9 inches

4 A square has side lengths in whole units. Which of these could be the perimeter of the square? Select all the possible answers.

☐ 14 inches ☐ 16 inches ☐ 18 inches

☐ 24 inches ☐ 26 inches ☐ 27 inches

☐ 35 inches ☐ 36 inches ☐ 39 inches

☐ 53 inches ☐ 75 inches ☐ 80 inches

5   Carly has two gift boxes. Each gift box has 8 sides of equal length. She wants to decorate them by placing ribbon around all the sides of each box, as shown below.

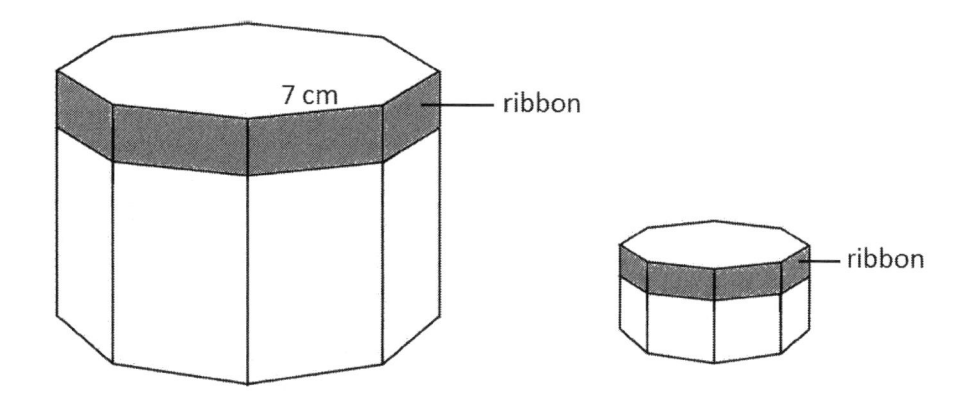

7 cm — ribbon

ribbon

The large box has side lengths of 7 centimeters. How much ribbon will she need to go around the large box exactly once?

Show your work.

Answer _____ cm

She uses 24 centimeters of ribbon to go around the small box exactly once. What is the length of each side of the small box?

Show your work.

Answer _____ cm

A roll of ribbon is 100 centimeters long. How many complete small boxes could she decorate with 1 roll of ribbon?

Show your work.

Answer _____ small boxes

6 Clarissa made four name tags with the shapes shown below.

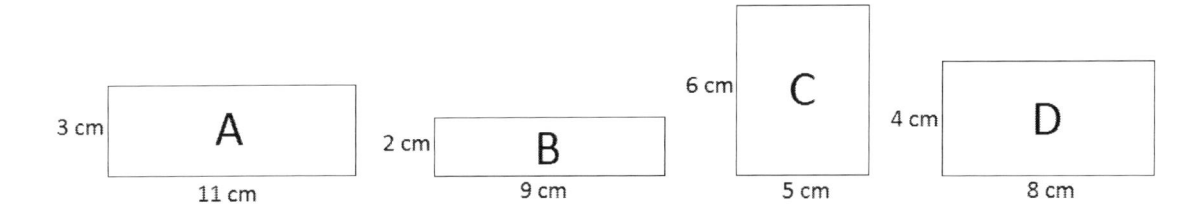

3 cm | A | 11 cm
2 cm | B | 9 cm
6 cm | C | 5 cm
4 cm | D | 8 cm

Clarissa wants to place ribbon around the edge of each name tag. The ribbon must go around the edge of each name tag without crossing over. Clarissa has 24 centimeters of ribbon. Answer the questions below by writing the letter or letters of the correct name tags.

For which name tag will she have exactly the right amount of ribbon? _____

Which two name tags will use the same amount of ribbon? _____ and _____

Which name tag does she not have enough ribbon for? _____

7 Gemma starts each soccer practice by running 3 laps around the edges of the soccer field. The diagram below shows the dimensions of the soccer field.

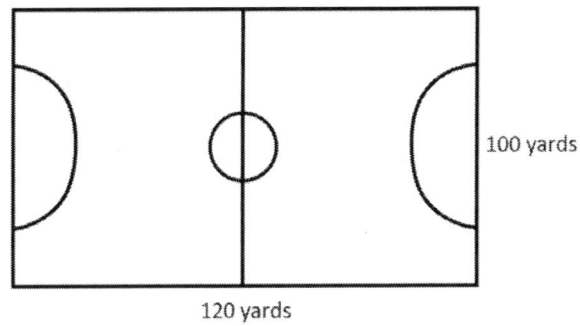

100 yards
120 yards

How far does Gemma run to complete the 3 laps?

Show your work.

Answer _____ yards

8 Jay is making masks for a play. He cut the mask below out of cardboard.

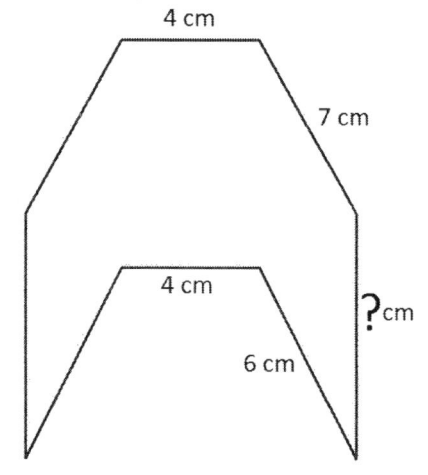

- 4 cm (top)
- 7 cm
- 4 cm
- ? cm
- 6 cm

The mask has a perimeter of 50 cm. What is the length of the missing side? Show your work or explain how you found your answer.

Answer _____ cm

9 The four shapes shown below each have equal sides.

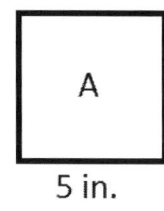

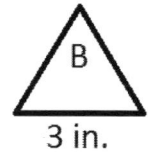

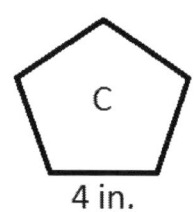

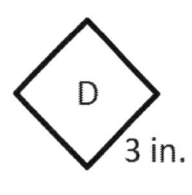

- A (square): 5 in.
- B (triangle): 3 in.
- C (pentagon): 4 in.
- D (diamond): 3 in.

Mike states that shapes B and D have equal side lengths and so have equal perimeters. Explain why this is incorrect.

_____

_____

_____

Which two shapes do have equal perimeters? _____ and _____

207

Quiz 53: Writing and Measuring Time

1. What time is shown on the clock below?

   Ⓐ 11:10 Ⓑ 1:55 Ⓒ 11:02 Ⓓ 2:05

2. Which of the following is closest to the time shown on the clock?

   Ⓐ 6:20 Ⓑ 4:30 Ⓒ 4:45 Ⓓ 9:00

3. Which of these is one way to write the time shown on the clock below?

   Ⓐ quarter past one Ⓑ ten past one
   Ⓒ five past three Ⓓ three fifteen

4. Harriet said she had a meeting at twenty to two in the afternoon. Which of these shows the time of the meeting?

   Ⓐ 1:40 a.m. Ⓑ 1:40 p.m. Ⓒ 2:20 a.m. Ⓓ 2:20 p.m.

5   Write the times listed below in number form.

quarter past one ____:____   ten to eleven ____:____

half past ten ____:____   quarter to nine ____:____

five to seven ____:____   ten past five ____:____

twenty past six ____:____   five past twelve ____:____

6   Write the time shown on each clock on the line below it.

____:____   ____:____   ____:____   ____:____   ____:____

7   Write the time shown on each clock to the nearest minute.

____:____   ____:____   ____:____   ____:____

____:____   ____:____   ____:____   ____:____

Quiz 54: Adding and Subtracting Time

1 David started reading at the time shown on the clock below.

He read for 42 minutes. What time did he finish reading?

Ⓐ 2:47 Ⓑ 3:07 Ⓒ 5:54 Ⓓ 6:04

2 Carly is meeting a friend at the library at 4:15 p.m. It takes Carly 25 minutes to walk to the library. She wants to arrive 5 minutes early. What time should she leave?

Ⓐ 3:25 p.m. Ⓑ 3:35 p.m. Ⓒ 3:45 p.m. Ⓓ 3:55 p.m.

3 Sawyer started riding to school at 8:45 a.m. It took him 35 minutes to get to school. What time did he get to school?

Ⓐ 9:00 a.m. Ⓑ 9:10 a.m. Ⓒ 9:15 a.m. Ⓓ 9:20 a.m.

4 Ricky started a guitar lesson at 3:40 p.m. The lesson finished at 5:05 p.m. How long did the guitar lesson go for?

Ⓐ 25 min Ⓑ 55 min Ⓒ 1 hr 25 min Ⓓ 1 hr 55 min

5 Hannah's flight was meant to leave at 12:42 p.m. The flight left at 1:06 p.m. How many minutes late was the flight?

Ⓐ 12 minutes Ⓑ 18 minutes Ⓒ 22 minutes Ⓓ 24 minutes

6 Bianca put a pie in the oven at 5:05 and baked it for 85 minutes. She let it cool for 25 minutes, and then served it. What time did she serve it?

Ⓐ 6:30 Ⓑ 6:40 Ⓒ 6:50 Ⓓ 7:00

7   Noah recorded the start and end time of the phone calls he made. Which phone calls went for more than 15 minutes? Select all the correct answers.

☐ 8:54 a.m. to 9:08 a.m.   ☐ 9:12 a.m. to 9:23 a.m.

☐ 7:03 p.m. to 7:20 p.m.   ☐ 11:48 a.m. to 12:01 p.m.

☐ 5:16 p.m. to 5:35 p.m.   ☐ 10:57 p.m. to 11:14 p.m.

8   The table below shows the start and end time of six movies. Complete the table by writing the length of each movie in hours and minutes.

Start Time	End Time	Length
9:45 a.m.	11:20 a.m.	
10:15 a.m.	12:10 p.m.	
11:20 a.m.	12:55 p.m.	
12:05 p.m.	2:30 p.m.	
1:35 p.m.	3:15 p.m.	
3:50 p.m.	5:40 p.m.	

9   The clocks show the time Jack started and finished work one evening.

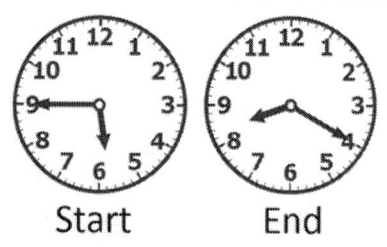

Start   End

What time did Jack work from? _____ to _____

How long did Jack work for? _____ hours, _____ minutes

Jack got home 40 minutes after work ended. What time did he get home? _____

10 Thomas drove to visit his uncle. He left home in the evening at the time shown on the first clock. He arrived at his uncle's house in the evening at the time shown on the second clock. How long did Thomas drive for?

Answer _____ hours, _____ minutes

11 Kobe got on a train at 1:45 p.m. He got off the train at 4:15 p.m. On the number line, plot the points to show when Kobe got on and off the train.

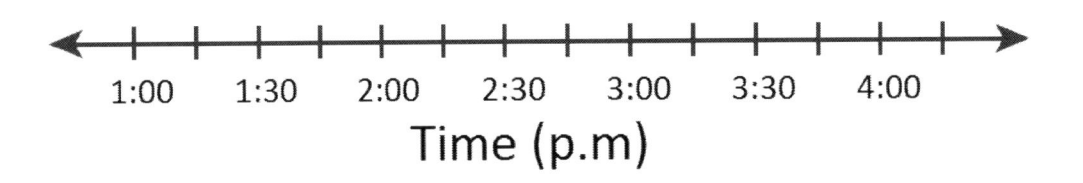

1:00   1:30   2:00   2:30   3:00   3:30   4:00
Time (p.m)

How long was Kobe on the train for? _____ hours, _____ minutes

12 Mia arrived at her restaurant job at 6:00 p.m. She worked for 1 hour and 30 minutes. Then she took a break of 15 minutes. She worked for another 1 hour and 45 minutes. Plot the following points on the number line below. Use the letter given to mark each point.

A – the time Mia started
C – the time Mia's break ended
B – the time Mia's break started
D – the time Mia finished work

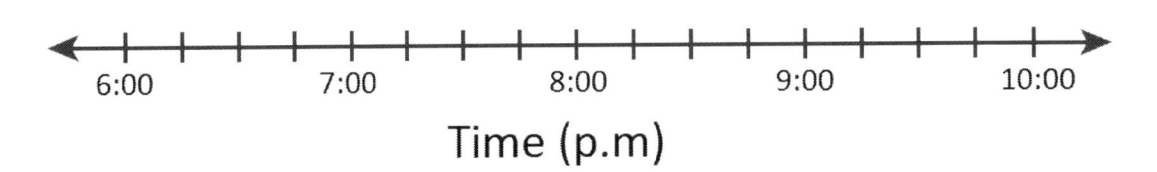

6:00   7:00   8:00   9:00   10:00
Time (p.m)

How long did Mia work for, including her break? _____ hours, _____ minutes

13 Students competed in a cycling race one morning. To avoid accidents, pairs of students started the race at different times. The table shows the results of the race. Complete the table with the missing information.

Student	Start Time	End Time	Total Time
Leyton	8:05	9:42	
Matt	8:05		1 hour 42 minutes
Omar	8:20		1 hour 35 minutes
Sean	8:20	9:48	
Perry	8:35	10:18	
Tim	8:35		1 hour 26 minutes
Sonny	8:50	10:39	
Ruben	8:50		1 hour 31 minutes

Who took the least time to finish the race? _____

Who took the most time to finish the race? _____

14 The table below shows a coach's plan for a basketball training session.

Task	Warm-up	Passing Practice	Dribbling Practice	Shooting Practice	Practice Game
Time (min)	5	14	12	18	45

The training session starts at 6:00 p.m. and ends at 7:40 p.m. How much time will be left over?

Show your work.

Answer _____ minutes

Quiz 55: Measuring and Estimating Liquid Volume

1. What is the most likely volume of the cooking pot shown below?

   Ⓐ 5 liters Ⓑ 50 liters Ⓒ 500 liters Ⓓ 5,000 liters

2. A store has the four fish tanks shown below for sale. Adam buys the tank with the greatest volume. Which tank did Adam buy?

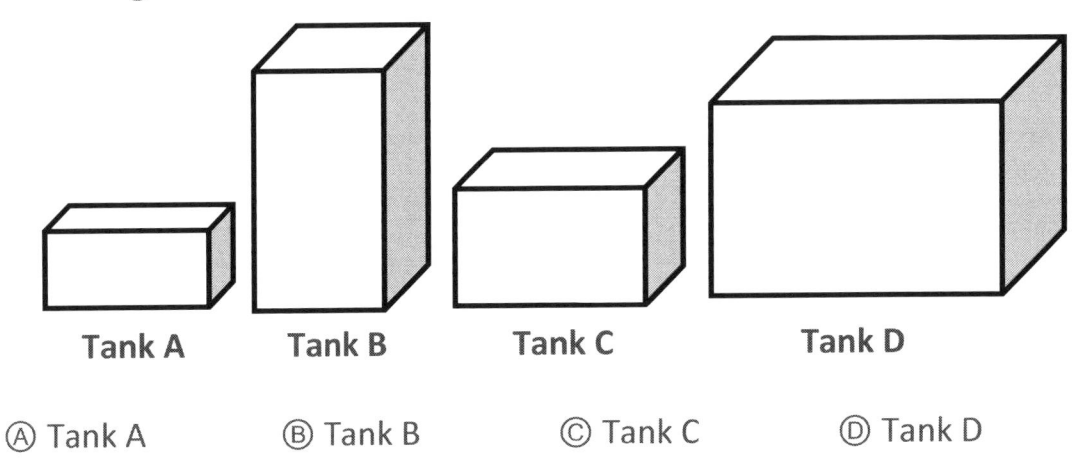

   Tank A **Tank B** **Tank C** **Tank D**

   Ⓐ Tank A Ⓑ Tank B Ⓒ Tank C Ⓓ Tank D

3. A 1-liter jug is filled with orange juice to the line shown.

   How much orange juice is in the jug?

   Ⓐ $\frac{1}{4}$ liter Ⓑ $\frac{1}{2}$ liter Ⓒ 2 liters Ⓓ 4 liters

4   Sara filled the container below with water.

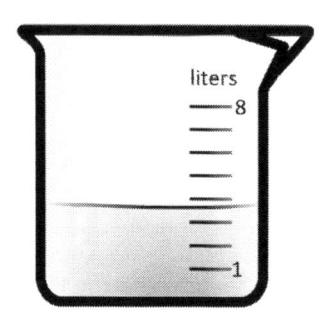

To the nearest liter, how much water did she fill the container with?

Answer _____ liters

5   Write the volume of water in each container on the line below it.

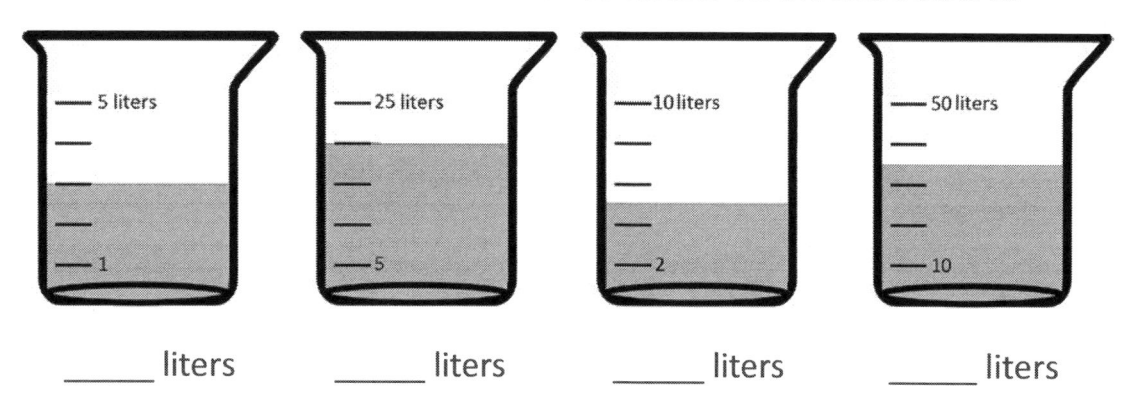

_____ liters   _____ liters   _____ liters   _____ liters

6   A 100 ml beaker is filled to the line below. The 150 ml and 250 ml beakers are then filled with the same amount of water. Draw lines to show the volume of water in the 150 ml and 250 ml beakers.

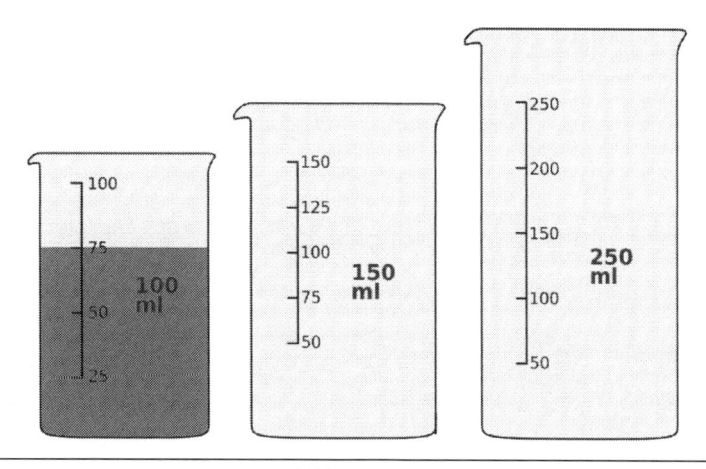

Quiz 56: Solving Word Problems Involving Liquid Volume

1 Jayden and Alana each have containers the same size, filled with different amounts of water.

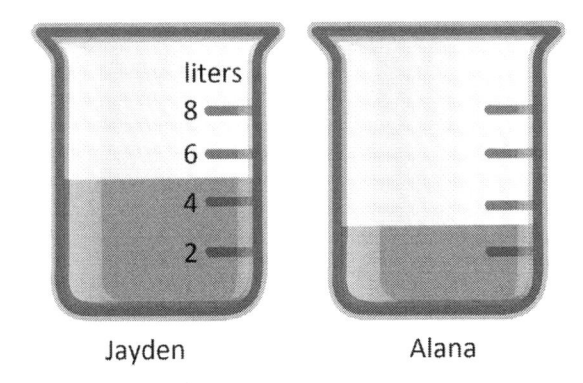

How much water is in Alana's container?

Ⓐ 2 liters Ⓑ 3 liters Ⓒ 4 liters Ⓓ 5 liters

2 Saxon buys a total of 2 liters of olive oil. The bottles of olive oil he bought are shown below.

How much olive oil is in each bottle?

Ⓐ $\frac{1}{4}$ liter Ⓑ $\frac{1}{2}$ liter Ⓒ 4 liters Ⓓ 8 liters

3 Anthony is filling a fish tank with water. He fills a 4-liter bucket with water and adds it to the tank. He does this a total of 6 times until the tank is full. How much water is in the tank when it is full?

Ⓐ 10 liters Ⓑ 24 liters Ⓒ 32 liters Ⓓ 60 liters

4 Donna was measuring out the ingredients for a cake. The diagram below shows the amount of milk and cream she needs.

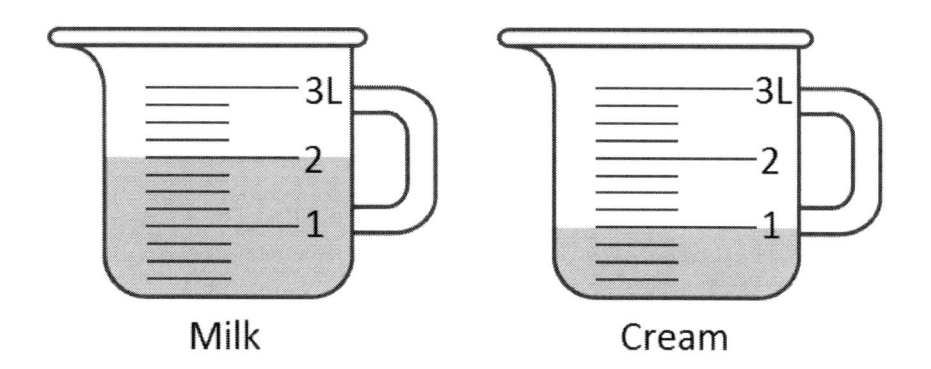

Milk   Cream

How much more milk than cream does she need? _____

How much milk and cream does she need in all? _____

5 The diagram below shows the volume of soil garden beds of different sizes can hold.

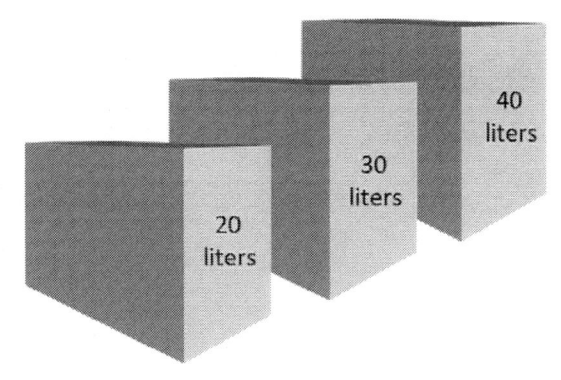

Don buys 5 bags of soil containing 20 liters of soil each. How much soil will Don have left after he fills all three garden beds?

Show your work.

Answer _____ liters

Quiz 57: Measuring and Estimating Weight

1 What is the most likely weight of a paperclip?

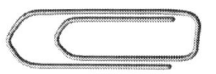

　Ⓐ 1 gram　　Ⓑ 100 grams　　Ⓒ 1 kilogram　　Ⓓ 100 kilograms

2 What is the most likely weight of the bicycle shown below?

　Ⓐ 1 g　　Ⓑ 100 g　　Ⓒ 10 kg　　Ⓓ 1000 kg

3 Which item in a kitchen is most likely to have a weight close to 10 grams?

　Ⓐ teaspoon　　Ⓑ toaster　　Ⓒ frying pan　　Ⓓ dinner plate

4 Match each item listed below to its most likely weight. Draw lines to connect the items.

strawberry　　　　　　　　　　　　　　　1 gram

olive　　　　　　　　　　　　　　　1 kilogram

watermelon　　　　　　　　　　　　　　　100 grams

banana　　　　　　　　　　　　　　　10 grams

5. For a school project, the students weighed items in the classroom. For each item listed below, select the correct unit of either grams or kilograms. Write kg or g on the blank line to show your choice.

Item	Weight
stapler	300 ___
desk	15 ___
pencil	40 ___
laptop	2 ___
whiteboard	12 ___
ruler	60 ___

6. When apples are placed on a scale, the scale has the reading shown.

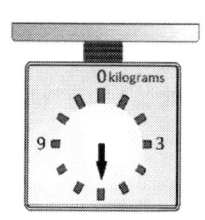

What is the weight of the apples? _____ kilograms

7. What reading is shown on the scale below? Write the answer in grams and kilograms.

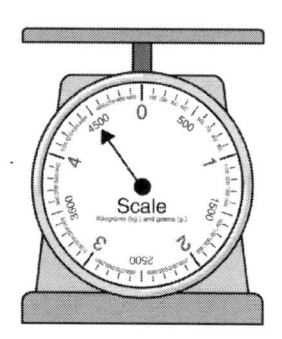

Answer _____ grams or _____ kilograms

Quiz 58: Solving Word Problems Involving Weight

1. A weightlifter places a 20 kilogram, 10 kilogram, and 5 kilogram weight on each end of a bar.

   What is the total weight of the weights added to the bar?

   Ⓐ 35 kg Ⓑ 45 kg Ⓒ 60 kg Ⓓ 70 kg

2. Soil is sold for $4 for each 10 kilogram bag. Rhys uses 60 kilograms of soil to fill the small garden. He uses twice as much soil to fill the large garden.

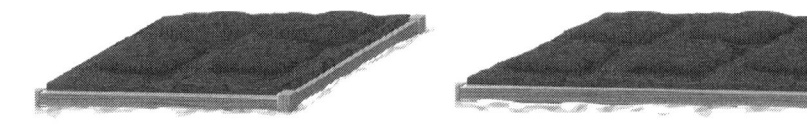

   How much would it cost to fill the large garden with soil?

   Ⓐ $24 Ⓑ $48 Ⓒ $60 Ⓓ $120

3. The diagram shows that a scale is balanced when a large notebook is placed on one side, and two small notebooks are placed on the other side.

   If the large notebook has a weight of 800 grams, which of these could be the weights of the small notebooks? Select all the possible answers.

   ☐ 200 grams and 600 grams ☐ 500 grams and 500 grams

   ☐ 750 grams and 250 grams ☐ 300 grams and 300 grams

   ☐ 400 grams and 400 grams ☐ 450 grams and 550 grams

4 What is the total weight of the weights shown below?

Answer _____ kilograms

5 An empty delivery van has a weight of 2,800 kilograms. After being loaded with 20 televisions of equal weight, the total weight is 3,100 kilograms. What is the weight of each television?

Show your work.

Answer _____ kilograms

6 Jenna made jars of strawberry jelly with the same weight. She placed three jars on a scale, as shown below.

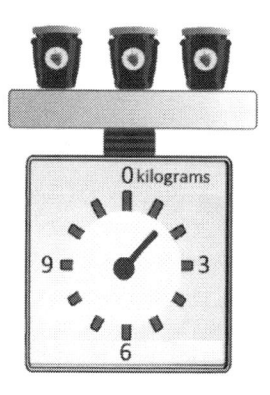

How many jars will have a total weight of 6 kilograms?

Show your work.

Answer _____ jars

Quizzes 59 to 66

Displaying and Interpreting Data

Directions

Read each question carefully. For each multiple-choice question, fill in the circle for the correct answer. For other types of questions, follow the directions given in the question.

You may use a ruler to help you answer questions. You should answer the questions without using a calculator.

MATHEMATICS SKILLS LIST
For Parents, Teachers, and Tutors

Quizzes 59 through 66 cover these skills from the Texas Essential Knowledge and Skills (TEKS).

Data Analysis

The student applies mathematical process standards to solve problems by collecting, organizing, displaying, and interpreting data.

The student is expected to be able to complete the following tasks.

- Summarize a data set with multiple categories using a frequency table, dot plot, pictograph, or bar graph with scaled intervals.

- Solve one- and two-step problems using categorical data represented with a frequency table, dot plot, pictograph, or bar graph with scaled intervals.

Quiz 59: Using Frequency Tables to Represent Data

1 Four classes at Chan's school collected cans for a food drive. The table shows how many cans each class collected.

Class	Number of Cans
Miss Powell	57
Mr. Sato	41
Mrs. Joshi	65
Miss Arthur	

The four classes collected a total of 200 cans. How many cans did Miss Arthur's class collect?

Ⓐ 37 Ⓑ 50 Ⓒ 60 Ⓓ 63

2 Leanne was given these scores from ten judges in a dancing contest.

7, 7, 7, 7, 7, 8, 8, 8, 9, 9

If the data was recorded in a frequency table, which number would describe the frequency for a score of 7?

Ⓐ 3 Ⓑ 5 Ⓒ 7 Ⓓ 10

3 Carmen tossed a coin 10 times. The coin landed on heads 6 times and tails 4 times. She wants to complete the tally chart below to show the results.

Heads	Tails

Which of these should Carmen place in the "Heads" column?

Ⓐ ||||
Ⓑ ||||
Ⓒ |||| |
Ⓓ |||| ||

4 The list below shows how many laps of a pool Mike swam in his training sessions each day for one month.

18, 12, 10, 14, 10, 14, 16, 11, 15, 16, 14, 14, 17, 20, 12, 13, 15, 11, 13, 17, 20, 14, 18, 19, 10, 15, 16, 18, 13, 11

Complete the frequency table below to represent the data.

Mike's Swimming Training

Number of Laps	Number of Times
10	
11	
12	
13	
14	
15	
16	
17	
18	
19	
20	

What was the most common number of laps swam? _____ laps

What was the least common number of laps swam? _____ laps

How many times did Mike swim 15 laps or more? _____ times

5. The list below shows the scores that 28 students in a class received on a science quiz.

$$6, 8, 11, 10, 12, 12, 7, 8, 6, 5, 12, 10, 8, 8,$$
$$10, 12, 5, 9, 10, 7, 11, 8, 12, 7, 10, 6, 5, 12$$

Complete the frequency table below to represent the data.

Science Quiz Scores

Score	Number of Students

What was the most common score? _____

What was the least common score? _____

How many students scored 7 or less? _____

How many students scored 10 or more? _____

How many more students scored 8 than scored 9? _____

6 The bar graph represents the number of students that have each type of pet.

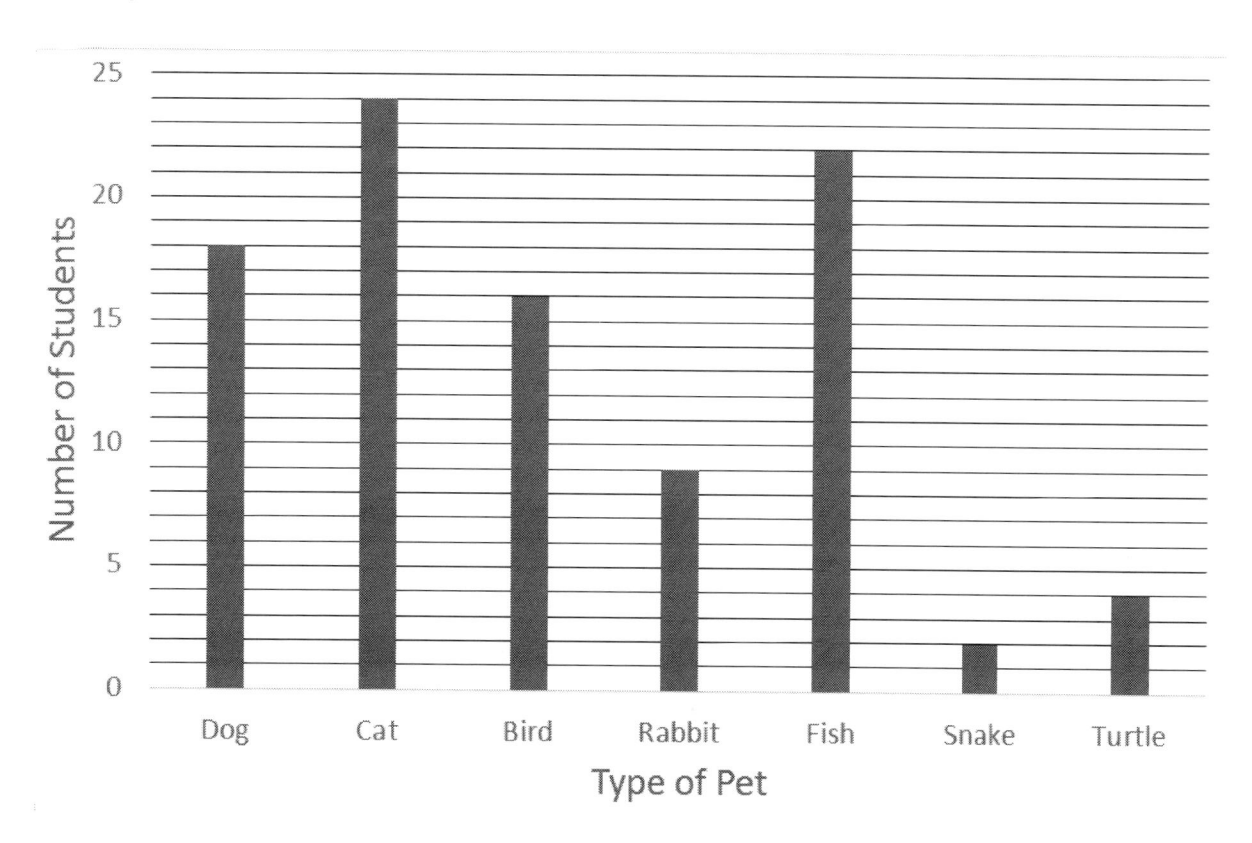

Complete the frequency table below with the data from the graph.

Type of Pet	Number of Students
Dog	
Cat	
Bird	
Rabbit	
Fish	
Snake	
Turtle	

Quiz 60: Using Dot Plots to Represent Data

1 Josie made the dot plot below to record the lengths of the carrots she picked from her garden.

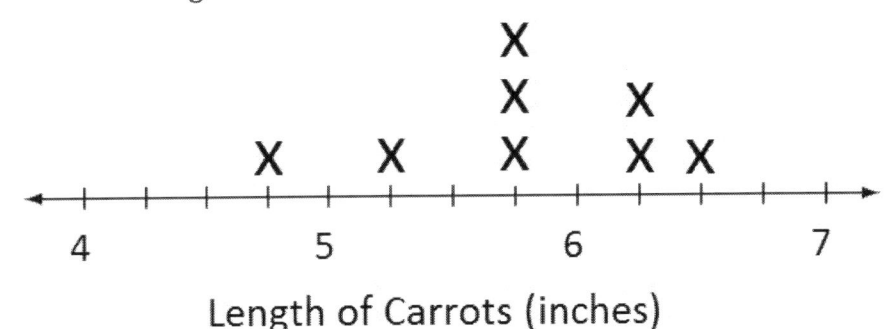

```
                    X
                    X     X
        X    X      X     X  X
     +--+--+--+--+--+--+--+--+--+-->
        4        5        6        7
           Length of Carrots (inches)
```

What was the most common carrot length?

Ⓐ $4\frac{3}{4}$ inches   Ⓑ $5\frac{3}{4}$ inches   Ⓒ $6\frac{1}{4}$ inches   Ⓓ $6\frac{1}{2}$ inches

2 The list shows the length of each fish that was caught on a fishing trip.

Length of Fish Caught (inches)

7, $7\frac{1}{2}$, $6\frac{1}{2}$, 6, 7, $8\frac{1}{2}$, 8, 6, $7\frac{1}{2}$, 8, 8, $6\frac{1}{2}$, $6\frac{1}{2}$, $8\frac{1}{2}$, 7, 6, $6\frac{1}{2}$, 8, $7\frac{1}{2}$

Randall made the dot plot below to represent the data, and completed the plot for 6 inches. Finish the dot plot by plotting the rest of the data.

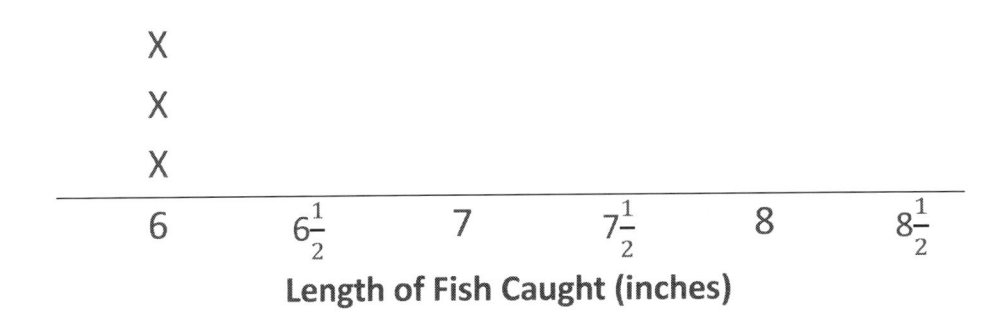

```
   X
   X
   X
   ——————————————————————————————
   6    6½    7    7½    8    8½
          Length of Fish Caught (inches)
```

228

3   The table shows the lengths of nine leaves.

Length of Leaves (inches)

Leaf 1	$4\frac{1}{2}$
Leaf 2	$5\frac{1}{2}$
Leaf 3	$4\frac{1}{4}$
Leaf 4	$4\frac{3}{4}$
Leaf 5	$4\frac{1}{2}$
Leaf 6	$4\frac{3}{4}$
Leaf 7	$4\frac{3}{4}$
Leaf 8	5
Leaf 9	$4\frac{3}{4}$

Use the data in the table to complete the dot plot below.

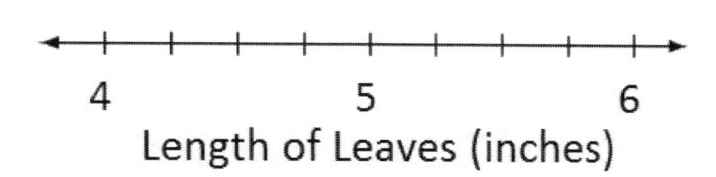

Length of Leaves (inches)

Student Quiz Book, STAAR Mathematics, Grade 3

4 Jordan measured the height of tomato plants after 2 weeks of growing. The data she collected is shown below.

Height of Plants (inches)

Plant 1	$2\frac{1}{2}$	Plant 7	$2\frac{3}{4}$
Plant 2	$2\frac{1}{4}$	Plant 8	2
Plant 3	$2\frac{1}{4}$	Plant 9	$1\frac{3}{4}$
Plant 4	$1\frac{3}{4}$	Plant 10	$2\frac{1}{2}$
Plant 5	$2\frac{1}{2}$	Plant 11	$2\frac{1}{4}$
Plant 6	$2\frac{3}{4}$	Plant 12	$1\frac{3}{4}$

Use the data in the table to complete the dot plot below.

$1\frac{1}{2}$ $1\frac{3}{4}$ 2 $2\frac{1}{4}$ $2\frac{1}{2}$ $2\frac{3}{4}$ 3

Height of Plants (inches)

How many plants had a height of 2 inches or more? _____ plants

Explain how you used the dot plot to find the answer.

_____

_____

5   The lengths of eight pencils are shown below.

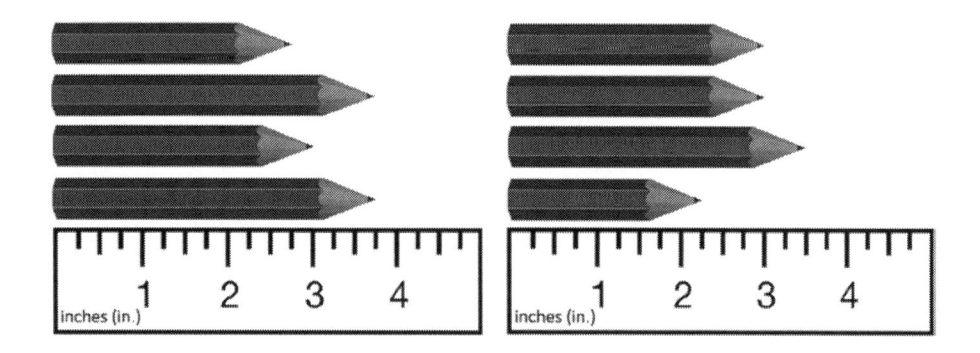

List the length of each pencil to the nearest quarter inch.

Length of Pencils (inches)

Use the data collected to complete the dot plot below.

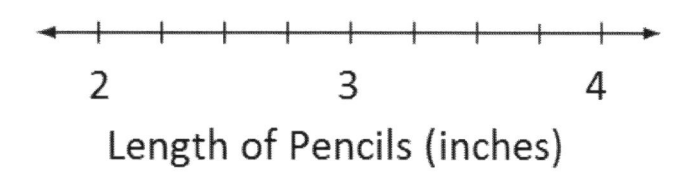

Length of Pencils (inches)

Which pencil length is the most common? _____ inches

Describe how the dot plot makes it easier to compare how common each length is.

_____

_____

_____

Quiz 61: Using Pictographs to Represent Data

1 The table below shows how many points Evan scored in the first eight games of the basketball season.

Evan's Points

Game	Points Scored
1	22
2	26
3	14
4	18
5	20
6	24
7	12
8	10

Complete the pictograph below to represent the data.

Evan's Points

Game	Points Scored
1	OOOOOOOOOOO
2	
3	
4	
5	
6	
7	
8	

Each O = 2 points

2. The table below shows how much money students raised on a fun run.

Money Raised on a Fun Run

Name	Amount Raised ($)
Terry	45
Arnold	25
Cato	50
Grant	20
Jorge	35
Payton	55
Pablo	40
Willis	15

Complete the pictograph below to represent the data.

Money Raised on a Fun Run

Name	Amount Raised ($)
Terry	
Arnold	
Cato	
Grant	
Jorge	
Payton	
Pablo	
Willis	

Each $ = $5

3 The table below shows the number of questions that seven students got correct on a science quiz.

Science Quiz Results

Name	Number of Correct Questions
Isha	14
Jess	18
Kassie	12
Lexis	8
Penny	20
Tessa	16
Renata	24

Choose a suitable scale for the pictograph below. Then complete the pictograph to represent the data.

Science Quiz Results

Each ✓ = _____ correct questions

Name	Number of Correct Questions
Isha	
Jess	
Kassie	
Lexis	
Penny	
Tessa	
Renata	

4. The table below shows how many pieces of pizza a store sold on each day of the week.

Pizza Sales

Day	Number of Pieces
Monday	80
Tuesday	110
Wednesday	90
Thursday	60
Friday	70
Saturday	130
Sunday	150

Choose a suitable scale for the pictograph below. Then complete the pictograph to represent the data.

Each ▷ = _____ pieces of pizza

Pizza Sales

Day	Number of Pieces
Monday	
Tuesday	
Wednesday	
Thursday	
Friday	
Saturday	
Sunday	

Quiz 62: Using Bar Graphs to Represent Data

1. The table below shows the score students received on a spelling quiz.

Spelling Quiz Scores

Name	Score
Ricky	18
Lucy	14
Chan	10
Jed	16
Corey	10
Bevan	12

Complete the bar graph below to represent the data.

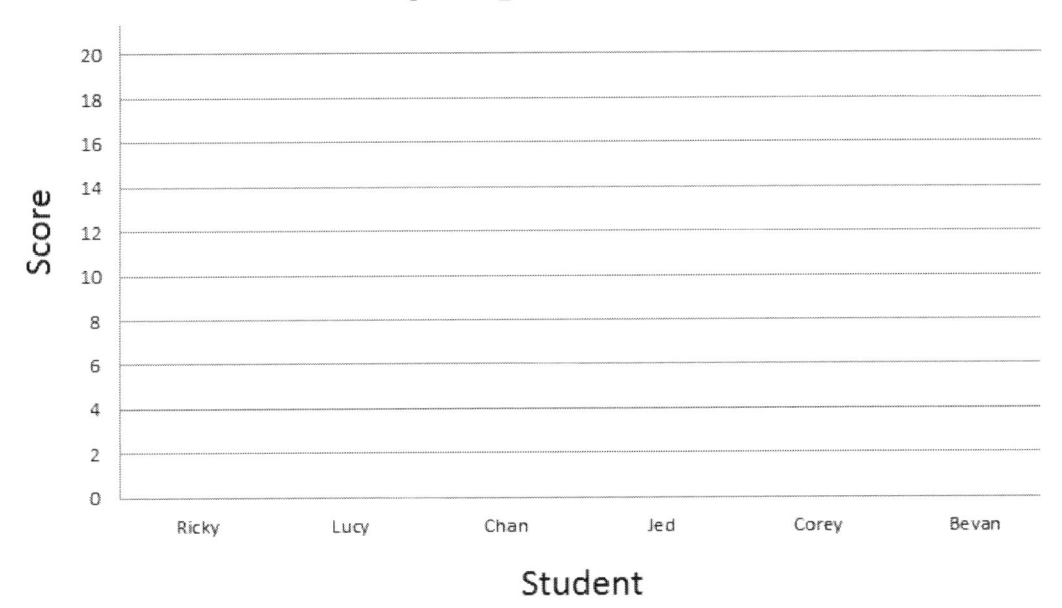

Spelling Quiz Scores

2. The table shows the time Margo spent studying math each week day.

Margo's Math Study Time

Day	Number of Minutes
Monday	60
Tuesday	45
Wednesday	45
Thursday	30
Friday	15

Complete the bar graph below to represent the data. Be sure to include a scale.

Margo's Math Study Time

3   A school has six sporting clubs. The table below shows the number of members each club has.

Sporting Clubs

Club	Number of Members
Baseball	45
Basketball	60
Volleyball	35
Lacrosse	25
Soccer	30
Hockey	40

Complete the bar graph below to represent the data. Be sure to include a scale.

Sporting Clubs

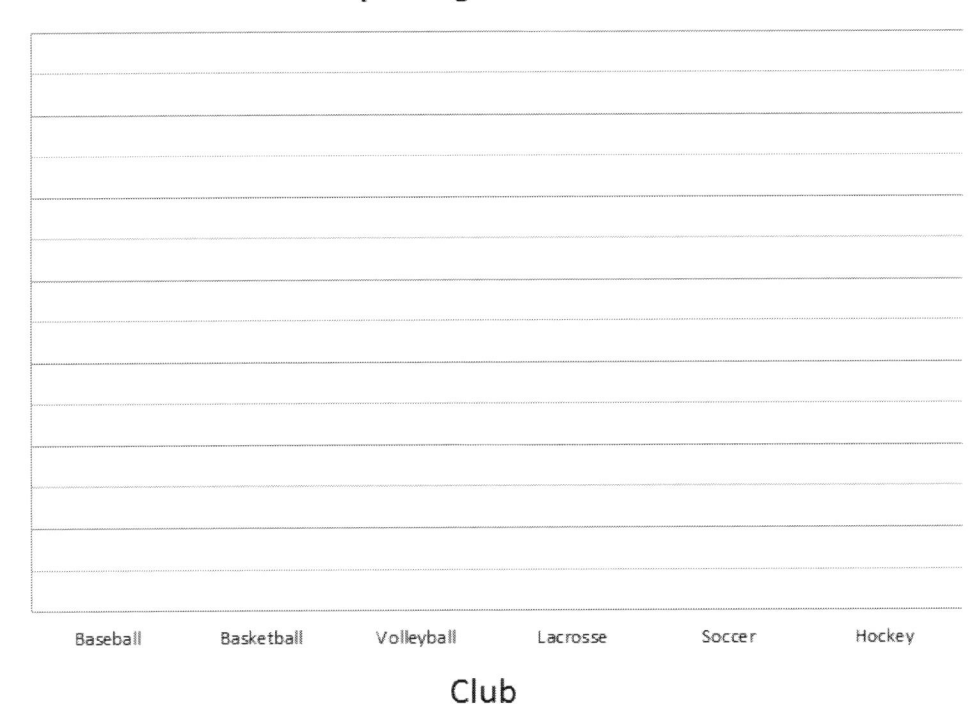

4 A football club had a vote to choose the color of a new mascot. The votes are shown below.

Votes for a New Mascot

Color	Number of Votes
Red	16
Green	18
Blue	14
Yellow	12
Pink	6
Purple	10

Complete the bar graph below to represent the data. Be sure to include a scale and labels on both axes.

Votes for a New Mascot

Quiz 63: Using Frequency Tables to Solve Problems

1 Mia has five groups of pennies. The table below shows the number of pennies in each group.

Group	Number of Pennies
J	26
K	12
L	24
M	17
N	23

Mia wants a group of exactly 40 pennies. Which two groups should Mia combine?

Ⓐ J and L   Ⓑ K and M   Ⓒ J and N   Ⓓ M and N

2 Anna recorded how many hours she worked at her part-time job each week. The frequency table shows her data.

Number of Hours	Number of Times
10	2
11	4
12	3
13	3
14	6
15	2

Anna earns $8 per hour. How many times did she earn over $100 in a week?

Show your work.

Answer _____ times

3 The table shows how many points players scored in a basketball match.

Points Scored in a Basketball Match

Name	Points Scored
Jason	15
Andy	17
Leroy	9
Jonah	14
Ryan	11
Pierre	3
Gabe	6

Who scored the most points? _____

Who scored the least points? _____

Who scored twice as many points as Pierre? _____

Who scored 1 less point than Jason? _____

Which two players scored a total of 25 points?

_____ and _____

How many more points did Ryan score than Leroy? _____

Which two players scored the same total number of points as Jonah?

_____ and _____

How many points were scored in all? _____

4   Amy makes bookmarks to sell at the markets. The table shows how many bookmarks of each color she sold in May.

Number of Bookmarks Sold in May

Color	Bookmarks Sold
Green	35
Red	15
Yellow	40
Pink	20
Blue	25
Purple	45

How many more yellow bookmarks than pink bookmarks did she sell?

Show your work.

Answer _____ bookmarks

How many fewer pink bookmarks did she sell than purple bookmarks?

Show your work.

Answer _____ bookmarks

How many bookmarks did she sell in all?

Show your work.

Answer _____ bookmarks

5. A manager kept a record of how many hours of overtime his employees worked one week. The table shows the results.

Amount of Overtime	Number of Employees
0 to 5 hours	15
6 to 10 hours	12
11 to 15 hours	9
Over 15 hours	4

How many employees worked overtime for 11 hours or more?

Show your work.

Answer _____ employees

How many employees worked overtime for 10 hours or less?

Show your work.

Answer _____ employees

The manager stated that over half the employees worked overtime for 5 hours or less. Is the manager correct? Explain your answer.

_____

_____

_____

_____

Quiz 64: Using Dot Plots to Solve Problems

1 The dot plot below shows how many goals each member of a soccer team scored in the season.

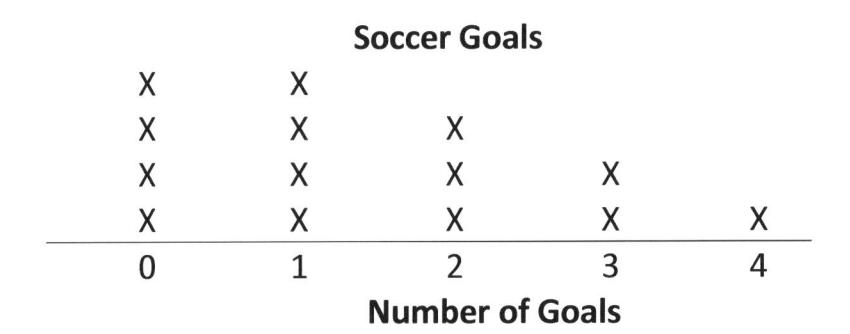

Soccer Goals

```
X   X
X   X   X
X   X   X   X
X   X   X   X   X
-------------------
0   1   2   3   4
```
Number of Goals

Which statement is true?

Ⓐ Each player scored at least 1 goal.

Ⓑ Only one player scored more than 3 goals.

Ⓒ The same number of players scored 2 goals as scored 3 goals.

Ⓓ More players scored 1 goal than scored no goals.

2 Valerie made the dot plot below to record the number of flowers on each rose bush in her garden.

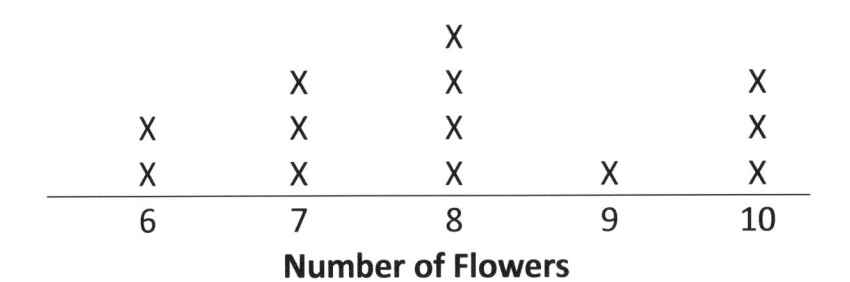

```
            X
        X   X       X
    X   X   X       X
    X   X   X   X   X
    ----------------------
    6   7   8   9   10
```
Number of Flowers

How many more rose bushes had 8 flowers than had 9 flowers?

Ⓐ 1   Ⓑ 3   Ⓒ 4   Ⓓ 5

3 Warren recorded the time he spent doing homework each day for two weeks. The dot plot shows the results.

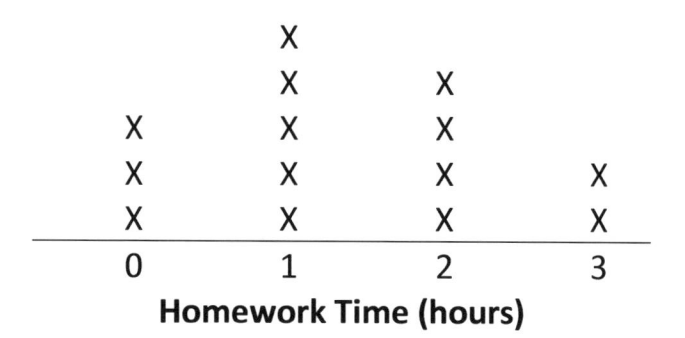

```
                  X
                  X       X
          X       X       X
          X       X       X       X
          X       X       X       X
         _____
          0       1       2       3
```
Homework Time (hours)

On how many days did he study for exactly 2 hours? _____ days

On how many days did he study for 1 hour or less? _____ days

What was the most amount of time he studied for in a day? _____ hours

How many hours did he study for in total over the two weeks?

Show your work.

Answer _____ hours

Warren's teacher states that all students should have 2 days rest each week where they do not do any homework. Is this true for Warren? Explain your answer.

_____

_____

_____

_____

4 A class made the dot plot below to show how students traveled to school.

Traveling to School

```
              X
  X           X
  X           X                   X
  X           X         X         X
  X           X         X         X
  X           X         X         X         X
  X           X         X         X         X
  X           X         X         X         X
  X           X         X         X         X
  X           X         X         X         X
  X           X         X         X         X
-----------------------------------------------
 Walk        Bus       Car       Bike      Train
```
Number of Students

How many students walked to school? _____

How many students took either a bus or a train? _____

How many more students traveled by bus than by car? _____

List the ways students traveled from most common to least common.

Most Common   Least Common

_____   _____   _____   _____   _____

Felicia stated that more students walk or travel by bike than travel by bus, car, or train. Is Felicia correct? Explain your answer.

_____

_____

_____

_____

5   Rex made the dot plot below to represent the coins in his money box.

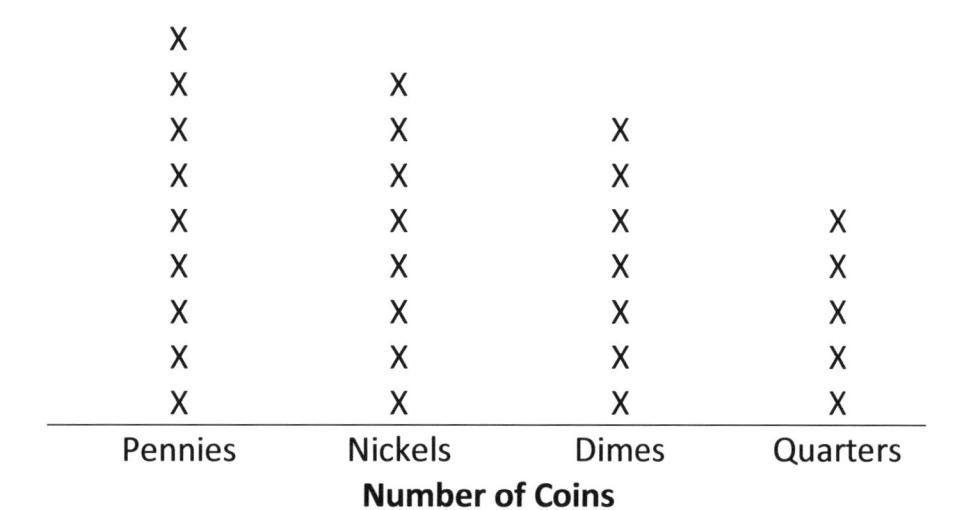

```
X
X       X
X       X       X
X       X       X
X       X       X       X
X       X       X       X
X       X       X       X
X       X       X       X
X       X       X       X
Pennies Nickels Dimes   Quarters
```
Number of Coins

What is the total value of the quarters that Rex has?

Show your work.

Answer _____ cents

How much more are all the dimes worth than all the nickels?

Show your work.

Answer _____ cents

Which type of coins could be divided into two equal groups? _____

What would be the value of the coins in each group?

Show your work.

Answer _____ cents

Quiz 65: Using Pictographs to Solve Problems

1 The pictograph shows how many emails Pam received each week day.

Pam's Emails

Day	Number of Emails
Monday	✉✉✉
Tuesday	✉✉
Wednesday	✉✉✉✉
Thursday	✉✉✉✉✉✉
Friday	✉✉✉✉✉✉✉✉

Each ✉ means 2 emails.

How many emails did Pam receive on Monday?

_____ emails

How many more emails did Pam receive on Wednesday than on Tuesday?

_____ emails

On which day did Pam receive 6 fewer emails than Thursday?

_____

On which two days did Pam receive a total of 10 emails?

_____ and _____

On which two days did Pam receive the same total number of emails as she received on Friday?

_____ and _____

How many emails were received in all?

_____ emails

2 The pictograph below shows how long Tammy spent at the computer each week day.

Tammy's Computer Time

Day	Computer Time
Monday	🖥️🖥️🖥️🖥️
Tuesday	🖥️🖥️🖥️🖥️🖥️🖥️
Wednesday	🖥️🖥️🖥️🖥️🖥️
Thursday	🖥️🖥️🖥️
Friday	🖥️🖥️🖥️🖥️🖥️🖥️🖥️

Each 🖥️ means 10 minutes.

How long did Tammy spend at the computer on Monday?

_____ minutes

On which day did Tammy spend 1 hour at the computer?

_____

How much longer did Tammy spend at the computer on Friday than on Thursday?

_____ minutes

How long did Tammy spend at the computer on Monday and Tuesday?

_____ minutes

On which two days did Tammy spend the same time at the computer as Monday and Tuesday combined?

_____ and _____

How long did Tammy spend at the computer in all?

_____ minutes

3 The pictograph shows how many votes seven students received in an election for class president.

Class President Election

Student	Number of Votes
Selena	☺☺☺☺☺☺☺☺
Riley	☺☺☺☺☺☺
Anton	☺☺☺☺
Tyra	☺☺☺☺☺☺☺☺☺☺
Gavin	☺☺☺☺☺
Jett	☺☺☺
Kimi	☺☺☺☺☺☺☺

Each ☺ means 5 votes.

Complete the equation to show how many votes Selena and Riley received in all. Then write the answer.

_____ + _____ = _____   **Answer** _____ votes

Complete the equation to show how many fewer votes Anton received than Tyra. Then write the answer.

_____ − _____ = _____   **Answer** _____ votes

Complete the equation to show how many votes Gavin and Jett received in all. Then write the answer.

_____ + _____ = _____   **Answer** _____ votes

Complete the equation to show how many more votes Kimi received than Jett. Then write the answer.

_____ − _____ = _____   **Answer** _____ votes

4 Kirsten collects pennies. The pictograph below shows how many pennies she added to the collection each month of the year.

Kirsten's Penny Collection

Month	Number of Pennies Added
January	●●●●●◐
February	●●●●◐
March	●●●
April	●●●●●●◐
May	●●●●●
June	●●●◐

Each ● means 10 pennies.

Write an equation to show how many more pennies Kirsten collected in January than in February. Then write the answer.

Answer _____ pennies

Write an equation to show how many fewer pennies Kirsten collected in June than in May. Then write the answer.

Answer _____ pennies

Write an equation to show how many pennies Kirsten collected in March and April. Then write the answer.

Answer _____ pennies

Quiz 66: Using Bar Graphs to Solve Problems

1 Mr. Morgan owns a diner. The graph below shows how many pieces of pie of each type he sold one week. Use the graph to answer the questions.

Pieces of Pie Sold

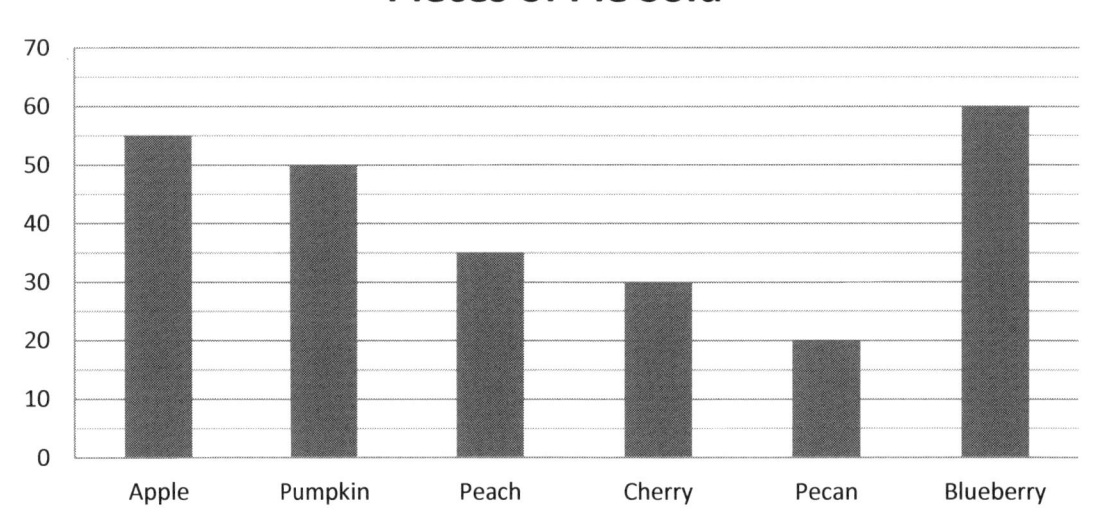

Pie	Pieces
Apple	55
Pumpkin	50
Peach	35
Cherry	30
Pecan	20
Blueberry	60

How many more pieces of pumpkin pie were sold than pecan pie? _____

Which type of pie sold 15 more pieces than peach pie? _____

Which type of pie sold 20 fewer pieces than pumpkin pie? _____

Which two types sold a total of 50 pieces? _____ and _____

How many pieces of pecan and blueberry pie were sold in all? _____

Which type of pie sold 3 times as many pieces as pecan pie? _____

Which two types of pie sold the same amount in total as apple pie?

_____ and _____

A piece of cherry pie sells for $3. How much was made from sales of cherry pie? _____

2 The graph below shows how many books seven students read in a month. Use the graph to answer the questions.

Number of Books Read

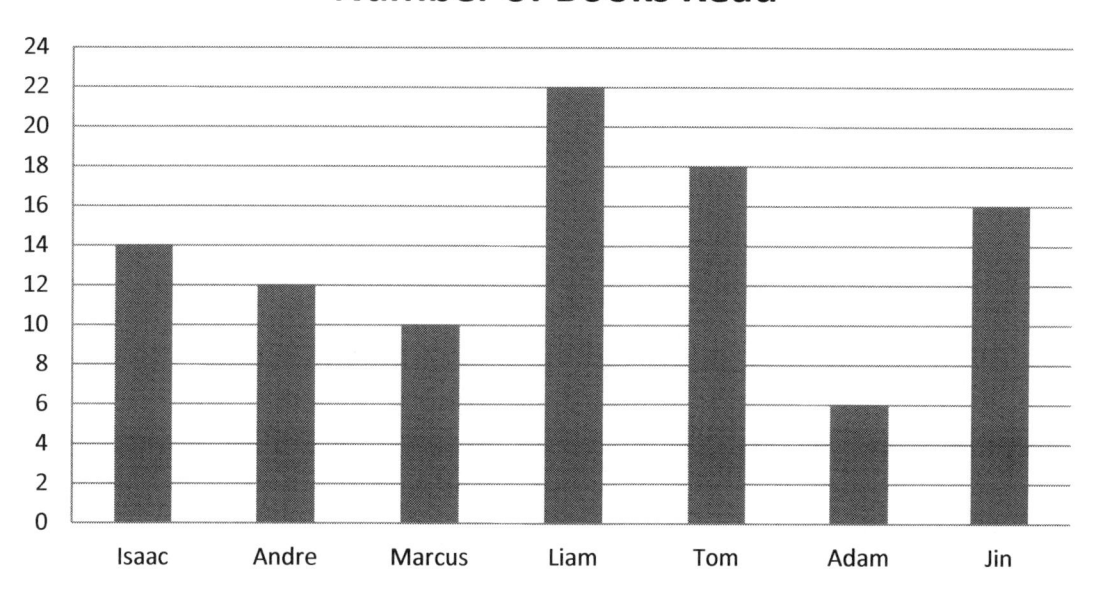

Student	Books
Isaac	14
Andre	12
Marcus	10
Liam	22
Tom	18
Adam	6
Jin	16

How many more books did Tom read than Marcus? _____

Who read 10 more books than Adam? _____

Which two students read a total of 20 books? _____ and _____

How many books did Isaac and Tom read in all? _____

Who read twice as many books as Adam? _____

How many fewer books did Andre read than Jin? _____

What is the difference between the most and the least books read? _____

List two pairs of students that read a total of 30 books.

1. _____ and _____   2. _____ and _____

3 The graph shows how long Cara spent practicing the piano each day.

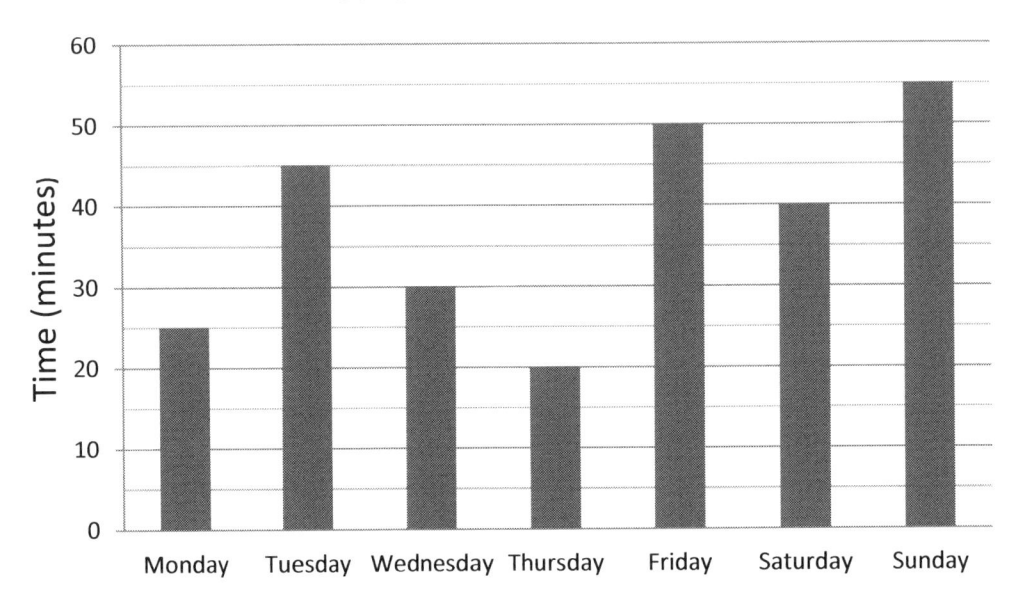

Cara's Piano Time

Complete the equation to show how long Cara practiced for on Saturday and Sunday. Then write the answer.

_____ + _____ = _____   **Answer** _____ minutes

Complete the equation to show how much longer Cara practiced for on Tuesday than on Monday. Then write the answer.

_____ − _____ = _____   **Answer** _____ minutes

Complete the equation to show how much longer Cara practiced for on Friday than on Thursday. Then write the answer.

_____ − _____ = _____   **Answer** _____ minutes

Complete the equation to show how long Cara practiced for on Monday, Tuesday, and Wednesday. Then write the answer.

_____ + _____ + _____ = _____   **Answer** _____ minutes

4 Jamie recorded the colors of the cars in a parking lot. The graph below shows the results.

Color of Cars in a Parking Lot

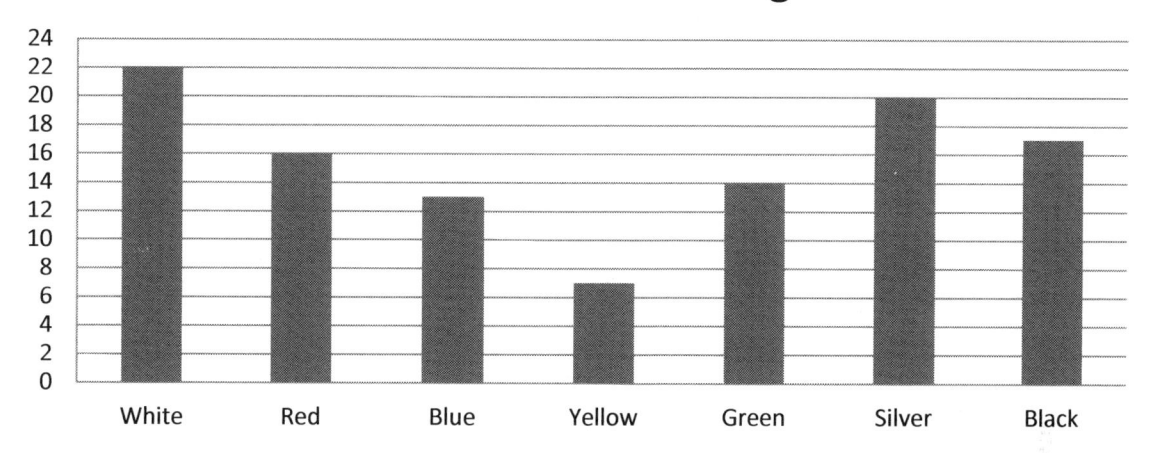

Color	Number
White	22
Red	16
Blue	13
Yellow	7
Green	14
Silver	20
Black	17

Write an equation to show how many more green cars there were than yellow cars. Then write the answer.

Answer _____ cars

Write an equation to show how many white, black, and silver cars there were in all. Then write the answer.

Answer _____ cars

Jamie says there were more white cars than blue and yellow combined. Is Jamie correct? Explain your answer.

_____

_____

_____

Quizzes 67 to 70

Developing Personal Financial Literacy

Directions

Read each question carefully. For each multiple-choice question, fill in the circle for the correct answer. For other types of questions, follow the directions given in the question.

You may use a ruler to help you answer questions. You should answer the questions without using a calculator.

MATHEMATICS SKILLS LIST
For Parents, Teachers, and Tutors

Quizzes 67 through 70 cover these skills from the Texas Essential Knowledge and Skills (TEKS).

Personal Financial Literacy

The student applies mathematical process standards to manage one's financial resources effectively for lifetime financial security.

The student is expected to be able to complete the following tasks.

- Explain the connection between human capital/labor and income.

- Describe the relationship between the availability or scarcity of resources and how that impacts cost.

- Explain that credit is used when wants or needs exceed the ability to pay and that it is the borrower's responsibility to pay it back to the lender, usually with interest.

- List reasons to save and explain the benefit of a savings plan, including for college.

Quiz 67: Understanding Labor and Income Relationships

1 Marilyn wants to increase the amount she earns each week. What two actions could Marilyn take to increase her earnings?

Ⓐ decrease her hourly wage and decrease the number of hours worked

Ⓑ decrease her hourly wage and increase the number of hours worked

Ⓒ increase her hourly wage and decrease the number of hours worked

Ⓓ increase her hourly wage and increase the number of hours worked

2 Kay is promoted from salesperson to store manager. The amount earned and wage for each position is listed below.

Position	Hours Worked	Wage (per hour)
Salesperson	35	$10
Store manager	40	$12

By how much per week would Kay's income increase when he is promoted?

Ⓐ $50 Ⓑ $60 Ⓒ $120 Ⓓ $130

3 Kendra and Jasmine work as waitresses at a diner. Kendra and Jasmine both work for 5 hours one night. Kendra earns $40 and Jasmine earns $45. Which statement best explains the difference in their earnings?

Ⓐ Jasmine earns more per hour than Kendra.

Ⓑ Jasmine enjoys her work more than Kendra.

Ⓒ Kendra has been a waitress longer than Jasmine.

Ⓓ Kendra is also studying, while Jasmine is not.

4 A website designer charges $40 for each hour she works on a website. How much would she charge for a website that takes 15 hours to complete?

Answer $ _____

5. The table below shows how much the staff of a restaurant made on Friday.

Name	Hours Worked	Total Wages ($)
Bruce	5	55
Emmett	5	65
Didi	4	48
Gwen	3	42
Donnie	4	56
Bianca	6	72

Who earns $11 per hour? _____

Who earns $12 per hour? _____ and _____

Who earns $13 per hour? _____

Who earns $14 per hour? _____ and _____

6. Jamal works as a basketball coach. He receives a base salary of $32,500 per year. He also receives a $250 bonus each week that his team wins. If his team wins 10 times, what is Jamal's total earnings for the year?

Show your work.

Answer $_____

7 The fees that a make-up artist charges for weddings are shown below.

- $45 for the bride
- $30 for each bridesmaid
- a flat fee of $50 for travel costs for each job

Wendy books the make-up artist to do make-up for 1 bride and 4 bridesmaids. What would be the total cost of the job?

Show your work.

Answer $_____

8 A plumber charges a flat fee of $75 for each job that he takes, as well as $35 for each hour the job takes. How much would the plumber charge for a job that takes 4 hours?

Show your work.

Answer $_____

The plumber finishes a job and charges $425. How long did the job take?

Show your work.

Answer _____ hours

9 Wade works as a mechanic. He works 40 hours a week and earns $16 per hour. He want to increase his income to $800 per week. If he worked the same number of hours, what would his wage need to be to make $800?

Show your work.

Answer $_____ per hour

If his wage stayed the same, how many hours would he need to work to make $800?

Show your work.

Answer _____ hours

10 The table below shows the hours worked and the hourly rate for four people working part-time at a bookstore. Complete the table with the total earnings for each person.

Name	Hours Worked	Hourly Rate ($)	Total Earnings ($)
Kylie	15	6	
Stefan	12	9	
Marcus	12	8	
Yuri	10	12	

Explain why Yuri earns more than everyone while working fewer hours.

_____

_____

Quiz 68: Understanding Scarcity and Cost Relationships

1 Good weather and high rainfall increased the crop of pumpkins on a farm. Which statement best describes the effect on the price?

Ⓐ The price will likely increase, because there are more pumpkins available.

Ⓑ The price will likely decrease, because there are more pumpkins available.

Ⓒ The price will likely increase, because there are fewer pumpkins available.

Ⓓ The price will likely decrease, because there are fewer pumpkins available.

2 A movie theater sells all tickets for half price on Tuesdays. What is the most likely purpose of this?

Ⓐ to increase demand and increase sales

Ⓑ to increase demand and decrease sales

Ⓒ to decrease demand and increase sales

Ⓓ to decrease demand and decrease sales

3 During September, the price of honey increased to almost twice the price of August. Which of the following would explain the increase in price? Select all the correct answers.

☐ A disease caused supplies of honey to be very low during September.

☐ A number of new suppliers increased the amount of honey for sale.

☐ Several news articles on the benefits of honey greatly increased demand for honey.

☐ Information published about honey being high in sugar made many people worried about consuming too much.

☐ Cooler than expected weather lowered the quality of the honey produced.

☐ A larger number of plants in the area provided food for the bees, which increased the amount of honey produced.

4 Gabby makes scented candles to sell at the markets. She can make a maximum of 40 candles each week, and always sells out in the first hour. Which of these would Gabby be best to do to decrease demand?

Ⓐ start advertising the candles

Ⓑ increase the price of each candle

Ⓒ reduce the number of candles she makes

Ⓓ offer customers two candles for the price of one

5 The table below shows the value of pennies of different years that were minted in Denver.

Value of Pennies Minted in Denver

Year	1922	1924	1931	1933
Value ($)	15	30	4	1

Which year listed is most likely to be the rarest penny?

Ⓐ 1922   Ⓑ 1924   Ⓒ 1931   Ⓓ 1933

6 A tuna fisherman sells the fish he catches each morning to the general public. On Saturday and Sunday, there are more people to sell his fish to. How would this most likely effect the price? Explain your answer.

_____

_____

On stormy days, he catches fewer fish. How would this most likely effect the price? Explain your answer.

_____

_____

7   The graph below represents the price that a store sells firewood for in each season.

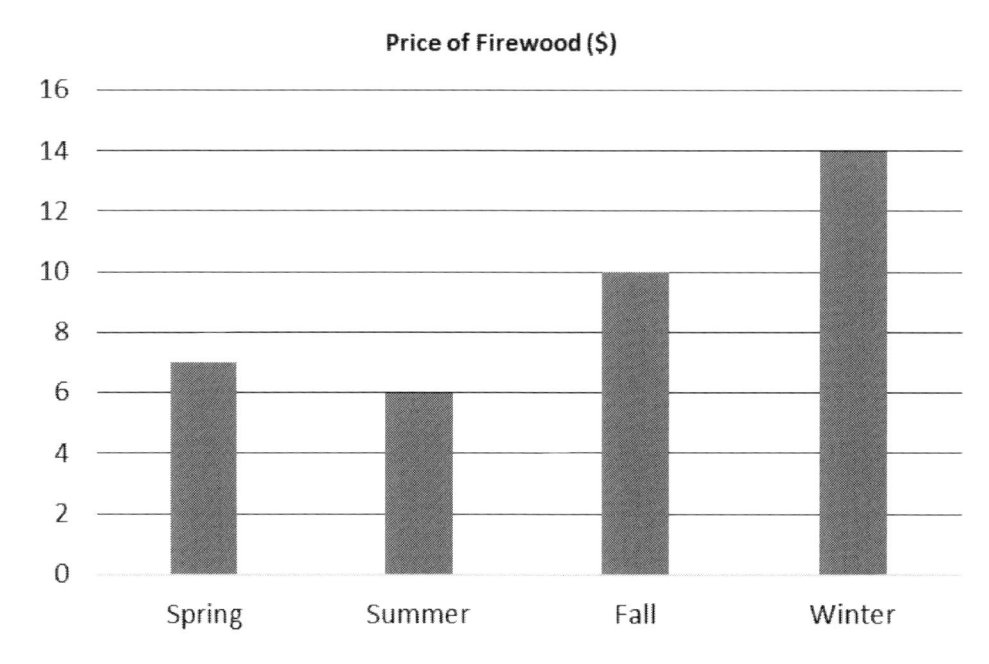

Price of Firewood ($)

Season	Price ($)
Spring	7
Summer	6
Fall	10
Winter	14

How much more is firewood sold for in winter than in summer?

Show your work.

Answer $_____

Describe how demand for firewood explains the price difference.

_____

_____

There is the same demand for firewood in spring as in fall, but the amount of firewood available influences the price. Based on the price, is there more firewood available in spring or in fall? Explain your answer.

_____

_____

8. Mangoes are grown in Mexico and imported to Texas. The table below shows the average cost of mangoes in each month of the growing season.

Average Cost of Mexican Mangoes in Texas

Month	Cost per Pound ($)
March	1.23
April	1.05
May	0.85
June	0.77
July	0.71
August	0.89
September	1.18

Describe what the price changes suggest about how many mangoes are available at the beginning of the season, in the middle of the season, and at the end of the season.

_____

_____

_____

_____

In one year, poor weather reduced the number of mangoes available. Would this be likely to increase or decrease the price? Explain your answer.

_____

_____

_____

Quiz 69: Understanding Credit and Interest

1 Jeffrey borrowed $80 from his father to go to a concert. His father stated that Jeffrey would have to pay the money back with interest. Which statement best explains what Jeffrey's father meant?

Ⓐ Jeffrey can keep the $80 and does not have to pay anything back.

Ⓑ Jeffrey must pay back $80 plus additional money as well.

Ⓒ Jeffrey must give his father back exactly $80.

Ⓓ Jeffrey can ask for another $80 at any time.

2 Alana got a new job and needed to buy a car to travel to work. She got a loan for $10,000 to buy the car with 5% interest. What is the main benefit of getting a loan?

Ⓐ Alana can buy the car now and pay for it over time.

Ⓑ Alana only has to pay 5% of the total cost of the car.

Ⓒ Alana gets a discount of 5% on the purchase price of the car.

Ⓓ Alana can stop paying for the car if she no longer needs it.

3 Baxter is comparing credit cards. The table below shows four options his bank is offering.

Credit Card	Annual Fee	Interest Rate
Basic Card	$99	11%
Rewards Card	$250	14%
Premium Card	$195	15%
Saver Card	$49	12%

Which card should Baxter choose if he wants to pay the least interest?

Ⓐ Basic Card   Ⓑ Rewards Card

Ⓒ Premium Card   Ⓓ Saver Card

4   Bianca takes out a personal loan to go on a holiday. She borrows $6,000 and is charged 15% interest. Which statement is true?

Ⓐ Bianca will have to pay back exactly $6,000.

Ⓑ Bianca will have to pay back less than $6,000.

Ⓒ Bianca will have to pay back more than $6,000.

Ⓓ Bianca will not have to pay back anything.

5   Kody borrows $45 from his sister to buy a pair of shoes. His sister states that he will have to pay back the $45, plus $2 extra for every week it takes him to pay it back. Kody pays back his sister in 6 weeks. What is the total amount he pays back to his sister?

Show your work.

Answer $_____

6   Yahir borrows $80 from a friend so he can buy textbooks. His friend states that Yahir will have to pay him interest. Yahir agrees to pay back his friend $8 a week for 12 weeks. What is the total amount of interest Yahir will pay?

Show your work.

Answer $_____

7 Janet's friend Margo wants to buy a skateboard for $85 but only has $25. Janet agrees to lend Margo the rest of the money if Margo pays her back $7 a month for one year. How much more than the amount borrowed will Margo pay back?

Show your work.

Answer $_____

8 Miguel pays for a new television using a credit card. He pays $1,400. He forgets to pay the money off and is charged interest. To pay off the debt, he makes monthly payments of $200 for 8 months and then a final payment of $150. Including the interest, how much did Miguel end up paying for the television?

Show your work.

Answer $_____

9 Oliver needs $900 to buy a new computer. His uncle offers to lend him the money and not charge any interest. What does this tell you about how much Oliver will need to pay back?

_____

_____

10 Lucy needs to purchase a new phone. The price of the phone is $599. Lucy's phone company offers payment plans, where Lucy can pay for part of the phone up-front and the rest of the phone with a payment each month for 12 months. The four deals available are described below.

Deal	Up-front Fee	Monthly Payment
A	$50	$60
B	$100	$50
C	$150	$40
D	$250	$30

What is the total price of each phone deal over 12 months?

Show your work.

Deal A $_____   Deal B $_____

Deal C $_____   Deal D $_____

Lucy only has $130 she can use for the up-front payment. What is the lowest cost deal she can afford? Show your work or explain how you found your answer.

Answer _____

Lucy takes the lowest cost deal she can afford. How much extra will she pay compared to paying the total price of the phone up-front?

Show your work.

Answer $_____

Quiz 70: Understanding Saving and Savings Plans

1 In which situation would starting a savings plan best solve the problem?

Ⓐ Christa wants to buy a computer game for $49, but her allowance is only $6 a week.

Ⓑ Tenille loaned $50 to her brother, but he is not paying her back as he promised to.

Ⓒ Curtis wants to buy 12 vanilla cupcakes, but the bakery only has 8 available.

Ⓓ Ezio is given $5 each time he washes his father's car, but he thinks the job is worth more than $5.

2 Ethan wants to buy a new backpack for $29 but he does not have enough money. He can either save the money or borrow the money from his sister and pay her back $35 over 7 weeks. Which statement explains the main reason he would be better to save for the backpack instead of borrowing money to buy it?

Ⓐ He can have the backpack right away.

Ⓑ He will not pay any interest.

Ⓒ He will pay less than $29.

Ⓓ He will have more money to get a better backpack.

3 Sarah wants to buy a watch for $80. Which of these describes Sarah saving for the watch?

Ⓐ She asks her mother to lend her $80.

Ⓑ She asks for the watch for her birthday.

Ⓒ She puts $5 of her allowance away every week until she has $80.

Ⓓ She takes the watch home and agrees to pay the store $10 a month for 12 months.

4 Judd receives $12 allowance every week. He spends $8 of his allowance and saves $4. Judd wants to increase the amount he saves. Which actions should he take?

Ⓐ spend more money and save more money

Ⓑ spend less money and save more money

Ⓒ spend more money and save less money

Ⓓ spend less money and save less money

5 Every time Kody gets paid, he puts $100 into a savings account. He uses the money in the account when he has to make large purchases. Kody wants to make changes to increase his savings. Which of these should Kody do? Select all the correct answers.

☐ put his money in an account that pays higher interest

☐ withdraw money from the account less often

☐ put a smaller amount of money in the account each time he gets paid

☐ add any extra money he does not need to the account

☐ take money out of the account any time he has more than $1,000

☐ add his savings to the account once a month instead of once a week

6 Rose added $6 to her savings account every week for 12 weeks. She also added another $40 when she was given money for her birthday. How much did Rose save over the 12 weeks?

Show your work.

Answer $_____

7 Sean's parents started a college savings plan for him when he was born. They started the savings plan with $2,000 and added $1,200 on each of Sean's birthdays. Not including any interest earned, how much money would they have saved in total over 20 years?

Show your work.

Answer $_____

8 Tegan makes $16 each week by doing jobs around the house, and saves half the money she earns every week. Tegan wants to save to buy a camera for $112. How many weeks would she have to save to have enough money to buy the camera?

Show your work.

Answer _____ weeks

Tegan wants to save more so that she can have enough for the camera in 7 weeks. How much will Tegan need to save each week?

Show your work.

Answer $_____

9   Wes started a new savings plan at the start of the year. He made the table below to show his total savings at the end of each month.

Month	Total Savings ($)
January	38
February	71
March	112
April	100
May	163
June	191

In which month did Wes spend some of his savings? _____

In which month did Wes save the most money?

Show your work.

Answer _____

10 Vince's parents earn about $50,000 each year. They expect that Vince will need about $80,000 to go to college. How does the difference between annual earnings and the cost of college help explain why a college savings plan is important?

_____

_____

_____

_____

ANSWER KEY

Quizzes 1 to 7: Understanding, Representing, and Comparing Whole Numbers

Quiz 1: Composing and Decomposing Whole Numbers

1. C **2.** D **3.** B **4.** 124 **5.** C **6.** D **7.** 8, 9; 6, 5; 4, 2; 9, 7, 5; 7, 0, 3; 5, 4, 0 **8.** 6, 8, 4; 7, 5, 9; 4, 0, 3; 1, 6, 0 **9.** 40,006; 40,060; 40,600; 46,000; 400,600; 460,000; 400,006; 406,000; 400,060 **10.** 1, 6, 8, 2; 3, 2, 9, 5; 4, 0, 8, 3; 6, 2, 8, 6, 7; 9, 1, 3, 0, 4; 8, 6, 5, 7, 0 **11.** 7,352; 6,848; 27,069; 81,608; 48,034; 305,825; 980,350; 565,007 **12.** 7, 30, 37

Quiz 2: Identifying Place Value

1. C **2.** C **3.** B **4.** A **5.** 4, 9 **6.** 67, 60, 365, 5,364 **7.** 1, 2, 8, 9; 6, 8, 5, 9; 1,356; 7,924 **8.** any two-digit number with a 6 in the tens place, such as 64; any three-digit number with a 2 in the hundreds place, such as 205; any four-digit number with a 7 in the hundreds place, such as 5,700; any four-digit number with a 1 in the thousands place, such as 1,254; any five-digit number with a 9 in the thousands place, such as 39,057; any five-digit number with a 5 in the ten thousands place, such as 52,346

Quiz 3: Understanding Place Value Relationships

1. C **2.** B **3.** C **4.** B **5.** D **6.** C **7.** 3rd, 4th, 6th **8.** 2nd, 7th **9.** 420, 4,200, 42,000; 6,850, 68,500, 685,000; 2,710, 27,100, 271,000; 35, 3,500, 35,000; 284, 28,400, 284,000; 3,095, 30,950, 3,095,000; 224, 2,240, 224,000 **10.** 10, 100, 10, 100, 100, 1,000, 100, 10, 10 **11.** 100, 6 × 100 = 600; 100, 24 × 100 = 2,400; 1,000, 11 × 1,000 = 11,000; 100, 680 × 100 = 68,000 **12.** 1,500 pennies (15 × 100 = 1,500) **13.** 12,000 safety pins (12 × 1,000 = 12,000) **14.** $3,200 (32 × 100 = 3,200) **15.** The student should explain that the 3 in 30,000 is 10 times greater than the 3 in 3,000.

Quiz 4: Using Place Value to Compare Numbers

1. B **2.** B **3.** B **4.** 369 **5.** 998, 133, 999, 743, 135, 655, 158, 659 **6.** 448, 565, 427, 177, 286, 563, 736, 908 **7.** 20, 400, 40, 300, 2, 600, 90, 70, 400, 30, 10, 5, 30, 30, 20 **8.** 367 and 376; the two smallest numbers have the lowest number in the hundreds place **9.** Monday, Friday, Wednesday, Thursday **10.** 2, 6, 5, 7, 3; 2, 6, 5, 73; 26, 5, 7, 3; 26, 57, 3 **11.** 800, 80, 30, 3, 70, 7; 800, 80, 30, 3, 70, 7

Quiz 5: Representing Numbers on Number Lines

1. A **2.** C **3.** 860 **4.** 46 **5.** 280 **6.** X at 55, Y at 95, Z at 25 **7.** J between the marks for 20 and 25, K between the marks for 40 and 45, L between the marks for 65 and 70, M between the marks for 95 and 100 **8.** A at 2,400, B at 2,560, C at 2,680, D at 2,820

Quiz 6: Rounding Whole Numbers

1. C **2.** D **3.** 652, 653, 647, 651 **4.** 842, 803, 848, 826, 817 **5.** 770, 800 **6.** 1,230, 1,200 **7.** 690, 700; 520, 500; 190, 200; 360, 400; 60, 100; 730, 700; 130, 100; 810, 800; 260, 300; 910, 900 **8.** Any number in the following ranges from top to bottom: 425 to 434, 85 to 94, 675 to 684, 125 to 134, 105 to 114, 185 to 194, 685 to 694, 455 to 464, 335 to 344, 705 to 714 **9.** 1, ones; 6, ones; 4, tens; 5, tens **10.** numbers 85 to 94 plotted **11.** 45, 54; 275, 284; 395, 404; 1,755, 1,764 **12.** 8,780, 8,800; The number 2 in the ones place is less than 5, and so the number is rounded down to the nearest ten. The number 8 in the tens place is more than 5, so the number is rounded up to the nearest hundred. **13.** 4 and 6; 1, 3, and 7; 64, The highest number that rounds to 60 is 64. Any number 65 or greater would be rounded to 70.; All the scores would be rounded up, so the estimate would be greater. **14.** Jessica did not realize that the number could be less than 700. The numbers 650 through 699 also round to 700.

Quiz 7: Comparing and Ordering Whole Numbers

1. C **2.** B **3.** C **4.** D **5.** 1st, 3rd, 4th **6.** 2, 3, 4, 1 **7.** 5,687, 24,537, 102,007, 2,175, 67,297, 333,647, 447,652, 999,827, 374,845, 445,710 **8.** 3,458, 8,543, 3,854, 5,483, 3,485, 8,354 or 8,534 **9.** drawing of two sets of 10 blocks and 8 individual blocks; 28 **10.** >, >, =, >, <, >, = **11.** 6; 6, 4; The student should explain that 60 and 64 have the same number of tens, but 64 has more ones. **12.** 3, 8, 5; 3, 4, 5; The student should explain that 345 has fewer tens than 385. **13.** 11,530 < 11,965 < 12,058 < 12,507 < 12,854; any four numbers between 11,530 and 11,965

Student Quiz Book, STAAR Mathematics, Grade 3

Quizzes 8 to 16: Representing and Using Fractions

Quiz 8: Representing Fractions with Diagrams

1. A **2.** C **3.** A **4.** D **5.** C **6.** 3rd, 4th, 6th **7.** $\frac{5}{6}$ **8.** B **9.** 9 of 18 squares shaded; 4 of 16 squares shaded; 5 of 15 squares shaded; 2 of 12 squares shaded; 4 of 32 squares shaded **10.** Italy, Hungary, and Chad circled; Monaco; Mauritius **11.** $\frac{1}{3}, \frac{2}{3}$

Quiz 9: Modeling Fractions

1. B **2.** D **3.** A **4.** 1st, 3rd, 4th **5.** each shape is divided into two equal triangles **6.** second circle divided into equal quarters, third circle divided into equal sixths, fourth circle divided into equal eighths **7.** rectangle divided into equal quarters, rectangle divided into equal sixths, rectangle divided into equal eighths **8.** divided into three 2 by 7 rectangles; divided into three 1 by 8 rectangles; divided into three 3 by 8 rectangles

Quiz 10: Representing Fractions on Number Lines

1. B **2.** D **3.** B **4.** $\frac{1}{4}, \frac{1}{2}, 1\frac{1}{4}$, and $1\frac{3}{4}$ plotted **5.** number line divided into thirds, $\frac{2}{3}$ plotted **6.** $\frac{1}{8}, \frac{4}{8}, \frac{5}{8}$, and $\frac{7}{8}$ plotted; $\frac{4}{8}$ and $\frac{5}{8}$; $\frac{7}{8}$; $\frac{4}{8}, \frac{1}{8}$ **7.** $\frac{1}{3}, 1\frac{1}{3}, 1\frac{2}{3}$, and $2\frac{1}{3}$ plotted; $1\frac{1}{3}$ and $1\frac{2}{3}$; 1; $1\frac{1}{3}; \frac{1}{3}$ and $1\frac{1}{3}; \frac{2}{3}$ **8.** $\frac{1}{6}, \frac{2}{6}, \frac{5}{6}, 1\frac{3}{6}$ and $1\frac{5}{6}$ plotted on the number line; $1\frac{3}{6}$ and $1\frac{5}{6}; \frac{5}{6}; \frac{2}{6}; 1\frac{3}{6}; \frac{2}{6}; \frac{5}{6}$ **9.** Kent Street; Maple Street; $\frac{1}{4}$ mile; $\frac{1}{2}$ mile; Butler Street **10.** the fractions plotted are $\frac{1}{2}$ or $\frac{3}{6}, \frac{2}{3}$ or $\frac{4}{6}, \frac{1}{6}, 1\frac{1}{3}$ or $1\frac{2}{6}$, and $1\frac{5}{6}$ **11.** $\frac{1}{8}$; The race is divided into 8 equal sections, and Checkpoint A is after 1 of the 8 parts.; D; Checkpoint D is at $\frac{4}{8}$ of the race, or you can see on the number line that it is half way.

Quiz 11: Understanding Unit Fractions

1. C **2.** A **3.** $\frac{1}{8}, \frac{3}{8}$ **4.** rectangle is divided into 3 equal parts; $\frac{1}{3}$ **5.** hexagon is divided into 6 equal parts; $\frac{1}{6}$ **6.** each shape is divided into two equal halves **7.** a 3 by 6 rectangle is shaded **8.** $\frac{1}{4}; \frac{1}{4}$; The number of candies is a quarter of the total, but the total number is different so the number in a quarter is different. OR A quarter of Sam's 16 candies is 4, while a quarter of Joseph's 20 candies is 5. **9.** The shape is divided into 2 parts, but the 2 parts are not equal. **10.** 3 of the 8 equal parts are shaded; 3 of the 4 equal parts are shaded; The fraction $\frac{3}{8}$ is less than $\frac{3}{4}$ because less of the whole shape is shaded. **11.** $\frac{1}{6}; \frac{1}{6}$; The shaded area is not equal because the two whole shapes do not have equal areas.

Student Quiz Book, STAAR Mathematics, Grade 3

Quiz 12: Composing and Decomposing Fractions

1. A **2.** A **3.** C **4.** 3rd, 5th **5.** $\frac{2}{6}, \frac{1}{8}, \frac{2}{3}, \frac{1}{6}, \frac{7}{10}, \frac{2}{5}$ **6.** $\frac{3}{6}, \frac{4}{10}, \frac{2}{4}, \frac{1}{5}, \frac{4}{8}, \frac{8}{10}$ **7.** 2 of 8 parts shaded, 1 of 4 parts shaded, $\frac{1}{8} + \frac{1}{8} = \frac{1}{4}$; 2 of 6 parts shaded, 1 of 3 parts shaded, $\frac{1}{6} + \frac{1}{6} = \frac{1}{3}$ **8.** 3 of 8 parts shaded, $\frac{3}{8}$ **9.** 2 of 4 parts shaded, 2 of 4 parts shaded, 4 of 4 parts shaded, $\frac{2}{4} + \frac{2}{4} = 1$; 1 of 4 parts shaded, 1 of 4 parts shaded, 1 of 4 parts shaded, 1 of 4 parts shaded, 4 of 4 parts shaded, $\frac{1}{4} + \frac{1}{4} + \frac{1}{4} + \frac{1}{4} = 1$ **10.** 3 of 6 parts shaded, 3 of 6 parts shaded, 6 of 6 parts shaded, $\frac{3}{6} + \frac{3}{6} = 1$; 2 of 6 parts shaded, 2 of 6 parts shaded, 2 of 6 parts shaded, 6 of 6 parts shaded, $\frac{2}{6} + \frac{2}{6} + \frac{2}{6} = 1$ **11.** $\frac{4}{10}$ or $\frac{2}{5}$ (6 of the 10 parts are shaded, 4 of the 10 parts remain) **12.** $\frac{5}{8}$ (5 of the 8 parts are shaded) **13.** 3 laps (The student may draw a diagram, write an equation, or explain in words that there are three $\frac{1}{3}$ in 1.)

Quiz 13: Using Fractions to Solve Problems

1. $\frac{1}{3}$ **2.** $\frac{1}{8}, \frac{2}{8}$ or $\frac{1}{4}$, 3 **3.** 8 serves **4.** 3 cars **5.** rectangle divided into 6 equal parts **6.** Reading; $\frac{1}{4}$; Math 30 minutes, Reading 15 minutes, Writing 45 minutes (The student may show calculations or may describe using the graph to compare the times.) **7.** Jane; $\frac{1}{6}, \frac{1}{4}, \frac{1}{2}, \frac{1}{6}$ (Jane painted 2 of 12 parts more, so $\frac{1}{6}$ more); $\frac{1}{6}$ (The student may use a diagram or give a written explanation.) **8.** $\frac{1}{3}$ (The student may use a diagram, simplify $\frac{4}{12}$, or give a written explanation.); 8 shots made, 4 shots missed (The student may use a diagram or give a written explanation.)

Quiz 14: Understanding Equivalent Fractions

1. $\frac{2}{6}, \frac{4}{6}, \frac{3}{6}$ **2.** 4 of 6 parts shaded; 2 of 3 parts shaded; $\frac{2}{3}$ **3.** $\frac{2}{4}, \frac{4}{8}, \frac{3}{6}$, and $\frac{1}{2}$ circled **4.** 2 of 4 parts shaded; 3 of 6 parts shaded; 4 of 8 parts shaded; $\frac{2}{4}, \frac{3}{6}, \frac{4}{8}$ **5.** 2 of 3 parts shaded; 4 of 6 parts shaded; 8 of 12 parts shaded; $\frac{4}{6}; \frac{8}{12}$ **6.** 1 of 4 parts shaded; 2 of 8 parts shaded; $\frac{2}{8}$ **7.** $\frac{2}{8} = \frac{1}{4}$ **8.** $\frac{2}{4}$ and $\frac{4}{8}, \frac{2}{8}$ and $\frac{1}{4}, \frac{6}{8}$ **9.** 1 of 2 parts shaded, 2 of 4 parts shaded, 4 of 8 parts shaded; The circles for each fraction have the same area of the circle shaded. **10.** 3 of 4 parts shaded, 6 of 8 parts shaded; The rectangles for the two fractions have the same area shaded.

Quiz 15: Representing Equivalent Fractions

1. A **2.** D **3.** B **4.** $\frac{1}{2}, \frac{3}{6}, \frac{2}{4}$ **5.** B **6.** D **7.** $\frac{1}{2}, \frac{2}{4}, \frac{3}{6}, \frac{4}{8}$ **8.** $\frac{2}{8}$ and $\frac{4}{16}$ **9.** $\frac{4}{12} = \frac{2}{6} = \frac{1}{3}$ **10.** 2 of 8 parts shaded and 4 of 16 parts shaded; $\frac{1}{4}$ **11.** 1 of 2 parts shaded, 3 of 6 parts shaded; 2 of 4 parts shaded; $\frac{2}{4}$ **12.** $\frac{2}{3}, \frac{1}{3}$; 5 plants (The student may draw a diagram or explain that there must be equal numbers of each plant for half to be parsley.) **13.** $\frac{1}{6}$ (The student may simplify $\frac{2}{12}$, use the diagram, or give a written explanation.)

Quiz 16: Comparing Fractions

1. D **2.** B **3.** B **4.** 2, 1, 3, 4 **5.** $\frac{5}{6}, \frac{2}{3}, \frac{6}{6}, \frac{4}{6}$ **6.** A, C, E; B, D; F, G **7.** 1 of 3 equal parts shaded; 1 of 6 equal parts shaded; $\frac{1}{3} > \frac{1}{6}$ circled **8.** 3 of 4 equal parts shaded, 1 of 2 equal parts shaded, 6 of 8 equal parts shaded, 1 of 4 equal parts shaded; $\frac{3}{4}, \frac{6}{8}; \frac{1}{2}, \frac{1}{4}; \frac{1}{4}; \frac{1}{4}$ **9.** 2 of 3 equal parts shaded, 5 of 6 equal parts shaded; $\frac{2}{3}$ is less than $\frac{5}{6}$ or $\frac{5}{6}$ is greater than $\frac{2}{3}$ **10.** 7 of 10 parts shaded, 8 of 10 parts shaded; $\frac{7}{10} < \frac{4}{5}$; The student may describe how $\frac{7}{10}$ has less area shaded than $\frac{4}{5}$, or how $\frac{7}{10}$ has 7 parts shaded and $\frac{4}{5}$ has 8 parts shaded. **11.** $\frac{5}{8} > \frac{1}{2}$

Quizzes 17 to 30: Computing with Whole Numbers

Quiz 17: Adding Whole Numbers

1. D **2.** B **3.** D **4.** 779, 914, 578, 410, 379, 830, 770, 700, 706, 909, 809, 840, 610, 600, 600, 860 **5.** 52 + 48, 3 + 82 + 15, 62 + 28 + 10 **6.** 244 + 213 **7.** 19, 12; 66, 89; 23, 55; 71, 27 **8.** 79 − 44 = 35, 79 − 35 = 44; 129 − 77 = 52, 129 − 52 = 77; 113 − 24 = 89, 113 − 89 = 24; 293 − 152 = 141, 293 − 141 = 152; 590 − 305 = 285, 590 − 285 = 305; 752 − 641 = 111, 752 − 111 = 641 **9.** 60 + 10 = 70, 3 + 9 = 12, 70 + 12 = 82; 20 + 40 = 60, 7 + 8 = 15, 60 + 15 = 75; 30 + 20 = 50, 1 + 6 = 7, 50 + 7 = 57; 70 + 10 = 80, 5 + 7 = 12, 80 + 12 = 92; 50 + 30 = 80, 8 + 8 = 16, 80 + 16 = 96 **10.** 49 miles (18 + 19 + 12 = 49) **11.** 1,007 visitors (586 + 421 = 1,007) **12.** 293 stamps (111 + 182 = 293); 404 stamps (293 + 111 = 404) **13.** 138 + 262 = 400, 400 + 85 = 485; The numbers 138 and 262 add to a whole hundred, and it is easier to add 85 to a whole hundred. **14.** 65 + 35 = 100, 100 + 47 = 147; 29 + 71 = 100, 100 + 34 = 134; 88 + 32 = 120, 120 + 67 = 187; 26 + 44 = 70, 70 + 57 = 127

Quiz 18: Subtracting Whole Numbers

1. B **2.** B **3.** B **4.** 542, 531, 403, 631, 325, 359, 400, 160, 179, 730, 355, 403, 655, 38, 478, 277 **5.** 289 − 285, 88 − 42 − 42, 100 − 64 − 32 **6.** 689 − 659 **7.** 549, 389, 349 **8.** (88 − 22) − 15, (175 − 67) − 39, (412 − 73) − 58 **9.** 86 + 73 = 159, 99 + 266 = 365, 96 + 178 = 274, 122 + 745 = 867, 769 + 138 = 907, 325 + 425 = 750 **10.** 120 centimeters (136 − 16 = 120) **11.** $640 (790 − 150 = 640) **12.** 218 students (247 − 29 = 218) **13.** $53 (500 − 259 − 188 = 53, or 259 + 188 = 447 and 500 − 447 = 53) **14.** $104 (128 − 6 − 6 − 6 − 6 = 104, or 6 × 4 = 24 and 128 − 24 = 104) **15.** 96 meals (213 − 117 = 96); 352 meals (1000 − 151 − 167 − 213 − 117 = 352, or 151 + 167 + 213 + 117 = 648 and 1000 − 648 = 352)

Quiz 19: Solving Word Problems Using Addition and Subtraction

1. A **2.** B **3.** D **4.** (100 + 35) + 6, 100 + 30 + (6 + 5) **5.** 3, 4, 2, 1 **6.** 1000 − 20 − 840 − 40 = 100; 1000 − (20 + 840 + 40) = 100 **7.** 320 drinks (36 + 49 + 57 + 39 + 68 + 71 = 320); 36 drinks (36 + 49 + 57 = 142, 39 + 68 + 71 = 178, 178 − 142 = 36) **8.** 48 pages (150 − 26 − 42 − 34 = 48, or 26 + 42 + 34 = 102 and 150 − 102 = 48) **9.** Tuesday and Thursday; Monday and Wednesday; 480 sales; 6 sales; 147 sales; 134 + 134 = 268 **10.** 68 beads (18 + 18 + 24 + 8 = 68); 32 beads (100 − 68 = 32); 1 necklace and 1 anklet or 4 anklets (24 + 8 = 32, 8 + 8 + 8 + 8 = 32); 4 necklaces (100 − 4 = 96, 24 + 24 + 24 + 24 = 96)

Quiz 20: Solving Two-Step Word Problems

1. A **2.** D **3.** C **4.** C **5.** Denzel and Colin; Denzel and Wes; 4 **6.** 240 apples (3 × 20 = 60, 60 × 4 = 240) **7.** $83 (8 × 6 = 48, 48 + 35 = 83) **8.** 42 pieces of pie (12 × 8 = 96, 96 - 54 = 42) **9.** 4 packs of nails (6 × 10 = 60, 60 ÷ 15 = 4) **10.** 7 weeks (The student could find the total amount each week by completing a list or a table, could use equations or show calculations, or could use a written explanation.) **11.** 410 grams (The student could show the work using a list, table, equations, calculations, or a written description.) **12.** 16 days (The student could show the work using a list, table, equations, calculations, or a written description.) **13.** 30 oranges (12 ÷ 4 = 3, 3 × 10 = 30); $27 (bananas 2 lots for $3 each, apples 3 lots for $2 each, pears 5 lots for $3 each, 6 + 6 + 15 = 27); 24 pears (20 – 8 = 12, $12 buys 4 lots of 6 pears each, 4 × 6 = 24); 20 oranges and 12 pears (20 oranges for $8, 12 pears for $6)

Quiz 21: Using Estimation and Rounding

1. D **2.** A **3.** C **4.** C **5.** B **6.** B **7.** 70 × 3 = 210, 80 × 3 = 240, between 210 and 240; 20 × 5 = 100, 30 × 5 = 150, between 100 and 150; 80 × 6 = 480, 90 × 6 = 540, between 480 and 540 **8.** 1800 – 1200 = 600, 600 books; 1800 – 1400 = 400, 400 books; 1400 + 1800 + 1200 = 4400, 4400 books **9.** $280, $220, $370; $130 (1000 – 280 – 220 – 370 = 130 or 1000 – (280 + 220 + 370) = 130) **10.** 60 miles (180 ÷ 3 = 60) **11.** 150 seats (500 – 350 = 150) **12.** 700 visitors (240 + 260 + 200 = 700; Sunday (The student may find 4000 ÷ 20 = 200 and state that Sunday's figure is closest to 200. The student could also estimate ticket sales for each day and find that Sunday's estimate is $4000.) **13.** He would have saved over $240. 8 × 30 = 240. 32 is greater than 30, so 8 × 32 is greater than 240. **14.** 4 × 10 = 40 and 9 is less than 10, so 4 × 9 is less than 40

Quiz 22: Finding the Value of Money

1. C **2.** B **3.** C **4.** $0.36 **5.** 56 cents **6.** C **7.** 19 nickels **8.** $5.50, $6.50

Quiz 23: Representing Multiplication

1. C **2.** D **3.** 2nd and 6th **4.** 64 pencils **5.** 6 × 5 = 30, 9 × 3 = 27, 8 × 10 = 80, 6 × 7 = 42, 5 × 8 = 40 **6.** Any four of the following: 2, 24; 24, 2; 3, 16; 16, 3; 4, 12; 12, 4; 6, 8; 8, 6.
7. Example: There were 7 boxes of water on a truck. Each box had 24 bottles in it. How many bottles were there?
8. Example: Davis had 3 basketball lessons. Each basketball lesson went for 60 minutes. How long were all the basketball lessons?
9. Example: Joe bought 15 notepads for $3 each. How much did he spend?
10. 2 / 2 × 6 / 12, 3 / 3 × 6 / 18, 4 / 4 × 6 / 24, 5 / 5 × 6 / 30 **11.** 2 rows of 8, 8 rows of 2, or 4 rows of 4; 2 × 8 = 16 or 4 × 4 = 16 **12.** 3 × 6 × 4 = 72; 72 stickers

Quiz 24: Using Multiplication Facts

1. B **2.** C **3.** A **4.** 42 ÷ __ = 7, 48 ÷ 8 = __, 10 × __ = 60 **5.** 16, 16 ÷ 2 = 8; 63, 63 ÷ 9 = 7; 20, 20 ÷ 4 = 5; 27, 27 ÷ 3 = 9 **6.** B **7.** 20, 24, 28, 32 should be circled; Only numbers that are multiples of 4 or can be divided evenly by 4 are possible.

Quiz 25: Solving Word Problems Using Multiplication

1. B **2.** C **3.** 3, 4, 2, 1 **4.** 1st and 4th **5.** 20, 36, 44, 52 circled; 40 pounds **6.** 6, 8; 48 people (6 × 8 = 48); 8 tables (48 ÷ 6 = 8) **7.** Paolo; Trey **8.** 4 / 24 / 12, 6 / 36 / 18, 8 / 48 / 24, 10 / 60 / 30 **9.** 24 roses **10.** $42 **11.** 15 planks of wood (5 × 3 = 15), 20 feet (5 × 4 = 20) **12.** 4 lettuces (work shows 6 rows of 4 lettuces and 4 left over)

Quiz 26: Representing Division

1. A **2.** C **3.** 1st and 3rd **4.** 30 ÷ 6 = 5, 28 ÷ 4 = 7, 72 ÷ 9 = 8, 32 ÷ 4 = 8 **5.** 40 ÷ 8 = 5
6. 4, 5, and 8 circled; 80 ÷ 4 = 20, 80 ÷ 5 = 16, 80 ÷ 8 = 10
7. Example: There are 24 students in a class. They are sorted into 6 teams. How many students are in each team?
8. Example: Morgan has 36 baseball cards. He puts 4 cards on each page of an album. How many pages does he fill?
9. Example: Anna has 50 candies. She divided them between 10 children. How many candies does each child get?
10. 5 lots of 4 apples circled; 4 apples **11.** diagram of 3 sets of 4 quarters; 12 ÷ 4 = 3
12. 18 ÷ 3 = 6; 6 tomatoes

Quiz 27: Using Division Facts

1. B **2.** D **3.** A **4.** 21 ÷ __ = 7, 3 ÷ 1 = __, 15 ÷ 5 = __, 10 × __ = 30, __ × 9 = 27 **5.** 8, 8 × 8 = 64; 9, 9 × 4 = 36; 7, 7 × 2 = 14; 8, 8 × 6 = 48 **6.** 32 ÷ 4 = 8, 70 ÷ 7 = 10, 18 ÷ 3 = 6, 56 ÷ 8 = 7, 27 ÷ 9 = 3 **7.** The student should explain that 8 is not a factor of 30 or that 8 does not divide evenly into 30. The student should give a way of dividing 30 evenly, such as 5 teams of 6 players each or 3 teams of 10 players each.

Quiz 28: Solving Word Problems Using Division

1. B **2.** D **3.** 1st, 4th, and 5th **4.** 8 pounds **5.** 12 fish tanks **6.** 5 cakes (80 ÷ (8 × 2) or 80 ÷ 2 ÷ 8)
7. $4 (8 × 3 = 24, 24 ÷ 6 = 4) **8.** $6 (12 × 4 = 48, 48 ÷ 8 = 6) **9.** 6, 4, 32, 3 **10.** 24 cups, 7 cartons, 8 cartons, 40 cups **11.** 18 ÷ 2 = 9, 18, 2, 9; 18 ÷ 3 = 6, 18, 6 **12.** Ivy, 10 tiles (50 ÷ 5 = 10 or 5 × 10 = 50); Amelia, 6 tiles (54 ÷ 9 = 6 or 9 × 6 = 54); Tori and Dina (8 × 8 = 64, 7 × 7 = 49)

Quiz 29: Identifying Even and Odd Numbers

1. C **2.** B **3.** B **4.** 17, 29, 41, 45, 49, 67, 91 **5.** groups of 2 and 16, 4 and 14, 6 and 12, or 8 and 10 **6.** Friday and Sunday **7.** The student should explain that 83 snow globes could not be divided into two equal groups because 83 is an odd number or because 83 cannot be divided evenly by 2.

Quiz 30: Using Properties of Numbers to Multiply and Divide

1. A **2.** A **3.** 24 ÷ 6 = 4, 24 ÷ 4 = 6; 42 ÷ 7 = 6, 42 ÷ 6 = 7; 27 ÷ 3 = 9, 27 ÷ 9 = 3; 32 ÷ 8 = 4, 32 ÷ 4 = 8; 35 ÷ 5 = 7, 35 ÷ 7 = 5; 72 ÷ 9 = 8, 72 ÷ 8 = 9 **4.** 4 × 9 = 36, 9 × 4 = 36; 4 × 5 = 20, 5 × 4 = 20; 2 × 9 = 18, 9 × 2 = 18; 8 × 6 = 48, 6 × 8 = 48; 6 × 5 = 30, 5 × 6 = 30; 4 × 7 = 28, 7 × 4 = 28 **5.** 6, 1, 6, 9, 4, 8, 5, 3, 7 **6.** 6 × 8, 48; 8 × 9, 72; 2 × 6, 12; 6 × 4, 24; 9 × 7, 63 **7.** (4 × 6) + (4 × 2), 32 **8.** 9 × (4 + 5) and (9 × 3) + (9 × 6) **9.** C **10.** (10 × 2) + (4 × 2) = 20 + 8 = 28; (10 × 4) + (8 × 4) = 40 + 32 = 72; (20 × 6) + (5 × 6) = 120 + 30 = 150; (30 × 3) + (6 × 3) = 90 + 18 = 108; (10 × 3) + (5 × 3) = 30 + 15 = 45; (40 × 5) + (3 × 5) = 200 + 15 = 215; (20 × 7) + (8 × 7) = 140 + 56 = 196; (50 × 7) + (2 × 7) = 350 + 14 = 364 **11.** 2 × 5 = 10, then 10 × 6 = 60; 2 × 6 = 12, then 12 × 5 = 60; 5 × 6 = 30, then 30 × 2 = 60 **12.** (2 × 10) + (2 × 6), 32 coins; the coins are divided into two groups of 16 coins each, (2 × 8) + (2 × 8) or (1 × 16) + (1 × 16), 32 coins

Student Quiz Book, STAAR Mathematics, Grade 3

Quizzes 31 to 39: Analyzing and Creating Patterns and Relationships

Quiz 31: Representing Word Problems with Equations

1. B **2.** B **3.** B **4.** D **5.** $72 \div n = 8$, $8 \times n = 72$, $72 \div 8 = n$, $n \times 8 = 72$ **6.** 1st and 3rd, 2nd and 4th, 3rd and 1st, 4th and 2nd **7.** __ $\times 5 = 45$, 9; __ $- 12 = 20$, 32; $20 \div$__ $= 4$, 5; __ $+ 13 = 30$, 17; __ $\div 10 = 5$, 50; __ $- 4 = 24$, 28; __ $\times 7 = 28$, 4 **8.** $6 \times 9 + 2 = c$ **9.** $62 + 48 - 85 = p$, 25 pennies **10.** $60 + 20 + m = 120$, 40 minutes **11.** $(80 - 30) \div 5 = d$, 10 days **12.** $380 - 170 - 140 = m$ or $170 + 140 + m = 380$, 70 miles **13.** $(36 + 28) \div 4 = b$, 16 boxes of tiles **14.** $22 + x = 86$ or $86 - 22 = x$, 64 points; $3 \times x = 120$ or $120 \div 3 = x$, 40 minutes; $12 - 9 = x$ or $9 + x = 12$, 3 free throws; $86 - 9 = x$ or $86 - x = 9$, 77 points

Quiz 32: Representing Word Problems with Diagrams

1. A **2.** number line shows counting by 8s, 48 **3.** number line shows counting by 15s, 6; number line shows counting by any factor of 90, such as 10 or 30, equation matches the number line completed, such as $10 \times 9 = 90$ or $30 \times 3 = 90$ **4.** number line has points at 15 and 70, 70 minutes **5.** number line shows counting by 20s to 80, $80 **6.** number line has points at 15, 50, and 70, 70 **7.** 4 notebooks; The student may describe counting by 3s to reach 12, or explain that 4 lots of 3 equals 12. **8.** 24, 36, and 48 are circled; The student should explain that the other numbers cannot be evenly divided by 6. **9.** $45 \div 3 = 15$, $45 \div 15 = 3$, $45 \div 5 = 9$, $45 \div 9 = 5$ **10.** 13, 26, 39, 52, 65, 78

Quiz 33: Representing Multiplication and Division with Arrays

1. C **2.** C **3.** C **4.** A **5.** $2 \times 9 = 18$, $4 \times 4 = 16$, $3 \times 5 = 15$, $2 \times 7 = 14$ **6.** 6 days **7.** drawing of a 4 by 3 array, 4 books

Quiz 34: Representing Multiplication and Division with Equations

1. B **2.** C **3.** $72 \div$ __ $= 9$, $72 \div 9 =$ __, $9 \times$ __ $= 72$, __ $\times 9 = 72$ **4.** A **5.** $30 \div$ __ $= 10$, 3; __ $\times 6 = 42$, 7; __ $\times 2 = 12$, 6; __ $\div 5 = 7$, 35 **6.** 6×2, 3×4; 8×2, 4×4; 9×2, 3×6; 10×2, 5×4; 12×2, 8×3, 6×4; 15×2, 10×3, 6×5; 20×2, 10×4, 8×5 **7.** $56 \div 8 = 7$, 7 pages; $7 \times 4 = 28$, 28 stickers **8.** $72 \div 8 = 9$, 9 bags; $9 \times 4 = 36$, $36 **9.** $28 \div 4 = 7$, 7 tables; $7 \times 3 = 21$, 21 sunflowers **10.** $27 \div 3 = 9$, 9 groups; $9 \times 5 = 45$, 45 leaves

Quiz 35: Understanding Multiplication as a Comparison

1. C **2.** A **3.** D **4.** C **5.** 2, 7, $14 = 2 \times 7$; 3, 7, $21 = 3 \times 7$; 5, 7, $35 = 5 \times 7$; 7, 7, $49 = 7 \times 7$; 11, 5, $55 = 11 \times 5$ **6.** 3, 9, 15, 3, 5, 42 miles **7.** addition, $14 + 3$, 17 years old; multiplication, 5×3, $15; multiplication, 6×5, 30 floors; addition, $80 + 15$, 95 students; multiplication, 18×4, 72 cameras

Quiz 36: Finding Missing Numbers in Equations

1. A **2.** C **3.** C **4.** C **5.** 4 **6.** 19 **7.** 21, 24, 16, 81, 28, 9, 30, 56, 42, 36, 4, 40, 24, 35, 12 **8.** 9, 3, 9, 10, 6, 5, 1, 8, 10, 6, 8, 5 **9.** 2 × 7, 3 × 9, 4 × 8, 5 × 7, 6 × 8, 7 × 9, 8 × 8, 6 × 9, 5 × 5 **10.** 6, 8, 7, 10, 6, 7, 7, 10, 9, 8, 5, 3, 9, 7, 9 **11.** 4, 4, 9, 21, 3, 9, 6, 9, 4, 9, 8, 25 **12.** 21, 30, 30, 16, 45, 4, 40, 48, 81

Quiz 37: Understanding Patterns

1. B **2.** A **3.** C **4.** D **5.** B **6.** 14, 18, 22, 26, 30, 34, 38 **7.** A **8.** 2, 3; 3, 2; 40, 4; 1, 5; 100, 11; 1, 4 **9.** 24, 27; 26, 30, $n + 4$; 18, 12, $n - 6$; 4, 2, $n ÷ 2$; 32, 64, $n × 2$ **10.** Odd A, E, G; Even C, H, J Odd and Even B, D, F, I **11.** 16, 6; 24, 9; 32, 12; 40, 15; 48, 18; The total number of rolls is always a multiple of 8 and 8 is even.; The total cost is a multiple of 3, which can be odd or even. **12.** 42, 48, 54, 60; There are 6 trees in each row, so the total amount must be able to be evenly divided by 6.

Quiz 38: Representing Real-World Relationships

1. D **2.** D **3.** C **4.** B **5.** $6, $9, $12, $15 **6.** A **7.** 24, 48, 60, 84 **8.** A **9.** 40, 48, 56, 64 **10.** A **11.** B **12.** × 6 **13.** A **14.** C **15.** $b × 4 = p$; 24 pounds (6 × 4 = 24) **16.** The student should explain that each lap of the track has a distance of 400 meters.

Quiz 39: Using Tables to Represent Relationships

1. 20, 40, 60, 80, 100, 120, 140 **2.** 10, 25, 50, 70, 100, 150 **3.** 12, 18, 30, 36, 45, 54 **4.** 24, 48, 64, 80, 120, 144, 200 **5.** B **6.** B **7.** D **8.** 6 apple trees **9.** 8, 16, 20, 36; $7 (28 ÷ 4 = 7 or 7 × 4 = 28)

Quizzes 40 to 50: Understanding and Analyzing the Properties of Shapes

Quiz 40: Classifying Two-Dimensional Shapes

1. B **2.** A **3.** D **4.** B **5.** C **6.** square, rhombus, rectangle **7.** (left to right, top to bottom) 2nd, 6th, 8th; All the octagons have 8 sides or 8 angles. **8.** square and triangle; rectangle and triangle; hexagon and rectangle; pentagon and rectangle; pentagon and triangle; hexagon and triangle **9.** C; 4 sides, equal side lengths, 2 pairs of parallel sides; A; 4 sides, a pair of parallel sides; F; 4 equal sides, 4 right angles

Quiz 41: Comparing and Sorting Two-Dimensional Shapes

1. C **2.** 3, 4, 2, 1 **3.** B **4.** D; A; B; C and D **5.** 4, 4; 4, 4; 4 or all, 4 or all; 2 pairs, 2 pairs; 4; 2 pairs; whether a shape has 4 equal sides or 2 pairs of equal sides **6.** Any three of the four similarities: They both have four sides. They both have equal side lengths. They both have 4 angles. They both have two pairs of parallel sides.; Squares have 4 equal angles. Squares have right angles. **7.** They are both quadrilaterals, both have 4 sides, or are both trapezoids.; The second shape has a right angle or does not have two sides with the same length. **8.** any 4-sided shape drawn; any 3-sided shape drawn **9.** a 4-sided shape with no equal side lengths; any 7-sided shape; any 6-sided shape; a 5-sided shape with no equal side lengths

Quiz 42: Understanding and Using the Properties of Shapes

1. A **2.** C **3.** 1st, 4th, 5th **4.** trapezoid; triangle and pentagon **5.** A, D, F, G; B, C, E, H; 5, 6 **6.** pentagon drawn; 5; 5; pentagon **7.** Annabelle is not correct because parallelograms have two pairs of parallel sides, and the trapezoid only has 1 pair. **8.** 1st, 3rd, 4th; square with side lengths of 4 units, rectangle with a height twice its width, trapezoid with a right angle and parallel sides 2 and 5 units long **9.** All the shapes have at least 1 right angle.; The first two shapes have 4 sides or are quadrilaterals. The last shape has 3 sides, or is a triangle.

Quiz 43: Classifying Three-Dimensional Shapes

1. C **2.** C **3.** C **4.** cone, cylinder **5.** beach ball is circled **6.** A **7.** D **8.** C **9.** second shape is circled **10.** cone **11.** cube, rectangular prism

Quiz 44: Comparing and Sorting Three-Dimensional Shapes

1. C **2.** A **3.** A **4.** C **5.** 2, 1, 4, 3 **6.** 5, 8, 5 **7.** 5, 6; triangle and rectangle, square and rectangle; 9, 12; 6, 8 **8.** Any two similarities are listed, such as having 6 faces, parallel faces, 8 vertices, or 12 edges.; Any two differences are listed, such as having different lengths, different heights, different widths, or the cube having square faces or 6 faces the same size. **9.** The student should identify that the sphere has no edges, the cone has 1 edge, and the cylinder has 2 edges. **10.** C; The student should describe how cubes have square faces. **11.** C and F, A, E, C

Quiz 45: Identifying and Drawing Quadrilaterals

1. B **2.** 2nd, 3rd, 6th **3.** square and rhombus drawn; square, rhombus **4.** 1 square, 1 parallelogram, 5 triangles; 1 square, 2 parallelograms, 3 triangles; 1 rectangle, 1 square, 1 parallelogram, 5 triangles; 1 square, 2 parallelograms, 3 triangles **5.** (left to right, top to bottom) 2nd, 6th, 8th, 10th; rhombus and rectangle; drawing of a square, square **6.** drawing of a 4 by 8 rectangle, rectangle; any trapezoid with a right angle, trapezoid; any rhombus, rhombus; square with side lengths of 5 units, square

Quiz 46: Finding the Area of Shapes

1. C **2.** B **3.** 1st and 4th **4.** 6, 8, 12, 12, 16, 16 **5.** 17, 22, 20, 19, 16; C, B, E, D **6.** rectangle 6 squares long and 3 squares high; 6 × 3 = 18, 6 + 6 + 6 = 18 **7.** (3 × 2) + (7 × 2); (3 × 9) - (7 × 1) **8.** 20 square meters (The student could use an expression like (4 × 2) + (6 × 2) or could describe counting squares.); 44 square meters (The student could use an expression like (8 × 8) - 20 or could describe counting squares.) **9.** 5 square units (The student could use an expression like 15 – (2 × 5) or could describe counting squares.)

Quiz 47: Finding the Area of Rectangles

1. D **2.** C **3.** B **4.** 32 square meters **5.** 1st, 4th, and 5th **6.** 35, 4, 3, 5, 7, 20, 3 **7.** 7 inches (7 × 8 = 56 or 56 ÷ 8 = 7) **8.** rectangles are drawn with the dimensions 4 by 6, 6 by 4, 8 by 3, and 3 by 8 **9.** 6 × 2 = 12; 4 by 3 or 3 by 4 rectangle shaded; 3 × 4 = 12 or 4 × 3 = 12 **10.** 27 square feet, 15 square feet, 12 square feet; Rectangles B and C combine to form a rectangle with the same length and height as Rectangle A. **11.** 4 squares (The student may use a diagram, an equation like 32 ÷ 8 = 4, or a written explanation.)

Quiz 48: Using Area to Solve Problems

1. B **2.** C **3.** 2nd and 3rd **4.** 2nd **5.** A; F; C and E; You could find the area of each banner by measuring it or tiling it. **6.** 36 square feet **7.** the rectangle is divided into 2 rows of 6 squares; 12; The area of the note paper is 12 square inches. **8.** rectangle 4 squares long and 6 squares high; rectangle 8 squares long and 5 squares high, Height = 5 cm; rectangle 9 squares long and 3 squares high, Length = 9 cm **9.** 18 square feet; The area of the large garden is 2 times the area of the small garden. 2 × 18 = 36; 6 feet (The student may draw a diagram, use an equation, or give a written explanation.)

Quiz 49: Finding the Area of Composite Shapes

1. C **2.** B **3.** C **4.** (1 × 2) + (8 × 5), (3 × 5) + (3 × 7), (2 × 5) + (5 × 3), (3 × 8) + (4 × 3) **5.** 6 by 2 and 4 by 3 rectangle combined in any way, 5 by 2 and 3 by 3 rectangle combined in any way, 8 by 1 and 2 by 4 rectangle combined in any way **6.** 5 by 4 and 8 by 2 rectangle combined in any way; 36 square feet **7.** $111 (The student may find the area and cost for each rectangle and add them [9 × 3 = 27, 27 × 3 = 81, 2 × 5 = 10, 10 × 3 = 30, 81 + 30 =111]. The student may find the combined area and then the cost [(9 × 3) + (5 × 2) = 37, 37 × 3 = 111]) **8.** 88 square meters (The student could use the equation (10 × 4) + (6 × 8) = 88, or could show finding the area of each rectangle separately and adding them.); 192 square meters (The student could use the equation (20 × 14) - 88 = 192, or could show finding the total area and then subtracting the area of the pool.) **9.** 32 square feet (The student could use the equation 4 × 8 = 32, could count by 4s, or could give a written explanation.)

Quiz 50: Dividing Shapes into Parts

1. B **2.** C **3.** D **4.** 6 pieces **5.** divided into equal halves, $\frac{1}{2}$ shaded; divided into equal quarters, $\frac{1}{4}$ shaded; divided into equal sixths, $\frac{1}{6}$ shaded; divided into equal fifths, $\frac{1}{5}$ shaded; divided into equal thirds, $\frac{1}{3}$ shaded **6.** Danny; 2, 1; 3, 4; Kasim **7.** Julie; Dana shaded 2 parts instead of 1. Emiko did not divide the rectangle into equal parts. Tiana divided the rectangle into 8 parts instead of 4. **8.** $\frac{1}{8}$ **9.** circle divided into equal thirds; Kate's circle has 3 parts, but they are not equal. The circle I divided has 3 equal parts. **10.** 8 by 2 rectangle shaded

Quizzes 51 to 58: Solving Measurement Problems

Quiz 51: Understanding and Measuring Perimeter

1. B **2.** A **3.** D **4.** 7 cm by 3 cm, 9 cm by 1 cm, 6 cm by 4 cm, 8 cm by 2 cm **5.** 4 + 3 + 2 + 4 + 2 + 7, 22 cm; 1 + 6 + 4 + 2 + 3 + 4, 20 cm; 2 + 6 + 2 + 2 + 4 + 8, 24 cm; 1 + 8 + 2 + 6 + 1 + 2, 20 cm **6.** 2 × (2 + 7) = 18, 2 + 2 + 7 + 7 = 18; 2 × (6 + 3) = 18, 6 + 6 + 3 + 3 = 18 **7.** 50 cm (6 + 13 + 3 + 4 + 15 + 9 = 50 **8.** 32 inches (The student could use the equation 8 + 8 + 8 + 8 = 32, use the diagram, or give a written explanation.) **9.** rectangle 8 squares long and 3 squares high, Perimeter = 22 cm; rectangle 10 squares long and 6 squares high, Height = 6 cm; rectangle 6 squares long and 7 squares high, Length = 6 cm **10.** Two rectangles are drawn with any of the following dimensions: 10 by 2, 9 by 3, 8 by 4, or 7 by 5. Matching perimeter equations are given, such as 2 × (10 + 2) = 24 or 9 + 3 + 9 + 3 = 24.

Quiz 52: Solving Problems Involving Perimeter

1. B **2.** C **3.** D **4.** 24 inches, 16 inches, 36 inches, 80 inches **5.** 56 cm (7 × 8 = 56 or 7 + 7 + 7 + 7 + 7 + 7 + 7 + 7 = 56); 3 cm (24 ÷ 8 = 3 or 3 + 3 + 3 + 3 + 3 + 3 + 3 + 3 = 28); 4 small boxes (4 × 24 = 96 or 24 + 24 + 24 + 24 = 96) **6.** D; B and C; A **7.** 1,320 yards (100 + 120 + 100 + 120 = 440, 440 × 3 = 1,320 or 440 + 440 + 440 = 1,320) **8.** 8 cm (The student may use an equation like 4 + 7 + 7 + 4 + 6 + 6 + __ + __ = 50 to find the missing side, could add all the dimensions to the diagram, or could give a written explanation.) **9.** B and D have different numbers of sides. B has a perimeter of 3 + 3 + 3 = 9. D has a perimeter of 3 + 3 + 3 + 3 = 12.; A and C

Quiz 53: Writing and Measuring Time

1. B **2.** B **3.** A **4.** B **5.** 1:15, 10:30, 6:55, 6:20, 10:50, 8:45, 5:10, 12:05 **6.** 7:00, 6:00, 5:00, 11:00, 9:00 **7.** 7:25, 11:47, 10:50, 4:07, 3:26, 8:48, 12:37, 7:15

Quiz 54: Adding and Subtracting Time

1. B **2.** C **3.** D **4.** C **5.** D **6.** C **7.** 1st, 2nd, 3rd, 6th **8.** 1 hr 35 min, 1 hr 55 min, 1 hr 35 min, 2 hrs 25 min, 1 hr 40 min, 1 hr 50 min **9.** 5:45 to 8:20; 2 hours, 35 minutes; 9:00 p.m. **10.** 3 hours, 55 minutes **11.** points plotted at 1:45 and 4:15; 2 hours, 30 minutes **12.** A at 6:00, B at 7:30, C at 7:45, D at 9:30; 3 hours, 30 minutes **13.** 1 hour 37 minutes, 9:47, 9:55, 1 hour 28 minutes, 1 hour 43 minutes, 10:01, 1 hour 49 minutes, 10:21; Tim; Sonny **14.** 6 minutes (The student may add the times to find the total time of 94 minutes, and then find that the time will be 7:34 after 94 minutes. The student may also find the time that each task ends to find the end time of 7:34.)

Quiz 55: Measuring and Estimating Liquid Volume

1. A **2.** D **3.** B **4.** 4 liters **5.** 3 liters, 20 liters, 5 liters, 35 liters **6.** lines drawn at the 75 ml mark

Quiz 56: Solving Word Problems Involving Liquid Volume

1. B **2.** B **3.** B **4.** 1 liter; 3 liters **5.** 10 liters (5 × 20 = 100, 100 − 20 − 30 − 40 = 10 or 100 − (20 + 30 + 40) = 10)

Quiz 57: Measuring and Estimating Weight

1. A **2.** C **3.** A **4.** strawberry 10 grams, olive 1 gram, watermelon 1 kilogram, banana 100 grams **5.** g, kg, g, kg, kg, g **6.** 6 kilograms **7.** 4500 grams or $4\frac{1}{2}$ kilograms

Quiz 58: Solving Word Problems Involving Weight

1. D **2.** B **3.** 1st and 3rd **4.** 23 kilograms **5.** 15 kilograms (3100 − 2800 = 300, 300 ÷ 20 = 15) **6.** 12 jars (4 lots of 3 will weigh 6 kilograms, 4 × 3 = 12)

Student Quiz Book, STAAR Mathematics, Grade 3

Quizzes 59 to 66: Displaying and Interpreting Data

Quiz 59: Using Frequency Tables to Represent Data

1. A **2.** B **3.** C **4.** 3, 3, 2, 3, 5, 3, 3, 2, 3, 1, 2; 14 laps; 19 laps; 14 times **5.** 5, 3 / 6, 3 / 7, 3 / 8, 5 / 9, 1 / 10, 5 / 11, 2 / 12, 6; 12; 9; 9; 13; 4 **6.** 18, 24, 16, 9, 22, 2, 4

Quiz 60: Using Dot Plots to Represent Data

1. B **2.** points plotted as follows: 4 points for $6\frac{1}{2}$, 3 points for 7, 3 points for $7\frac{1}{2}$, 4 points for 8, 2 points for $8\frac{1}{2}$ **3.** points plotted as follows: 1 point for $4\frac{1}{4}$, 2 points for $4\frac{1}{2}$, 4 points for $4\frac{3}{4}$, 1 point for 5, 1 point for $5\frac{1}{2}$ **4.** points plotted as follows: 3 points for $1\frac{3}{4}$, 1 point for 2, 3 points for $2\frac{1}{4}$, 3 points for $2\frac{1}{2}$, 2 points for $2\frac{3}{4}$; 9 plants; The student should describe counting the number of points for 2 or more. **5.** $2\frac{3}{4}$, $3\frac{3}{4}$, 3, $3\frac{3}{4}$, 3, 3, $3\frac{1}{2}$, $2\frac{1}{4}$; points plotted as follows: 1 point for $2\frac{1}{4}$, 1 point for $2\frac{3}{4}$, 3 points for 3, 1 point for $3\frac{1}{2}$, 2 points for $3\frac{3}{4}$; 3 inches; The student should describe how you can compare how many points are plotted for each length.

Quiz 61: Using Pictographs to Represent Data

1. circles from top to bottom: 13, 7, 9, 10, 12, 6, 5 **2.** $ from top to bottom: 9, 5, 10, 4, 7, 11, 8, 3 **3.** ✓ = 2 correct questions; ✓ from top to bottom: 7, 9, 6, 4, 10, 8, 12 **4.** ▷ = 10 pieces of pizza; triangles from top to bottom: 8, 11, 9, 6, 7, 13, 15

Quiz 62: Using Bar Graphs to Represent Data

1. all bars drawn to correct heights **2.** scale in units of 15, all bars drawn to correct heights **3.** scale in units of 5, all bars drawn to correct heights **4.** horizontal axis is labeled "Color" with the colors listed, vertical axis is labeled "Number of Votes" with a scale in units of 2, all bars drawn to correct heights

Quiz 63: Using Frequency Tables to Solve Problems

1. D **2.** 11 times (The work should show an understanding that she earned over $100 when she worked 13, 14, or 15 hours, and add 3, 6, and 2.) **3.** Andy; Pierre; Gabe; Jonah; Jonah and Ryan; 2; Ryan and Pierre; 75 **4.** 20 bookmarks (40 − 20 = 20); 25 bookmarks (45 − 20 = 25); 180 bookmarks (35 + 15 + 40 + 20 + 25 + 45 = 180) **5.** 13 employees (9 + 4 = 13); 27 employees (15 + 12 = 27; The student should explain that the manager is not correct because 15 employees worked 5 hours or less and 25 employees worked more than 5 hours.

Quiz 64: Using Dot Plots to Solve Problems

1. B **2.** B **3.** 4 days; 8 days; 3 hours; 19 hours (0 × 3 + 1 × 5 + 2 × 4 + 3 × 2 = 19); The student should explain that 2 rest days with no homework each week means 4 rest days in total, and identify that Warren only has 3 days with no homework. **4.** 10; 17; 3; Bus, Walk, Bike, Car, Train; The student should state that Felicia is incorrect. The student should describe how 19 students walk or travel by bike, while 26 students travel by bus, car, or train. **5.** 125 cents (5 × 25 = 125); 30 cents (7 × 10 − 8 × 5 = 30); nickels; 20 cents (8 ÷ 2 = 4, 4 × 5 = 20)

Quiz 65: Using Pictographs to Solve Problems

1. 6 emails; 4 emails; Monday; Monday and Tuesday; Thursday and Monday; 48 emails **2.** 40 minutes; Tuesday; 40 minutes; 100 minutes; Thursday and Friday; 250 minutes **3.** 45 + 30 = 75, 75 votes; 60 − 20 = 40, 40 votes; 25 + 15 = 40, 40 votes; 40 − 15 = 25, 25 votes **4.** 10 pennies (55 − 45 = 10); 15 pennies (50 − 35 = 15); 105 pennies (40 + 65 = 105)

Quiz 66: Using Bar Graphs to Solve Problems

1. 30; pumpkin; cherry; cherry and pecan; 80; blueberry; peach and pecan; $90 **2.** 8; Jin; Isaac and Adam; 32; Andre; 4; 16; Isaac and Jin, Andre and Tom **3.** 40 + 55 = 95, 95 minutes; 45 − 25 = 20, 20 minutes; 50 - 20 = 30, 30 minutes; 25 + 45 + 30 = 100, 100 minutes **4.** 14 − 7 = 7, 7 cars; 22 + 17 + 20 = 59, 59 cars; Jamie is correct. There are 22 white cars. There are 13 + 7 = 20 blue and yellow cars combined.

Student Quiz Book, STAAR Mathematics, Grade 3

Quizzes 67 to 70: Developing Personal Financial Literacy

Quiz 67: Understanding Labor and Income Relationships

1. D **2.** D **3.** A **4.** $600 **5.** Bruce; Didi and Bianca; Emmett; Gwen and Donnie **6.** $35,000 (32,500 + 250 × 10 = 35,000) **7.** $215 (45 + 30 × 4 + 50 = 215) **8.** $215 (75 + 35 × 4 = 215); 10 hours (425 − 75 = 350, 350 ÷ 35 = 10, or the student may list the costs for jobs of 1 hour, 2 hours, 3 hours, and so on up to 10 hours.) **9.** $20 per hour (800 ÷ 40 = 20 or 20 × 40 = 800); 50 hours (800 ÷ 16 = 50 or 16 × 50 = 800) **10.** 90, 108, 96, 120; Yuri earns more per hour, so he can make more in total by working fewer hours.

Quiz 68: Understanding Scarcity and Cost Relationships

1. B **2.** A **3.** 1st and 3rd **4.** B **5.** B **6.** The student should explain that more customers means more demand for fish, which would make the price higher.; The student should explain that there would be less fish available, which would make the price higher. **7.** $8 (14 − 6 = 8); The student should explain that there would be more demand for firewood in winter, which would cause the price to be higher.; The student should identify that the price is lower in spring, and should state that there must be more firewood available in spring than in fall. **8.** The student should describe how there must be fewer mangoes available at the beginning of the season, more available in the middle of the season, and less available again at the end of the season.; The student should identify that the price would increase, and explain that mangoes being rare would cause the price of the mangoes to rise.

Quiz 69: Understanding Credit and Interest

1. B **2.** A **3.** A **4.** C **5.** $57 (45 + 2 × 6 = 57) **6.** $16 (8 × 12 = 96, 96 − 80 = 16) **7.** $24 (Margo will borrow 85 − 25 = 60, Margo will pay back 7 × 12 = 84, Margo will pay back 84 − 60 = 24 more.) **8.** $1,750 (200 × 8 + 150 = 1,750) **9.** The student should explain that not paying interest means that Oliver will pay back exactly the same amount he borrowed, which is $900. **10.** Deal A $770, Deal B $700, Deal C $630, Deal D $610 (12 × 60 + 50 = 770, 12 × 50 + 100 = 700, 12 × 40 + 150 = 630, 12 × 30 + 250 = 610); Deal B (With $130 for the up-front payment, she can only afford Deal A or B, and Deal B costs less than Deal A.); $101 (700 − 599 = 101)

Quiz 70: Understanding Saving and Savings Plans

1. A **2.** B **3.** C **4.** B **5.** 1st, 2nd, 4th **6.** $112 (6 × 12 + 40 = 112) **7.** $26,000 (2,000 + 1,200 × 20 = 26,000, or the student could list the amount at year 1, 2, 3 and so on up to year 20) **8.** 14 weeks (16 ÷ 2 = 8, 112 ÷ 8 = 14); $16 (112 ÷ 7 = 16) **9.** April; May (saved $38 in January, saved $71 − $38 = $33 in February, saved $112 − $71 = $41 in March, spent $112 − $100 = $12 in April, saved $163 − $100 = $63 in May, saved $191 − $163 = $28 in June) **10.** The student should explain that Vince's parents would need more than they earn in a year, and so would need to save part of the money over time to have enough.

Made in the USA
Lexington, KY
16 February 2018